'...announce me to the world
by the style and title of
WILLIAM COWPER, ESQ.
of the Inner Temple.'

Letter to JOHN NEWTON, 5 *March 1781*

WILLIAM COWPER

OF THE INNER TEMPLE, ESQ.

A STUDY OF HIS LIFE AND WORKS
TO THE YEAR 1768

BY

CHARLES RYSKAMP

CAMBRIDGE
AT THE UNIVERSITY PRESS
1959

PUBLISHED BY
THE SYNDICS OF THE CAMBRIDGE UNIVERSITY PRESS
Bentley House, 200 Euston Road, London, N.W. 1
American Branch: 32 East 57th Street, New York 22, N.Y.

Printed in Great Britain at the University Press, Cambridge
(Brooke Crutchley, University Printer)

FOR
MY FATHER AND
MOTHER

CONTENTS

LIST OF PLATES

The illustration on the title-page is a pen drawing of a wax impression (here enlarged) taken from the carnelian intaglio ring presented by Theadora Cowper to William Cowper. The ring is in the possession of the Rev. Wilfrid Cowper Johnson, Norwich. The drawing originally appeared in J. C. Bailey's edition of *The Poems of William Cowper* (London: Methuen, 1905).

SHORT TITLES AND ABBREVIATIONS

Add. MSS.—Additional Manuscripts, the British Museum, London.

Alumni Dublin.—G. D. Burtchaell and T. U. Sadleir, *Alumni Dublinenses*, new ed. (Dublin, 1935).

B.M.—The British Museum.

Bn—Baron.

Bodleian MSS.—MSS. in the Bodleian Library, Oxford.

Boswell, *Johnson*—James Boswell, *Life of Johnson*, ed. G. B. Hill and L. F. Powell (Oxford, 1934–50).

Clutterbuck—Robert Clutterbuck, *The History and Antiquities of the County of Hertford* (London, 1815–27).

Cowper Mus., Olney—The Cowper Museum, Olney, Buckinghamshire.

Cowper's *Homer* (Subscribers)—'List of Subscribers' in William Cowper, *The Iliad and Odyssey... Translated into English Blank Verse* (London, 1791), vol. i.

Cowper's *Memoir*—*Memoir of the Early Life of William Cowper, Esq.* (London: R. Edwards, 1816).

Cussans—John Edwin Cussans, *History of Hertfordshire* (London, 1870–81).

D.—Duke.

dau.—daughter.

D.N.B.—*The Dictionary of National Biography.*

E.—Earl.

Early Poems—*Poems, The Early Productions of William Cowper*, ed. James Croft (London, 1825).

Eton Reg.—Richard Arthur Austen-Leigh, *The Eton College Register 1698-1752* (Eton, 1927).

Fitzwilliam MSS.—MSS. in the Fitzwilliam Museum, Cambridge.

Forster MSS.—MSS. in the possession of E. M. Forster, Esq., C.H., King's College, Cambridge.

G.E.C.—[G. E. Cokayne] and V. Gibbs, *The Complete Peerage* (London, 1910–).

G.M.—*Gentleman's Magazine.*

Gray's *Corr.*—Thomas Gray, *Correspondence*, ed. Paget Toynbee and Leonard Whibley (Oxford, 1935).

Greatheed's *Sermon on Cowper*—Samuel Greatheed, *A Practical Improvement of the Divine Counsel... in a Sermon... at Olney, 18 May 1800* (Newport Pagnel, [1800]).

Grimshawe's *Cowper*—William Cowper, *Works*, ed. T. S. Grimshawe, 2nd ed. (London, 1836).

Hayley (1803)—William Hayley, *The Life and Posthumous Writings of William Cowper, Esq.* (Chichester, 1803–4).

Hayley's *Memoirs*—William Hayley, *Memoirs of the Life and Writings of William Hayley, Esq.*, ed. John Johnson (London, 1823).

Hayley's *Memoirs* (MS.)—MS. of William Hayley's 'Anecdotes of the Family, Life, and Writings of William Hayley', vols. i, iii, iv, vi, with occasional pages missing [MS. of Hayley's *Memoirs*, with many pages not included by John Johnson]: Yale University Library.

Hayley's *Vindication* (MS.)—William Hayley, 'A Vindication of Hayleys Life of Cowper': MS. formerly in the possession of the late Mr William Nelson, Paterson, New Jersey; sold Parke-Bernet Galleries, New York, 22–3 October 1940 (Catalogue 220, lot 200); information from a transcription of the MS. in the possession of Professor Madison C. Bates, The Newark Colleges of Rutgers University, Newark, New Jersey.

Hesketh, *Letters*—*Letters of Lady Hesketh to the Rev. John Johnson*, ed. Catharine Bodham Donne (London, 1901).

Inner Temp. Rec.—F. A. Inderwick and R. A. Roberts, eds. *A Calendar of the Inner Temple Records* (London, 1896–1936).

I.T.—The Inner Temple, London.

I.T. MSS.—MSS. in the Inner Temple, London.

Johnson's England—A. S. Turberville, ed. *Johnson's England* (Oxford, 1933).

Journals of the House of Lords or *Jnls. H. of L.*—[Great Britain, Parliament, House of Lords], *Journals of the House of Lords* ([c. 1777]–1891).

Keynes Coll.—MSS. in the collection of Sir Geoffrey Keynes, Lammas House, Brinkley, Newmarket, Suffolk.

Letters—*The Correspondence of William Cowper*, ed. Thomas Wright (London, 1904).

m.—married.

M.—Marquis.

Madan Family—Falconer Madan, *The Madan Family* (Oxford, 1933).

Mid. Temp. Reg.—H. A. C. Sturgess, ed. *Register of Admissions to the...Middle Temple* (London, 1949).

M.T.—The Middle Temple, London.

M.T. MSS.—MSS. in the Middle Temple, London.

Morgan MSS.—MSS. in the Pierpont Morgan Library, New York.

Nichols, *Anecdotes*—John Nichols, *Literary Anecdotes of the Eighteenth Century* (London, 1812–16).

Nichols, *Illustrations*—John Nichols and John Bowyer Nichols, *Illustrations of the Literary History of the Eighteenth Century* (London, 1817–58).

Nichols, *Poems*—John Nichols, ed. *A Select Collection of Poems* (London, 1780–2).

O.E.D.—*The Oxford English Dictionary.*

Panshanger Coll.—MSS. from the collection of Lady Salmond, formerly at Panshanger House, Hertford; now deposited at the County Record Office, Hertford, Hertfordshire.

Poems—*The Poetical Works of William Cowper*, ed. H. S. Milford, 4th ed. (Oxford, 1934).

Poems (1815)—*Poems by William Cowper*, ed. John Johnson (London, 1815).

Poems (Bailey)—*The Poems of William Cowper*, ed. J. C. Bailey (London, 1905).

Private Correspondence—*Private Correspondence of William Cowper*, ed. John Johnson (London, 1824).

Rec. Old Westm.—G. F. R. Barker and A. H. Stenning, *The Record of Old Westminsters* (London, 1928).

Rec. Old Westm., Suppl.—J. B. Whitmore and G. R. Y. Raddiffe, *A Supplementary Volume to the Record of Old Westminsters* (London, [1938]).

s.—son.

Southey's *Cowper*—William Cowper, *Works*, ed. Robert Southey (London, 1836–7).

U. & U.—*The Unpublished and Uncollected Letters of William Cowper*, ed. Thomas Wright (London, 1925).

V.C.H.—*The Victoria History of the Counties of England*, ed. H. A. Doubleday and William Page (London, 1901–).

V.C.H.....*Herts*—*The Victoria History of the County of Hertford*, ed. William Page (Westminster, 1902–23).

Vct—Viscount.

Westminster MSS.—MSS. in the archives of Westminster School, London.

Wright, *Life* (1892)—Thomas Wright, *The Life of William Cowper* (London, 1892).

Wright, *Life* (1921)—Thomas Wright, *The Life of William Cowper*, 2nd ed. (London, 1921).

PREFACE

To write another biography of William Cowper may seem superfluous. In the century following his death (1800) there were at least thirty biographies, many of course little more than the customary nineteenth-century 'memoirs'. There can be no doubt concerning the enormous interest in the poet and the man, especially during the first half of those hundred years. In 1849 Lord Carlisle recorded in his diary some 'good talk' over dinner at The Club, in which Cowper was 'talked of as having been called the most popular of English poets'. There were, however, some 'doubts whether he still holds that position'. Present were the Lord President of the Council (Lansdowne), the Earl of Ellesmere, Philip Henry Stanhope, Sir David Dundas, Henry Holland, Milman, Macaulay, Henry Hallam, and others. In the twentieth century Cowper's reputation and the common knowledge of his poetry have not been so great, though they seem to be increasing. He continues to influence our thought and patterns of speech, even if he is unrecognized. The compilers of the latest edition of *The Oxford Dictionary of Quotations* indicate that Cowper is one of the twelve most quoted writers in the English language. And in the past thirty years four men have written full biographies of him, and there have been a number of shorter investigations into his life besides critical considerations of his work. Lord David Cecil's *The Stricken Deer* reached the status of a 'best-seller'.

But if we put aside the writers who knew him—William Hayley, John Johnson, and Samuel Greatheed—and two later biographers, Southey and Thomas Wright, few of these men have added much to our factual knowledge of

Cowper. Most have been interested in interpreting what was already known. In particular the religious problems and the psychopathic disorders have fascinated biographers. Readers of my study may feel that I have not taken a special perspective on the poet, that I have not chosen a centre from which to view the life. I have done this purposely. I have not tried to create a unity when I did not find one; the various elements and patterns are displayed but not drawn into a synthesis which would distort the data available to us. When one considers the history of Cowper's biography, it seems to me unusually important that at this time a life—not a portrait—be presented. So far as the facts were discoverable, I have set them down. Others may come again to form more colourful conclusions.

The work is, like Sir Herbert Grierson's life of Scott, 'a new life supplementary to, and corrective of' earlier biographies and critical studies. Or to use Dr R. W. Chapman's phrase, it might have the subtitle, 'Facts and Problems'. Nevertheless all previously known materials are used in the study, which I hope is a comprehensive early life of Cowper. Many of these materials are here documented for the first time. I believe the notation of the sources to be an important part of the work, for in the century and a half since Cowper's death the origins of the chains of information and myth have become so obscure and complex that it has become extremely difficult to separate later interpretation from the evidence of Cowper himself, or from that of his contemporaries. Wherever possible the various sources for a paragraph are combined to form a single note, in order to reduce interruption from the text and to conserve space. A list of supplementary information concerning some of Cowper's more significant friends and relatives may be found at the end of this book, preceding the index.

The title is taken from Cowper's customary description

of himself on the title-pages of his publications. It suggests that throughout his life he attached importance to the years in the Temple. It points to one of the focuses of this study: his life, connections, and literary activities while a templar. It indicates his stress on the *Esquire*, and my treatment of that facet of the personality of William Cowper, gentleman. My biography makes no attempt to cover thoroughly his relations with the Evangelical movement, with the Unwins, or with the town of Olney. It ends as this period, the late and mature period, begins.

Cowper's later life is well known from his own letters; of his early years very little has been discovered. I have not been able to illuminate all the parts of these years that I should like, but I have found enough to show him an animated, rather worldly young man, in contrast to the piety of his later years, and of his life as a whole according to some traditional biographies. There is a considerable amount of new information about his life at Westminster School (numerous friendships there and in the Temple are here discussed for the first time), his engagement to Theadora Cowper, his alleged hermaphroditism, his failure at the House of Lords, his insanity. There are many indications that the man famous as a recluse was at one time directly or indirectly associated with a large number of the literary and political figures of his day. In the chapters on Westminster School and the Temple I have tried not only to show Cowper's life, but also to establish a perspective on the lives of his friends, particularly the young writers, in relation to two of the most important nurseries of eighteenth-century English literature.

More than twenty letters and essays (or parts of them) from the period 1750–67 are collected for the first time. Nine new poems, early and late, are attributed to Cowper, and several first printings are given. 'The only large work' of his years in the Temple, a translation in couplets of

Voltaire's *Henriade*, is for the first time definitely identified. Five new reviews (1789–93) are shown to be his, and two letters to the *Gentleman's Magazine* (1790–1) are reprinted for the first time. These are of interest in connection with the early life. But if we seek in all of these works the 'strokes of genius and of art that distinguish the true poet [or essayist] from the poet made such only by the desire to be one' (the words come from one of Cowper's late reviews), we shall seldom find them.

Eccentricities of spelling may be regarded as those of the original manuscripts or books. I have appended comments such as *sic* in brackets only when the apparent incorrectness seemed especially confusing. When no authorship of a letter is given in the footnote references, the writer is Cowper (for example, To Lady Hesketh, 4 June 1786); otherwise the writer and the recipient are given (for example, Wilkes to Colman, 25 March 1765).

I wish to acknowledge assistance of one kind or another from the following: Mrs Lloyd Almirall; Edward Arnold Ltd; Professor Madison C. Bates; the late Dr Charles H. Bennett; Mrs Leland G. Birch; Mr Percy C. Birtchnell; the Bodleian Library; Mr M. F. Bond; the British Museum; Mrs Charles G. Brocklebank; the Rev. R. S. Brown; Mrs Ray H. Bryan; Miss Catherine M. Bull; Mr J. P. T. Bury; Mrs J. Busby; the University Library, Cambridge; Mr John Carleton; Lord David Cecil; the Columbia University Press; Professor Rosemary E. Cowler; the Cowper Museum, Olney; the Master and Fellows of Corpus Christi College, Cambridge; the Earl of Crawford and Balcarres; the late Mrs Andrew De Graaf; the Rev. M. B. Dewey; the Syndics of the Fitzwilliam Museum, Cambridge; Mr E. M. Forster; Dr Hoosag K. Gregory; Mrs Frank Hafenmaier; Dr Neilson Campbell Hannay; Harcourt, Brace and Company, Inc.; Professor Lodwick Hartley; the Library of Harvard University; the Hertford-

shire County Record Office; Professor F. W. Hilles;
Mr M. J. C. Hodgart; the Rev. Philip Hopkinson;
Mr Arthur A. Houghton, Jr; the Henry E. Huntington
Library; Mr and Mrs Donald F. Hyde; the Inner Temple
Library; Mrs Barham Johnson; Miss Mary Barham John-
son; the Rev. and Mrs Wilfrid Cowper Johnson; the
University of Kansas Press; the late Mrs George T. Kendal;
Sir Geoffrey and Lady Keynes; Dr Milo Keynes; King's
College Library, Cambridge; Alfred A. Knopf, Inc.;
Dr George L. Lam; the Lancashire County Record Office;
Colonel William Le Hardy; Mr Wilmarth S. Lewis; the
Library and the Record Office of the House of Lords;
the Macclesfield Public Library; Professor Maynard Mack;
Mrs Malcolm McGougan; Methuen and Company Ltd;
Dr Robert F. Metzdorf; the Middle Temple Library;
Mrs Marshall Miner; the University of Minnesota Press;
the Pierpont Morgan Library; Mrs Joann Ryan Morse;
Mr James Moss; Mr Arnold Muirhead; Mr A. N. L.
Munby; the New York Public Library; Pembroke College
Library, Cambridge; Mrs Marion S. Pottle; Mr Littleton
C. Powys; the Princeton University Library; the Princeton
University Press; the Private Papers of James Boswell
(excerpts reprinted by permission of Yale University, the
McGraw-Hill Book Company, Inc., and William Heine-
man Ltd); Professor Richard L. Purdy; Professor Maurice
J. Quinlan; Mr and Mrs T. T. Radmore; Sir S. C. Roberts;
Professor Edward Robertson; Lord Rothschild; Mrs Norma
Russell; the John Rylands Library; Mr C. F. L. St George;
St John's College Library, Cambridge; Lady Salmond;
Miss Barbara Damon Simison; Miss Jean Chandler Smith;
Dr Warren Hunting Smith; Mr John Sparrow; Mr Brian
Spiller; Mrs Stanley Sultan; Mr Herbert L. Sussman;
Mr Lawrence E. Tanner; Mr Robert H. Taylor; Viscount
Templewood; Professor John Timmerman; Professor
Chauncey B. Tinker; Trinity College Library, Cambridge;

Westminster School; the Wigan Public Library; Professor William K. Wimsatt, Jr; Miss Marjorie Gray Wynne; the Yale University Library; the Yale University Press; the late Professor Henry Zylstra.

I stand much indebted to Professor F. A. Pottle and Mr Kenneth Povey for their knowledge and kind advice; they deserve special thanks. I am similarly grateful to the University Research Committee at Princeton for generous support in the publication of this study. In a slightly different form it was a dissertation, presented for the degree of Doctor of Philosophy in Yale University.

C. A. R.

PRINCETON UNIVERSITY

September 1958

I

BERKHAMSTED

*I profess to write, not his panegyrick, which must be all praise, but his
Life; which, great and good as he was, must not be supposed to be entirely
perfect.*   BOSWELL, *Life of Johnson*

WHERE a thin slip of Hertfordshire reaches into
Buckingham, the Chilterns pile up quietly into a
theatre of soft hills. The enclosures have an unusual
elegance; the bright green grass seems richer, perhaps
because of the contrasts of white and pale grey and dark
green, which come from the white flocks on the slopes, and
the beech woods which crown the hills. The turf is thick
and the hillsides sunny; the avenues of limes vault gracefully, protectively through the parks of ancient manors and
new estates. But in the woods, where in 1066 William the
Conqueror brought Edgar Atheling to submission, there
are still awful shades of darkness. In the eighteenth century,
within these hills, nature reveals her most carefully regulated moods. The landscape has gentility—and simplicity,
for divisions are straightforward and plain, yet easy.

At the base of this finger of county, twenty-six miles
from London, is Berkhamsted. The town had had many
splendid associations (the honour, castle, and manor of
Berkhamsted belonged to the Crown until the middle of the
nineteenth century), but in 1731 when William Cowper
was born in the Rectory, only about fifteen hundred people
were living there, in a few hundred houses. There were
three or four lanes and two principal streets: the High, part
of an old Roman road, which was half a mile long and ran
parallel to the small still River Bulbourne; and the other,
Castle Street, which led to the ruins of the Conqueror's
castle. Here Chaucer had been Clerk of the Works, but

now little was left except grassy mounds and crumbling bricks. In the Prince of Wales's manor house there had been tenants for many years. The royal glories of the place had faded; Berkhamsted had become a small but prosperous agricultural centre with a thriving market.

On either side of the river the hills rise rather steeply, and along the summit of those to the north-east of the town was a large tract of brushwood, the Frith, where the poor went to cut wood for fuel. Berkhamsted's church, St Peter's, stood at the centre of the town and its square embattled tower dominated the valley. The body of the church had been built for the most part before 1300, but during its many years St Peter's had accumulated a variety of styles. The reconstruction of the fabric of the church was one of the first duties of the Reverend John Cowper, who had come to the Rectory in 1722, six years before his marriage. A few years before his son William was born he had directed the uncovering of the medieval paintings (whitewashed by the Puritans) on the pillars of the nave.

John Cowper had come from one of the great families of the county. The estates of the Cowpers spread over ten thousand acres in the centre of Hertfordshire. He was the son of Spencer Cowper the Judge, who at the end of his life was a Justice of the Common Pleas, and his uncle was William, first Earl Cowper, twice Lord Chancellor of Great Britain. This high distinction to the family came after several generations in which various Cowpers had risen from Sheriff of London (1551) and Alderman to become baronets (1642). Sir William, the first holder of the family title, was also the first to be remembered for his poetry. He wrote verses on the death of Richard Hooker and erected the monument to his memory in Bourne Church. From then on almost every Cowper was connected with both politics and poetry. Even John, in addition to being Rector, and Chaplain to the King, was after 1731 joint patentee for

2

making out commissions in bankruptcy. He was a Free-mason and a staunch Whig, whose patriotic enthusiasm was released in political songs. He was the typical eighteenth-century gentleman-versifier and encouraged his sons to write popular occasional poetry after the manner of Congreve, Rowe, and Prior. According to his oldest son William, he had the qualities needed for writing ballads—insight into country tastes, droll humour, simplicity and ease of style—and 'succeeded well in it...at a time when the best pieces in that way were produced'.[1]

Both of his sons testified that John was a 'most indulgent father'. 'He was everything that was excellent and Praise-worthy towards Man', said his son William, who sometimes during his most Evangelical years doubted whether his father had the sincerity and fervour and the Christocentric beliefs of the Evangelical ideal. Nonetheless, at this very time, in an emotional outburst which frequently charac-terized his personality then, William wrote that he had 'such a tender Recollection of my dear Father and all his Kindness to me, the Aimiableness and Sweetness of his Temper & Character, that I went out into the Orchard and burst forth into Praise and Thanksgiving to God for having made me the Son of a Parent whose Remembrance was so sweet to me'.[2] In part this was a result of the regrets of a man in his thirties for the errors of adolescence.

> At a thoughtless age, allur'd
> By ev'ry gilded folly, we renounc'd
> His shelt'ring side, and wilfully forewent
> That converse which we now in vain regret.
> How gladly would the man recall to life
> The boy's neglected sire![3]

---

[1] G.E.C.: Cowper; John Bruce, 'Memoir', Poetical Works of William Cowper (London, [1863]), i, ix–xiv; G.M. xxv (1755), 572; Madan Family, p. 74; Letters, i, 398–9; ii, 91–2; iii, 440.

[2] Letters, iii, 241; Nichols, Anecdotes, viii, 561; U. & U. p. 18.

[3] Task, vi, 38–43, and just below, ll. 43–4.

3   1-2

'A mother too', he went on to say, 'that softer friend, perhaps more gladly still.' She had died when he lacked two days of being six years old, yet he told his friend Joseph Hill a half century later: 'I can truly say, that not a week passes (perhaps I might with equal veracity say a day), in which I do not think of her. Such was the impression her tenderness made upon me, though the opportunity she had for showing it was so short.' When, a few years after the writing of this letter, he received his mother's portrait from his cousin in Norfolk, his happiness was inordinate. He recalled vividly 'a multitude of the maternal tendernesses' which he had received. 'Everybody loved her', he said, 'and with an amiable character so impressed upon all her features, everybody was sure to do so.'[1] She was 'an angelick woman', his cousin Lady Hesketh said, and 'was Idoliz'd by all her Husbands family; and not without reason as I have heard my Father say; who himself lov'd her much and always consider'd her as a most amiable Being'.[2] Cowper's own recollections of his mother, in his poem 'On the Receipt of My Mother's Picture out of Norfolk', are almost as famous as the man himself. In this he recalls her nightly visits to his chamber and her love and lovely person—her dresses with

> tissued flow'rs,
> The violet, the pink, and jessamine.

It seems unlikely that William, in spite of his clear and tender recollections, saw a great deal of his mother during these six years. The kind of home—upper-middle class and gentle—would preclude a constant intimate relation between child and mother. During most of the day he saw maids and his nurse, and was in the nursery, where the children were raised. His poem on his 'Mother's Picture'

---

[1] *Letters*, II, 267–8; III, 433; see also III, 434–5, 443, 445.
[2] Hesketh, *Letters*, p. 103 and Lady Hesketh to Hayley, 9 April 1802: Add. MSS. 30803 B, f. 26.

suggests a situation typical in such a home: visits to his parents at appointed hours. In addition, many of the days of these years were for his father and mother taken up by sickness and death. In the nine years in which she was married, Ann Donne Cowper had six pregnancies. Spencer, her first child, born in 1729, died after five weeks. Nine months after his death, Ann and John, twins, were born and died within two days. William, the poet, was born at Berkhamsted between three and four o'clock in the morning on 15 November 1731 O.S.[1] After him, came Theodora Judith, about a year and a half younger, who died at the age of two. Thomas was born on 9 October 1734 O.S., and died on the twenty-third of that month. The birth of John, the seventh child, who lived to become a Fellow of Corpus Christi College, Cambridge, caused the death of his mother six days later, 13 November 1737 O.S. Outside the nursery, life in the Rectory must have caused some sense of anxiety and grief even in so young a child as William.

In the town, as he himself said, he was a sort of principal figure.[2] This was because of his father's family and position, but his mother was of almost as distinguished ancestry. The Donnes claimed to have descended from Henry III, King of England, by four different lines, including that of Mary Boleyn, sister of Queen Anne Boleyn, and the noble houses of Carey, Howard, and Mowbray. According to the pedigree of the Donne family, granted in 1793 to William Cowper by the College of Arms, his great-grandfather, William Donne, of Letheringsett, Norfolk, Gent. (1645–84), was 'supposed to be descended from Dr. Donne the Dean of St. Paul's'; but such descent was probably collateral.[3]

---

[1] He was baptized on 13 Dec. 1731 O.S. The information concerning the birthdays of the Cowper children is taken from the Rev. John Cowper's notes in the Cowper family Bible, now in Cowper Mus., Olney.

[2] Letters, III, 335.

[3] John Johnson, 'Life of Cowper', Poems (1815), p. xii; Bruce, 'Memoir', I, xiv–xv; Catharine B. Johnson, William Bodham Donne and hi :Friends (London, 1905), pp. viii and 344. It has not been proved that either of John Donne's sons had male offspring.

5

Nevertheless, for William and for his cousins, the tradition of that ancestry was real: John Donne belonged to them as a venerable forefather. And William Cowper believed himself to be more Donne than Cowper. 'The bond of nature', he said, drew him 'vehemently' to that side. In his childhood his face was supposed to resemble his mother's in many ways, and in old age he had a little of the irritability of the Donnes, and he hoped, some of their good nature.[1]

As a small boy he posed for a portrait, perhaps by D. Heins, who had painted his mother's. He was shown armed with a bow and arrow, 'waging war either with a *cock sparrow* or a *bumble-bee* as they call it'.[2] (Sixty years afterwards he again sat in archer's costume for a portrait— that by Lemuel Abbott, now hanging in the National Portrait Gallery.) With his mother's love of all the details of nature, he inspected the gardens of his home and the countryside about the town. 'There was neither tree, nor gate, nor stile, in all that country, to which I did not feel a relation', he wrote thirty years after he had left Berkhamsted, 'and the house itself I preferred to a palace.' Not until his father's death, however, when he was forced to part from those Hertfordshire fields and woods forever, was he truly 'sensible of their beauties'.[3]

After his mother died, the Donne family in particular helped to make William's life more pleasant. His childhood before he went away to school was essentially happy—they were 'happy days', he said, 'compared with most I have seen since'—though not untroubled with greater cares than

---

[1] *Letters*, III, 434–5; 'To John Johnson': *Poems*, p. 422.
[2] Letter from Cowper's cousin John Johnson to William Hayley, 13 Oct. 1801: Bodleian MS. Eng. misc. d. 134, f. 83. The picture of William has never been located. According to Samuel Greatheed it was 'of the natural size': letter to Hayley, 26 Aug. 1800: Fitzwilliam MSS.
[3] *Letters*, III, 167–8. A comment exactly contrary to these words was expressed to John Duncombe shortly after the leave-taking (Appendix A, p. 184), but it was probably made in false heartiness, to bolster himself in the face of loneliness and regret.

PLATE I. ANN DONNE COWPER (1703–37)

Miniature ($6\frac{1}{4} \times 5$ in.) in oil on copper, by D. Heins, *c.* 1723; in the possession of Miss Mary Barham Johnson, Norwich

PLATE II. JOHN COWPER (1737–70)

Etching, by Michael Tyson (1740–80); in the Fitzwilliam Museum, Cambridge.
In a collection of Tyson's work, where it is identified as '——Cowper M.A. Fellow
of Bennet College Cambridge'. Reproduced by permission of the Syndics of the
Fitzwilliam Museum, Cambridge. Tyson 'owed much to the friendship and
acquaintance of Mr. John Cowper', who had given him a 'thorough knowledge
and insight into the Greek language'. 'Out of gratitude to his memory, [Tyson]
has etched a drawing of him, which is very like him, and which will be a curiosity,
as so few copies were taken from the Plate'—according to William Cole,
Add. MSS. 5886, f. 25, quoted in Nichols, *Anecdotes*, VIII, 204. The etching was
the subject of considerable correspondence between Tyson and Richard Gough
(Nichols, *Anecdotes*, VIII, 628–9), and between Horace Walpole, who was eager
to have a print of it, and William Cole: Yale edition of *Horace Walpole's
Correspondence* (New Haven, 1937), II, 302, 307–9.

most children know. The children of his Uncle Roger Donne, the Rector of Catfield in Norfolk, brought him laughter and joy and games when they came to Berkhamsted, or later when he went to Norfolk. He wrote: 'Of all places in the earth I love Catfield...where I passed some of the happiest days of my youth, in company with those whom I loved and by whom I *was* beloved.' One he loved especially: Harriot Rival Donne, 'an unaffected, plain-dressing, good-tempered, cheerful' cousin and playmate.[1]

He started going to school. The gardener Robert (Robin) Pope first drew him to school each day in his 'bauble coach' along the public way.[2] Then he went to Aldbury, where he was placed under the care of his father's friend the Reverend William Davis, who was Rector of that parish.[3] Aldbury, a few miles from Berkhamsted, is famous as one of the most beautiful villages in England. Here the Chiltern Hills drop abruptly to an idyllic valley and village of thatched cottages, manor-like houses, and an unusually fine church. Aldbury was the seat of the Harcourts, whose manor of Pendley was near by. Young Dick Harcourt was a special friend of William Cowper, and his brother John a special nuisance to him.[4] However, William was not sent away to school because of the death of his mother, or in order to associate with the more prominent people of the neighbourhood, but probably because of the miserable conditions in the school at Berkhamsted. The situation called for a suit in chancery which began in 1735 and lasted for over a hundred years. By 1743 there were only five boys attending the once prosperous foundation. The quarrels

---

[1] *Letters*, iv, 2, 82; portion of a letter to John Buchanan, 5 Sept. 1795: printed in Sotheby Cat., 12–13 Feb. 1951, lot 290.

[2] 'Mother's Picture', ll. 48–51: *Poems*, p. 395; it is not certain what kind of school that in Berkhamsted was, but it was most likely a dame-school.

[3] Clutterbuck, i, 316. John Cowper and William Davis (1679–1754) were associated on various boards of trustees: R. A. Norris, *A Short Account of Thomas Bourne* (Berkhamsted, 1929), p. 13.

[4] Appendix A, pp. 191–2; *Poems* (Bailey), p. xxxix.

7

between master and usher had become a scandal in the community, and the buildings were in such a ruinous condition that they were unfit for school purposes.[1]

Cowper remained at Aldbury for only a very short time; in his sixth year he was sent to 'a considerable school in Bedfordshire'—at Markyate Street on the Hertfordshire and Bedfordshire border. The boarding school was in the 'Old Vicarage', under the mastership of the Reverend William Pittman, who held the chapelry at Markyate Street and the curacy of Caddington. Pittman was, like Davis, well known to William's father, and was celebrated in that area as a classical scholar, and as schoolmaster. Nonetheless, one tormentor in the school escaped his surveillance, a bully of about fifteen years of age, who persecuted Cowper 'in so secret a manner that no creature suspected it'. He had by his savage treatment 'impressed such a dread of his figure' upon Cowper's mind, that he said many years later, 'I well remember being afraid to lift up my eyes upon him, higher than his knees; and that I knew him by his shoe-buckles, better than any other part of his dress'. At length, however, the bully was discovered and expelled from the school, and Cowper taken from it.[2]

From Markyate Street, at the age of eight, William was sent to the home of Mrs Disney, an eminent oculist, where he lived for two years.[3] This was done in an attempt to cure

---

[1] The Rev. John Cowper and the churchwardens brought one suit against the master and usher in 1742; a decree was made on this by the Court of Chancery, 30 Oct. 1754: *G.M.* LXXXIII (1813), 287–8; Cussans, III, 78; *V.C.H....Herts*, II, 77.

[2] Cowper's *Memoir*, pp. 1–3.

[3] Cowper's *Memoir*, p. 4 reads: 'Mr. D. an eminent surgeon and oculist...I continued a year in this family....' Cowper to Hayley, 6 April 1792, reads: 'a female oculist of great renown at that time, in whose house I abode two years, but to no good purpose' (Hayley (1803), I, 7–8). Southey, without giving any evidence for his decision, concluded that Cowper had been sent to 'the house of an eminent oculist, whose wife also had obtained great celebrity in the same branch of medical science' (Southey's *Cowper*, I, 9); this was accepted by Wright, *Life* (1921), pp. 6–7. However, the only MS. copies of the *Memoir* known to exist (they are not in C's hand: see *M.P.* LIII (1955), 70) give this reading of the passage: 'Mrs. D. an eminent oculist.' I believe that it was a female oculist, and that Cowper stayed at her home *two* years, because in

8

the 'specks' on his eyes, which threatened to cover one of them in particular, so that he was in danger of losing his sight.[1] His stay with Mrs Disney profited him little, either in health or in knowledge. Not until he left her home for Westminster School and life in London did his formal education become stable, and his learning progress in earnest.

Early stimulations to read and think came from his father, and from similar interests in his younger brother John, and from John Duncombe, whose family had a seat at Stocks, an estate a short distance north of Aldbury Church. With his brother, William engaged in a rhyming correspondence. And after John reached Felsted School (c. 1751) and Corpus Christi College, Cambridge (1754), William could profit from his brother's learning, which was phenomenal. By the time he was twenty-five or thirty, John's facility in Latin, Greek, Hebrew, French, and Italian drew excited comments from his contemporaries at the university, and already in his youth his studious bent and the brilliance of his learning were known to many.[2]

When John died at the age of thirty-three, the Bishop of Cloyne wrote to Samuel Parr: 'We have lost the best classic and most liberal thinker in our University.'[3] 'A very profound and distinguished scholar', the Gentleman's Magazine said; 'a man of great acquirements and various learning,

---

the *Memoir* and in the letter he says that he moved from the oculist's house to Westminster. We know that he entered that school at the age of ten. The first change of 'D' to Disney appears to have been in Bruce (1863, vol. I, p. xix).

[1] With so little information, it is not possible to determine the nature of the 'specks'. Eighteenth-century diagnoses, such as those by Robert James and William Heberden, are too general to be of much help. Heberden uses the term 'specks' only in connection with the strumous (scrofulous) inflammation of the eyelids, which, he says, may continue 'for a year, or longer, without ending in blindness; though it will often leave films, or specks upon the eye, which hurt the sight if they be upon the cornea, and in any other part are a deformity' (*Commentaries on the History and Cure of Diseases* (London, 1802), p. 327).

[2] *Letters*, I, 122–3; III, 303; William Cowper, *Adelphi* in H. P. Stokes, *Cowper Memorials* (Olney, 1904), p. 68.

[3] William Bennett, Bishop of Cloyne, to Samuel Parr, 18 April 1770: *The Works of Samuel Parr*, ed. John Johnstone (London, 1828), VII, 75–6.

9

as well as of talents'.[1] John had merited a share of the university's honours: the chief award in classical studies (1759) —one of the Chancellor's Medals for commencing bachelors and the first of the Member's Prizes for the best dissertation in Latin prose (1760). He wrote panegyrics for Cambridge University collections on the death of George II and the accession of George III, on George III's marriage, and on the birth of the Prince of Wales (1762); verses for the *Gentleman's Magazine*, and translations of four books of the *Henriade* for Smollett's edition of Voltaire. He became a Fellow of his college in 1763, and was appointed its Prælector (1765) and Bursar (1767).[2]

After he became a Fellow, John was known in Cambridge for his severe application to scholarship and college administration; yet he was also, as his brother said, 'a man of most candid and ingenuous spirit; his temper remarkably sweet'. William Cole described him as 'a short, thick, well-set man', who 'seemed to be of a robust constitution'.[3] But in the last year of his life his health failed rapidly, and some two or three months before his death it became clear that recovery would not be possible. The illness, which manifested itself as a dropsy, was thought to be a disease of the liver. During all of these months he was in addition 'nervously affected to such a degree y^t he w^d latterly break out into ye most violent Screams like hysterics with^t any external effect: but to ye last appear^d in high health & went off rather suddenly in ye night'.[4] The strain of John's illness on William—such terrifying scenes, and then his death—was so great that he could not be present at the burial at Foxton,

[1] *G.M.* N.S. III (1835), 564.
[2] Stokes, pp. 14–16, 27–9, 118–19; *G.M.* LIII, Pt i (1783), 152; Nichols, *Anecdotes*, VI, 615; Bodleian MSS. Gough Camb. 80; Corpus Christi Coll. MSS.: 'College Order Book: 1752–82.'
[3] *G.M.* LXXII, Pt i (1802), 335; *Adelphi*, Stokes, pp. 68, 130.
[4] MS. note by Richard Gough, a close friend, in Gough's copy of Robert Masters, *The History of the College of Corpus Christi* (Cambridge, 1753), among notes bound up with vol. II: Bodleian MSS. Gough Camb. 83.

seven miles from Cambridge, where John had been Vicar since 1765. He was 'so much affected with the loss' of his brother that the Master and Fellows of Corpus Christi advised him to leave Cambridge before the funeral, and without settling his brother's estate.[1] Later he would recall John in tranquillity:

> I had a brother once—
> Peace to the mem'ry of a man of worth,
> A man of letters, and of manners too!
> Of manners sweet as virtue always wears,
> When gay good-nature dresses her in smiles.
> He grac'd a college, in which order yet
> Was sacred; and was honour'd, lov'd, and wept,
> By more than one, themselves conspicuous there.[2]

A characteristic picture of the inhabitants of the Rectory at Berkhamsted and their most familiar guests, would show Mr Cowper and his two sons, Mr William Duncombe and son John, and Dr Jones Redman, the Berkhamsted physician. They would be talking about poetry, classical and modern, because that was for each of them a chief non-professional interest. Redman was of Eton and King's College, where he had been a Fellow and later Master of King's College School. His agreeable company and medical skill afterwards recommended him to a large practice and general esteem in Berkhamsted. The Duncombes, father and son, were widely known as men of letters. In 1725, at the age of thirty-five, William had quit his place at the navy office in order to spend the rest of his life among his friends and his books in literary leisure. He sent his son to Felsted School and later to Corpus Christi, Cambridge, where he became a close friend of two other alumni of the school: John Cowper (William's brother) and John Sawrey Morritt, of Christ's. At school John Duncombe had been

---

[1] William Colman, President of Corpus Christi, to Richard Gough, 9 April 1770: Nichols, *Illustrations*, IV, 713–14.
[2] *Task*, II, 780–7.

the first scholar and captain. He gained the very highest reputation for scholarship, and by his pleasant temperament and manners made strong friendships with his masters and fellow-students. Duncombe's knowledge of the classical languages was remarkable even before he was sixteen, so that he became the delight of his father, who took pride in his own efforts at translating the ancients, especially his favourite, Horace. Father and son collaborated in the publication of these Horatian odes (1757 and 1759), in which they were assisted by several friends, among them William Cowper.[1]

John Duncombe also turned very early to studies preparatory to the taking of Holy Orders. His 'inclination, virtuous turn of mind, and unquestionable abilities, concurred to render him peculiarly qualified' for the ministry. In Duncombe, William and John Cowper had a friend who, like them, was absorbed in Latin and Greek studies, and was becoming increasingly interested in religious matters. He wrote many original poetical compositions, and was an essayist and reviewer of merit. For years he undertook the department of the 'Review of Books' in the *Gentleman's Magazine*, and in this editorial capacity it was he who most probably reviewed William Cowper's books for the *Magazine* —the most important reviews to Cowper. Duncombe's appearance was not as attractive as his personality. Sir Egerton Brydges described him in later life as 'a sort of general *littérateur*—very multifarious in his erudition, but not very exact; neglected and uncouth in his person, and awkward in his manner; a long face, with only one eye, and a shambling figure; his pockets stuffed with pamphlets; his manner hurried, and his articulation indistinct'.[2]

---

[1] According to 'D' [John Duncombe], Nichols, *Poems*, VI, 304; Andrew Kippis, *Biographia Britannica* (London, 1793), V, 505, 509; *Nichols Anecdotes*, VIII, 270.

[2] Kippis, V, 509–11; John Nichols, *General Index* (to the *G.M.* 1787–1818), Pt I (London, 1821), pp. lviii and lxvi; *Letters*, III, 267; Sir Egerton Brydges, *Autobiography* (London, 1834), I, 51–2.

PLATE III. JOHN DUNCOMBE (1729–86)

Oil painting, by Joseph Highmore in 1766; in the Hall, Corpus Christi College, Cambridge. Identified by the College authorities. Reproduced by permission of the Master and Fellows of Corpus Christi College, Cambridge.

During the Berkhamsted years, whenever William Cowper was with John Duncombe, or with his own brother John, or with his Donne cousins from Norfolk, he found a large measure of peace and happiness, and he grew in the knowledge of language, literature, and religion. These occasions provided an exception to the usual flux of his life, and created a semblance of normal order and stability that was in conformity with the natural world of Berkhamsted: the regulated hills and gardens about the town. 'Hertfordshire is England at its quietest', says Mr E. M. Forster; 'it is England meditative.' Nature was and would always be for William Cowper a restorer to peace; the world of relations with men would continue to be, for the most part, a mass of entanglements and disruptions which forced him from gentle living and a scholar's meditations.

II

WESTMINSTER

The meek and bashful boy will soon be taught
To be as bold and forward as he ought;
The rude will scuffle through with ease enough,
Great schools suit best the sturdy and the rough.
'Tirocinium', ll. 338–41

WILLIAM's school would be Westminster, of course. It had been his father's school and his grandfather Spencer Cowper's, and that of the grandfather's two namesakes: his nephew the Hon. Spencer, second son of the first Earl, and his grandson Spencer, whose elder brother William had preceded him there. This youngest Spencer was in his last year when his cousin, William Cowper of Berkhamsted, enrolled in April 1742.[1] Three of the Madans, Martin, Spencer, and John, also his cousins, were there with him, and Spencer Madan's son and grandsons and great-grandsons would come hereafter, but 1742 was the last year in which a Cowper would matriculate at Westminster.

William's father was a steadfast Whig,[2] closely allied to one of the families of the rising Whig aristocracy. Westminster, then ruling with Eton as one of the two schools high above all others, opposed its Tory rival as the seat of this ascendant oligarchy. The school could be relied upon to foster the political ideals which were important to the father, and would be to the son. The father, kindly and soft-spoken, was nevertheless ambitious. He had seen the glory of his uncle, the Lord Chancellor and Earl, and he had similar dreams of glory for his son. He 'intended to beget a chan-

---

[1] *Rec. Old Westm.* I, 224–5; II, 612–13; facing I, 224 is a reproduction of a page of Nicoll's admission book, showing the entry of William Cowper in 1742.
[2] *Letters*, I, 398; III, 440.

14

cellor, and he begat instead, a Translator of Homer. It is impossible for the effect to differ more from the intention.'[1] He dreamed, as fathers desiring honour were prone to do,

> of little Charles or William grac'd
> With wig prolix, down-flowing to his waist;
> ...the oracle of law![2]

The first step towards success in law, or in any career, was an education at a public school. At this moment the first school in the land was Westminster, and so a most important step was made. In boyhood William felt the pushing of his father as a personal problem; later, in 'Tirocinium', he would criticize it as a common failing.

Eton had been and would be in the future the most continuously popular of the public schools. But Westminster twice rose to a greatness almost unknown in the history of English education. It happened first under Richard Busby, who, as Head Master for over fifty years during the Restoration, moulded the opinion of the land for all time. He established the belief in the well-born that it was necessary for their sons to have a public-school education. The palmy days came again in the middle of the eighteenth century because of a quietly pre-eminent Head Master, John Nicoll (1733–53), and never had a school seen such a large assemblage of sons of peers, or so many men who would win fame.[3] During Nicoll's administration there came two boys who would become prime ministers, Rockingham and Portland; two future admirals, Howe and Keppel; Warren Hastings and Elijah Impey; Cowper, Churchill, Colman, Lloyd, and Thornton; Gibbon and Cumberland; the reserved Cracherode, the munificent collector, and the courtly tenth Earl of Huntingdon; Philip Stanhope and

---

[1] To Miss Frances (Fanny) Hill, 21 April 1786: Panshanger Coll.
[2] 'Tirocinium', ll. 360–3.
[3] Edward C. Mack, *Public Schools and British Opinion 1780 to 1860* (London, 1938), pp. 17–18, 23; John Sargeaunt, *Annals of Westminster School* (London, 1898), p. 166.

Lord March, later the third Duke of Richmond; Hervey and Hobart, afterwards Earls of Bristol and Buckinghamshire, and Thomas Harley, the son of the Earl of Oxford, who became Lord Mayor of London.

They came to ancient monastic buildings beside the Abbey, and to the new dormitory for the scholars which an Old Westminster, Sir Christopher Wren, had designed and Lord Burlington had modified. The school was just above the notorious Thieving-lane, but on the other side, between Westminster and Chelsea stretched Tothill Fields. Here was a large open area of field and marsh where the boys could take their airings and play cricket and football. It was here that the truant boy who 'lov'd the rural walk' would ramble along the banks of the Thames. And when William Cowper's small slice of pocket money was spent, he would come here to supplement the meagre diet of the houses. 'Still hung'ring, pennyless and far from home', he fed in the fields on scarlet hips and haws, crabs and bramble berries.[1] And he had time to be alone, to read and think in peace.

There were 354 boys in the school when William came in 1742.[2] The Town Boys, those who were not among the forty scholars in the College, lived in fifteen or twenty boarding-houses in the neighbourhood. Many of the houses were in the two Dean's Yards. Usually they were kept by 'Dames', occasionally by masters, and the numbers in each varied from six to perhaps twenty-four or more. The common fee was £25 a year, if the boy went home during the vacations; £30 if he did not.[3] But the fees might be considerably higher for 'quality children' who had single rooms and came with their own tutors and servants. There were additional bills for the cleaning of shoes and the wash-

[1] *Task*, I, 119 ff.   [2] *Rec. Old Westm.* II, 1094.
[3] See the letter written by Archibald Campbell 'to a friend' in 1735; quoted in Tanner, *Westminster School* (1951), p. 49. I am indebted to Tanner's book, pp. 49–51, for the information in the first part of this paragraph.

ing and mending of linen; for paper, pens, and books; for candles and the fire; and even 'for the rods'. The house had to be selected with care, according to the kind of boarders, whether noble or poor, and the kind of family owning the house. Only too frequently an aged Dame kept a boarding-house in order to remain alive. She lived very much by herself in her own quarters, and life above stairs—the high jinks and revelry, fighting and bullying—turned night after night into a wild mêlée. Perhaps she engaged a master to keep order, but he could not be expected to do more than pop his head inside the door now and then.[1]

William was in some ways fortunate; he came to 'Madam Playford's'.[2] Her narrow, four-storey house was on the north side of Little Dean's Yard (the site of the present Bursary).[3] It could not have held many boys, and its location at the very heart of the school was ideal. The house was inside the small and quiet Yard, so at night Cowper did not suffer as Cumberland did at Edmund Ashby's house, from the 'yells and howlings of the crews of the depredators, which infested that infamous quarter, and sometimes even roused and alarmed us by their pilfering attacks'. This was the considerable price which Cumberland had to pay for a room to himself, normally a luxury reserved only for sons of peers and the enormously wealthy. When he was in the same house with Cowper (1746), he was not so lucky.[4] Ten years later at Mrs Morrell's, Lord

<hr />

[1] A. M. W. Stirling, *The Hothams* (London, 1918), II, 1–2; J. D. Carleton, *Westminster* (London, 1938), p. 27, and from Mr Carleton in conversation.

[2] Reproduction of the page of Nicoll's admission book: 'Wm Cowper—Playford—[age] 10—1[st form]': *Rec. Old Westm.* I, 224.

[3] Tanner, *Westminster School* (1951), p. 49. The house was known as 'Singleton's' in the early part of the nineteenth century. It was pulled down in 1841. Tanner, *Westminster School: Its Buildings and Associations* (London, 1923), p. 14. The house is shown at the extreme right in a rare print of the school, *c.* 1830; reproduced in a plate facing p. 26.

[4] Richard Cumberland, *Memoirs* (London, 1806), pp. 48, 58–60; Bentham's conversation, in John Bowring, *Memoirs of Bentham*, vol. x, *The Works of Jeremy Bentham* (Edinburgh, 1843), p. 27.

Edward Cavendish-Bentinck (afterwards third Duke of Portland) had 'as many as two, if not three, rooms', while poor Jeremy Bentham slept in a room with three beds. 'One of these', he told Bowring,

I shared with different bedfellows; who, in the course of a dozen months, were changed perhaps half as many times. This bed was on one side of two windows, between which was stationed a bureau, belonging to one of us; and on the other side of the farthest windows was another bed, occupied by two boys, who were from two to four years older than I. One of them was named Mitford...the son of an opulent country gentleman....His bedfellow was a boy of the name of Cotton; one of the Cottons of Cheshire.[1]

If the opulent William Mitford and the son of Sir Lynch Salusbury Cotton, Bart., M.P., had to share a bed, it is almost certain that the son of the proud, but much poorer, Rector of Berkhamsted must have done the same, at least during his first years at the school.

So William was not especially fortunate. And coming as he did to a Dame's house, he would not have a family to live with as some boys did. At the age of ten he moved into the boarding-house of Mrs Ann Playford, a woman of seventy-one. She could scarcely be much of a comfort to the lonely boy, or exercise control over the pranks and wrangles of the lodgers in the house. It was, apparently, a typical Dame's house, with all the traditional attendant evils, with this exception, that Madam Playford was not keeping a boarding-house because of poverty. When she died as the school was being dismissed at the end of William's first year, she was able to bequeath several considerable legacies. Presumably this money came through the estate of her husband. He was Henry Playford, only surviving son of John Playford, the celebrated music publisher in the Temple, near the church door. During the Commonwealth, and for some years of Charles II's reign, 'Honest John Playford' con-

---

[1] *Memoirs of Bentham*, p. 27.

trolled the publishing of music in England; he had no rival. He became famous for his many publications of songs and catches, and his shop was the meeting-place of musical enthusiasts. Pepys knew him well, and when in the Temple it was his custom to go to Playford's 'to look over a book or two'. After John Playford's death, Henry, the godson of Henry Lawes, succeeded to the family business. And when Henry died he left a legacy to Henry Purcell and the bulk of his property to Ann, his wife. Sometime before 1730 she moved to the house in Little Dean's Yard. In the year that William knew her she may therefore have told him of Lawes and Purcell and Pepys, and of Oxford, where she was born and lived until her marriage.

She was succeeded by her nephew and niece, Thomas and Ann Ludford, who must have brought some kind of family life to the house. He, the keeper, was a man about thirty-five, and his wife about ten years older. Their son Edward Taylor Ludford entered the school at this time, became a King's Scholar at the age of thirteen, and in 1756 was elected head to Christ Church. Mrs Ludford died in May 1748 and shortly afterwards Mr Ludford seems to have left, perhaps before Cowper went down from the school in 1749. It is to be hoped that the cantankerousness of his later life was not evident while the boys boarded 'up Ludford's'. He died leaving his estate to others, alleging that his family had disowned him. There was this proviso, however, that these people too would forfeit everything if they ever spoke to someone whom he called 'that infernal hussey Suett'.[1]

To go to his classes—'up School' in the language of the Westminster, who has always spoken in the 'up' and 'down' fashion—William Cowper merely had to cross Little Dean's

---

[1] Thomas Ludford left several 'freehold estates at Hayes and at Westminster' and leasehold property in Ireland. His son was not named in the will, but may have died before this time (1776). Joseph L. Chester, ed. *The Marriage, Baptismal, and Burial Registers of...St Peter, Westminster* (London, 1876), pp. 375, 421.

Yard. The Playford-Ludford house was on the left when entering the Yard; in front, at the end, is the stone gateway built in 1734 (it was new in Cowper's day) by Lord Burlington as the entrance to 'School' and to 'College'. On either side of the gateway are the 'Mon. Os.' stones, on which a Monitor Ostii stands daily, now as in Cowper's time, to cap the masters as they come 'down School' after Latin prayers. Inside the entrance the steps lead first to the Busby Library, or the Museum, as it was then called, the classroom of the Head Master's seventh form. The room built for the great Head Master in 1659 had richly carved bookcases, and cherubs and foliage and fruit entwined in the plaster ceiling around the dome. There were books in the cases in the splendid library, but it was difficult, if not impossible, for anyone below the sixth form to get permission to use the room. However, there were almost no books which younger boys would want to read. Very few were in English, though those in Latin and Greek would not long have been a problem for Will Cowper. Some for their age (fifteenth-century and earlier manuscripts) would have fascinated him; but those in Hebrew and Arabic, and the mysterious languages learned later by Jones, had lost currency after Busby.[1]

Beyond was the School, one enormous room where all the boys were taught from Elizabethan times until 1884. There was one division: a curtain which hung from a bar separated the Upper School from the Under School. The School had eleventh-century walls and a spectacular hammer-beam roof (1450). At the northern end was the 'Shell', an alcove scooped from the wall in the time of Cromwell and decorated with pilasters and mouldings just two years before Cowper's arrival. Before the Shell the

---

[1] John Sargeaunt, 'Cowper's School Days at Westminster', *Cowper in London* (London, 1907), p. 15; Tanner, *Westminster School* (1951), pp. 111, 128, and *Westminster ...Buildings* (1923), pp. 28, 48; D. C. Simpson, 'The Scott Library, 1883 to 1933', *Westminster Library*, no. 1 (1933), pp. 7–8.

Shell form met, the form between the fifth and the sixth. (The name, which originated at Westminster, spread to many of the public schools.) Behind the Shell was the Rod Room, where the College juniors made the birch rods for floggings.

For the 350 boys there were two masters, an Upper (Head) and an Under Master, and six ushers.[1] The chances of effective teaching can in part be imagined from the ratio of one man to fifty boys. James Johnson was Under Master (1733–48) when Cowper arrived. During this period he was the principal disciplinarian at the school. For the masters of the upper forms were notoriously ineffective in maintaining order, especially Vincent Bourne and also Pierson Lloyd (father of Robert the poet) who took the fourth form. According to Bentham, Lloyd was one of the teachers who were 'distinguished by their aptitude for some one or other trifle which was valueless'. He, 'the son of a tapster, and thence called Tappy Lloyd, was wholly occupied in teaching prosody; "a miserable invention", said Bentham, "for consuming time"'. Bentham's experiences at the school were mainly unpleasant, and he laid a large part of the blame on several of the masters 'who were perfect sinecurists. They were paid fees for doing nothing; and Bentham's impression generally was, that the higher their rank, the less their efficiency.'[2] Cowper did not share Bentham's attitude towards prosody, nor did he reflect his feeling towards Lloyd. He took pleasure in translating the verses of Dr William Vincent (who succeeded Lloyd as Under Master), 'To the Memory of Dr Lloyd'. 'Affection for the memory of the worthy man whom they celebrate', Cowper wrote, 'alone prompted me to this endeavour.' The reasons why were obvious: for his humour —'second in harmless pleasantry to none'—his many

---

[1] George Reeves, *A New History of London*, 2nd ed. (London, 1764), p. 183.
[2] Bowring, *Memoirs of Bentham*, p. 34.

stories, and his simplicity; 'he was kind, and gentle, hating strife'.[1]

These were qualities especially strong in Cowper himself, and which he always sought in other people. He loved 'Vinny' Bourne for similar reasons. Bourne was his master after he had crossed to the far side of the curtain, to the fifth form. 'He was so good-natured', Cowper later wrote to his friend Unwin, 'and so indolent, that I lost more than I got by him; for he made me as idle as himself. He was such a sloven, as if he had trusted to his genius as a cloak for every thing that could disgust you in his person.' The boys continually took advantage of Bourne's good nature. Cowper recalled the pathetically funny scene when Lord March 'set fire to his greasy locks' and boxed his ears to put the fire out again. Bourne's own humour was 'entirely original', and in all his drollery there was a 'mixture of rational, and even religious reflection at times'. There was the 'pleasantry, good-nature, and humanity' which was in Cowper himself, and both had as a chief joy to be 'always entertaining, and yet always harmless'. In the purest happiness of recollection Cowper could compare Bourne with Ovid and Tibullus and find Vinny's ballads 'infinitely surpassing'.[2] His excellence as poet was not so much in the elegance of his Latinity, though that was admirable— 'most classical, and at the same time, most English, of the Latinists', Lamb said[3]—but in his 'genial optimism and homely touches of quiet pathos. He had quick sympathy for his fellow-men and loving tenderness towards all domestic animals.'[4] These words of A. H. Bullen might as well have been written about the student as the master. And one would almost think that Charles Lamb, so much

---

[1] Hayley (1803), II, 386; 'Translation of the Verses to the Memory of Dr. Lloyd' and 'Another Version': Poems, pp. 561–2.

[2] Letters, I, 310–11. See also, II, 92; III, 332.

[3] Charles Lamb, 'A Complaint of the Decay of Beggars in the Metropolis', The Essays of Elia.　　　　　　　　　　　　[4] A. H. Bullen, D.N.B.: Bourne.

like Cowper, had Cowper in mind as well as Wordsworth, when he wrote: 'What a heart that man [Bourne] had, all laid out upon town scenes, a proper counterpoise to *some people's* rural extravaganzas. . .what a sweet unpretending, pretty-mannered *matter-ful* creature, sucking from every flower, making a flower of every thing' (to Wordsworth, 7 April 1815).[1]

But formal schooling was not to be had from Lloyd and Bourne. Sargeaunt, the historian of Westminster, has said that there was no period in the history of the school 'when less knowledge was imparted, and few when more was acquired'.[2] The excess of freedom resulted sometimes in barbaric treatment by boy to boy; but also in single and co-operative reading and writing such as Cowper's study of Homer with Dick Sutton, Cumberland's translations of the Georgics, and Colman's early poems. These private studies of the boys were encouraged and supervised by the Head Master, John Nicoll. It was his principle, said Cumberland, 'to cherish every spark of genius, which he could discover in his scholars'. He 'seemed determined so to exercise his authority, that our best motives for obeying him should spring from the affection, that we entertained for him'. He was the Head Master, rare at the time, who knew when to spare the rod. He could win the love of the culprit, as he did of Cumberland, after misbehaviour: 'the offence was highly reprehensible, and when my turn came to be called up to the master, I presume he saw my contrition, when, turning a mild look upon me, he said aloud—*Erubuit, salva est res,*—and sent me back to my seat.'[3] Cowper years afterwards could remember Nicoll's comments: 'habit has endued me with that sort of fortitude which I remember my old schoolmaster Dr. Nicol used to call the passive valour

---

[1] Charles and Mary Lamb, *Letters*, ed. E. V. Lucas (New Haven, 1935), II, 154.
[2] *Annals of Westminster School*, p. 175.
[3] Cumberland, *Memoirs*, pp. 52–4. Terence, *Adelphoe*, 643.

of an ass'. Cowper recalled his Head Master with respect, even in his most captious Evangelical period, because of the pains he had taken with the boys in preparing them for confirmation. 'I believe most of us were struck by his manner, and affected by his exhortation. For my own part, I then, for the first time, attempted prayer in secret.'[1]

The classics were the basis of Westminster study; they were in fact almost the only education offered at the public schools until the nineteenth century.[2] This meant that in the classroom the boys learned the rules of Latin and Greek by heart, and large portions of Cicero, Horace, Virgil, Ovid, Terence, Tibullus, Propertius, Ausonius, and Aesop. They wrote Latin verses. They memorized the dates of ancient history, as modern boys do those of modern history. If Cowper had come to Orwell's Crossgates in 1911, in this respect he would not have found a very considerable change. 'I recall positive orgies of dates,' Orwell wrote, 'with the keener boys leaping up and down in their places in their eagerness to shout out the right answers, and at the same time not feeling the faintest interest in the meaning of the mysterious events they were naming.

"1587?"
"Massacre of St Bartholomew!"[3]
"1707?"
"Death of Aurangzeeb!"'[4]

Substitute 431 and 331 B.C. and you have a picture of Westminster in the 1740's.

At too early an age the boys were taught to construe the classics, and were weary of them before their minds were able to comprehend their meaning. This was Cowper's

[1] *Letters*, III, 341; Cowper's *Memoir*, p. 6.
[2] Mack, *op. cit.* p. 26. Frederick Reynolds, at Westminster 1776–81, wrote: 'Latin, Latin—Greek, Greek, and the measurement of verses were our sole themes, morning, noon, and night.' *The Life and Times of Frederick Reynolds* (London, 1826), I, 53.
[3] Orwell seems to have lost some of his own early keenness here: the date is 1572.
[4] George Orwell, *Such, Such Were the Joys* (New York, 1953), p. 21.

belief. He wrote to Unwin: if they begin 'Latin and Greek at eight, or even at nine years of age, it is surely soon enough. Seven years, the usual allowance for those acquisitions, are more than sufficient for the purpose'.[1] His schoolbooks were of the preceding century or earlier, and the grammars were still filled with hair-splitting dissections and classifications. Nevertheless, William found Busby's Grammars 'compendious and perspicuous' after the tortures of his introduction to Latin in Lyly. On the whole he believed that the matter and method of a Westminster education was satisfactory, and later even claimed it to be the best he had observed.[2]

It was with a formal knowledge of the ancient languages that Cowper would leave Westminster. This was the official legacy of the school. 'Tolerably furnished with grammatical knowledge', he said. Or, what was really closer to the truth, he went down a typical Westminster-classical snob. At eighteen he 'valued a man according to his proficiency and taste in classical literature, and had the meanest opinion of all other accomplishments unaccompanied by that'.[3] He had been head of his house and third in the sixth form.[4] But he soon found that there were 'other attainments which would carry a man more handsomely through life than a mere knowledge of what Homer and Virgil had left behind them. In measure, as my attachment to these gentry wore off, I found a more welcome reception among those whose acquaintance it was more my interest to cultivate.'[5] These were the literati, but that story comes later.

[1] *Letters*, 1, 236.

[2] In the Forster Library, South Kensington Mus. (48. D. 10), is a 'singularly beautiful' (note by Dawson Turner on end-leaf) MS. treatise on logic in Latin which Cowper had at Westminster. The calligraphy is the kind of black-letter 'usually called Church-text'. Compendium [*black-letter*] | LOGICÆ | Conimbricensis [*black-letter*] | TRADITVM | Sapientissimo, et re-[*black-letter*] | VERENDISSIMO | P. Francisco d Amaral [*black-letter*] | Societatis [*black-letter*]. | JESV. | Anno Domini. 1625. *Letters*, 1, 491-2: 'I am no friend to Lily's [*sic*] Grammar'; also 1, 137.

[3] Cowper's *Memoir*, p. 8; *Letters*, 1, 271.

[4] Tanner, *Westminster School* (1951), p. 50.   [5] *Letters*, 1, 271.

Honours came to him while in the school. The desire for prizes, engrained in every English schoolboy's heart, was in his also. In 'Tirocinium' he would blast the scholars' emulous desire for prizes:

> Each vainly magnifies his own success,
> Resents his fellow's, wishes it were less,...
> And labours to surpass him day and night,
> Less for improvement than to tickle spite.[1]

But on a different day—light and dark are never far apart in Cowper, and what he sternly warns against he can also visualize in golden warmth—he would dream that he was still in the sixth form, in high favour with his master, receiving a silver groat. He saw his exercise pass 'from form to form, for the admiration of all who were able to understand it'. The grandeur of the sixth form—'a period of life', he wrote, 'in which, if I had never tasted true happiness, I was at least equally unacquainted with its contrary'.[2]

> At Westminster, where little poets strive
> To set a distich upon six and five,
> Where discipline helps op'ning buds of sense,
> And makes his pupils proud with silver pence
> I was a poet too.[3]

Obviously, at Westminster all the glory did not go to the athletes. There was in the school, Cumberland said, 'a kind of taste and character, peculiar to itself, and handed down perhaps from times long past, which seems to mark it out for a distinction, that it may indisputably claim, that of having been above all others the most favoured cradle of the Muses'.[4] Many of the famous in English literature had been there: Udall, Hakluyt, Camden, King, Jonson, Herbert, Cowley, Locke, Dryden, Prior, Rowe.

Besides, some of the athletic distinctions were Cowper's.

---

[1] 'Tirocinium', ll. 476–81. [2] *Letters*, III, 80–1.
[3] 'Table Talk', ll. 506–10. [4] Cumberland, *Memoirs*, p. 57.

As an Under-School boy he played the games of the two Yards. He pitched and drove the ball, which was good preparation for the games at which he later excelled, cricket and football. Cricket had just then emerged at both Eton and Westminster as a serious sport. By 1744 the King's Scholars and the Town Boys of Westminster had definite places for their games in Tothill Fields, and their annual match was one of the chief events of the cricketing season. But one sport important to the English gentry was not appreciated by Cowper, and never would be; that was horsemanship. 'If all men were of my mind,' he said, 'there would be an end of all jockeyship for ever.'[1] And so the story that inspired 'John Gilpin' was especially appealing; Cowper to an unusual extent experienced sympathetically John's ludicrous situation.

When he was not at games or scribbling poetry or reading Homer, he might be in his room caring for a smuggled pet. From his childhood Cowper was extraordinarily fond of animals. When Lady Hesketh visited him many years later, she reported that he had at one time five rabbits, three hares, two dogs, two guinea-pigs, two goldfinches, two canary birds, a magpie, a jay, a starling, and a squirrel.[2] At school he had to be content with one tame mouse in his bureau-drawer. 'I kept it', he said, 'till it produced six young ones, and my transports when I first discovered them cannot easily be conceived,—any more than my mortification, when going to visit my little family, I found that mouse herself had eaten them! I turned her loose, in indignation, and vowed never to keep a mouse again.'[3]

He was not, however, one disposed to stay inside the boarding-house. Close by was the Abbey, where the boys worshipped three times a week, and which was continually

---

[1] *Letters*, I, 314; Tanner, *Westminster School* (1951), pp. 122–3.
[2] *Early Poems*, p. 74.
[3] *Letters*, II, 448–9; *G.M.* LV, Pt ii (1785), 987.

fascinating to them. The hundreds of monuments and marvellous relics became a part of Cowper's daily life; most of the statues were fixed in his memory forever. Sometimes he prowled in the church-yard of St Margaret's beside the Abbey. Late one evening he watched a grave-digger at work and the sight of a freshly dug-up skull brought to him the knowledge of mortality. Other times he crossed the street to the House of Commons to join his school-fellows in listening to the debates. Here, according to ancient privilege, they sat in seats reserved for members of the school. Occasionally he would go off to see the sights of London. He and his friends could visit the treasures of the Tower, and, like Charles Lamb and the boys of Christ's Hospital forty years later, see the great curiosity of the city —the wild beasts kept inside the outer gate. In the spirit of the times he took a jaunt to Bedlam with others on holiday. He gazed with the throng at the 'poor captives' and was amused by their 'whimsical freaks'; not altogether insensible of their misery, yet entertained, and afterwards angry with himself for being so.[1]

In this way his idle time was spent. When the perennially lonely week-ends came, he was fortunate in having many relatives to visit in the city. And fortunate in being at a school where it had become the custom for the boys to go home, if that were possible, or stay with friends and relatives from Saturday to Monday.

He was happy at Westminster. This was in spite of occasional lowness of spirits and his fears of consumption. He kept these to himself, considering 'any bodily infirmity a disgrace, especially a consumption'. His attack of small-pox at twelve or thirteen must have added to these fears, for he was in imminent danger during the illness.[2] All his

[1] *Letters*, I, 150, 168–9; II, 116, 229; Cowper's *Memoir*, pp. 4–5; also Greatheed to Hayley, 26 Aug. 1800: Fitzwilliam MSS. The name 'John Gilpin' may have been recalled by Cowper from a gravestone in the same church-yard: *Letters*, II, 16, n. 1.
[2] Cowper's *Memoir*, pp. 5–7.

life he was subject to inflammation of the eyes, but before he had the smallpox he had 'specks' on both eyes which threatened to cover them. After this severe illness the spots were completely removed, though the inflammation continued to plague him.[1] In later years the irritation caused his eyes to be almost constantly bloodshot, which made his 'wild and piercing' eyes the dominant feature of his face.[2]

He was comfortable at Westminster notwithstanding the miseries of the fagging system. That is to say, he was relatively comfortable or mainly happy. 'No one', George Orwell has said, 'can look back on his schooldays and say with truth that they were altogether unhappy.' Nor altogether happy. It is a difficult thing to penetrate the miasma or the rose-coloured mists that surround most recollections of schooldays, then and now. Cowper himself tried to cut through the false haze which characterizes the stories of school told by fathers to sons.

> Be it a weakness, it deserves some praise;
> We love the play-place of our early days.[3]

He lightly ridiculed the Old Boys' sentimentality. Yet this same romanticism appears again and again in the references to Westminster which are scattered through Cowper's letters. His attitude towards the school is revealed in two quite different ways: as the Evangelical moralist of Huntingdon who condemned the school for keeping the boys ignorant in all points of religion—an attitude which was expanded in a more benevolent and also a more satiric fashion in the three letters on education to Unwin and in 'Tirocinium';[4] and as the letter-writer by the fireside, relishing a choice anecdote of youthful humour.

---

[1] Hayley (1803), I, 7–8.
[2] Anonymous review of Greatheed's *Sermon on Cowper*: *Anti-Jacobin Rev.* VIII (1801), 272. There was some improvement in Cowper's vision in 1782: *Letters*, II, 24, 34.
[3] 'Tirocinium', ll. 296–7; see also ll. 290–340.
[4] Cowper's *Memoir*, p. 8, and to Unwin, 7 and 17 Sept., 5 Oct. 1780: *Letters*, I, 234–42.

His strongest criticism, and a little of his kindliest, occurs in 'Tirocinium'. The evils he portrays there form an important part of a true picture of the public schools in the eighteenth century. 'The whole poem is worth the attention of the student of social history', Trevelyan writes.[1] In a school full of young peers one might expect to find the sins peculiar to the aristocracy. Here was the excessive self-indulgence and dissipation of the young rakes; haunting of taverns, gambling, visits to harlots.

> Would you your son should be a sot or dunce,
> Lascivious, headstrong; or all these at once?

Send him to a public school then, Cowper said. His model in virtue will be the 'waiter Dick, with Bacchanalian lays', or the strong, handsome, swaggering School Captain, hero of a hundred wild escapades.[2] What made matters worse, these same boys were to mould their own and their fellow-students' education. Owing to the small number of masters and the failure of these few to exercise discipline, education was what the student body made it, what the boys gave to boys or what the boys learned from struggling against obstacles placed by other boys. The individual could remain an individual if he could withstand the slavish following of custom by the herd, and the capricious behaviour of the powerful. Cruelty and bullying 'were almost universal occurrences at all the schools', says Mack, the principal historian of the school system.[3] The 'horrid despotism' of Westminster boys enraged Bentham whenever he thought of the school. Oppression was everywhere, he said; it could not be escaped.[4]

It was no wonder then that pious parents cautioned one

---

[1] G. M. Trevelyan, *English Social History* (New York, 1942), p. 520, n. 4.
[2] 'Tirocinium', ll. 201–2; see ll. 201–90; also A. S. Turberville, *The House of Lords in the Eighteenth Century* (Oxford, 1927), p. 431.
[3] Mack, pp. 42–3.
[4] *Memoirs of Bentham*, p. 34.

another against sending their sons to the public schools. Almost all of the Evangelicals were opposed to them. Hannah More accepted their training in the classics, but urged that the boys remain at home to protect them from the evils which were the result of too much freedom.[1] When Martin Madan, William Cowper's cousin, told Henry Venn to send his son John to Westminster, Henry replied: 'I know too well the state of the scholars there ever upon any worldly consideration to have him amongst them.'[2] Parson Adams, hardly a member of the Evangelical party, said to Joseph Andrews: 'I have found it; I have discovered the cause of all the misfortunes which befell him [Mr Wilson]: a public school.... Public schools are the nurseries of all vice and immorality. All the wicked fellows whom I remember at the university, were bred at them....they called them King's Scholars, I forget why—very wicked fellows! Joseph, you may thank the Lord you were not bred at a public school.'

The Evangelicals objected to the public schools first of all because of the abatement of confidence and intimacy between the boys and their parents to which their education almost necessarily led.[3] This was also Cowper's feeling: from the moment in which a boy goes to boarding-school, he becomes a stranger in his father's house, and each year he grows more detached from his family. Absence will chill his love into respect. He becomes bashful with older people, especially with women, whom he scarcely knows except as maids. How is he to catch the love of virtue, the love of holiness, when the schools have given up the teaching of religion?[4]

---

[1] See M. G. Jones, *Hannah More* (Cambridge, 1952), p. 220; L. E. Elliott-Binns, *The Early Evangelicals* (London, 1953), p. 67.

[2] Henry Venn to James Kershaw, c. 1770: John Venn, *Annals of a Clerical Family* (London, 1904), p. 113.

[3] 'Memoir of Henry Thornton', L. M. Forster's Copybook, p. 11: Forster MSS.

[4] *Letters*, I, 237–41; 'Tirocinium', ll. 563–90.

Cowper in this criticism moved from the particular faults of his own time to the everlasting sores in the public-school system. The public schools train men for a world of public-school men, of upper-class Englishmen. They therefore frequently enter a world beyond Westminster or Eton of a variation and a complexity for which they are wholly unprepared. Today, Mr E. M. Forster writes: 'They go forth into it with well-developed bodies, fairly developed minds, and undeveloped hearts.... An undeveloped heart —not a cold one.'[1] Men before Cowper, notably Locke and Steele, had attacked the superficiality of the public schools, but had never moved the public conscience to any considerable extent. Nor had the subtler evils and uglinesses previously been shown with similar effect. Gibbon pontificated: 'I shall always be ready to joyn in the common opinion, that our public schools, which have produced so many eminent characters, are the best adapted to the Genius and constitution of the English people.'[2] But after Cowper's day not many men of letters endorse the system whole-heartedly. The Gibbons of English school-memoirs are few.

As the published personal memoirs become more personal, they reinforce Cowper's description of school life. His story can no longer be seen as it once was: that of a morbidly sensitive Evangelical. The pathos of his story of the school at Markyate Street was not excessive. In 1786 Frederick Reynolds, aged eleven, wrote home after his first day and night at Westminster—'after suffering the several torments of every...species of manual wit':

---

[1] E. M. Forster, 'Notes on the English Character', *Abinger Harvest* (London, 1936), p. 5.
[2] Edward Gibbon, *The Autobiographies*, ed. John Murray (London, 1896), p. 51. Gibbon was at school (Jan. 1748–Aug. 1750) with Cowper, but probably never knew him. He had much to say about the advantages of the public schools, but little to show whether he himself was happy or unhappy while he attended one. D. M. Low, 'Introduction', *Gibbon's Journal to January 28th, 1763* (London, 1929), pp. xlii and xliv, n. 3.

My dear, dear Mother,

If you don't let me come home, I die—I am all over ink, and my fine clothes have been spoilt—I have been tost in a blanket, and seen a ghost.

I remain my dear, dear mother,
Your dutiful, and most unhappy son,

FREDDY.

P.S. Remember me to my father.[1]

For some, life became a game of how to escape—a flogging from the master, or a drubbing from the boys. Philip Thicknesse's *Memoirs* contain tales of horror at Westminster. To his dying day he could show marks on his hands from the elegant sadist, 'that truly beautiful nobleman the present Earl of—'. The marks were earned in order to pay for candles for light by exposing the backs of his hands to 'a yard and a half of doubled wax candle, at so *much a* cut'.[2] Anthony Trollope a century later spoke of his 'daily purgatory' at Harrow. It was by the masters' ferules that he knew them. 'How well I remember all the agonies of my young heart; how I considered whether I should always be alone; whether I could not find my way up to the top of that college tower, and from thence put an end to everything?'[3] Always in fear, yet always afraid to be a sneak: it was again and again like Cowper and the bully at the school in Bedfordshire. Or like David Copperfield and his schoolfellows. When Steerforth said there was nothing of the sneak in Traddles, they felt that to be high praise.

Brutality, barbarism; the beauty of the holy service; the desperate scramble to be the best, to be successful; the flashy learning and the pompous teaching; the squalor behind every crook of the ancient buildings; the constant

---

[1] Frederick Reynolds, *The Life and Times*, I, 59; see also I, 52–112.
[2] Philip Thicknesse, *Memoirs and Anecdotes* ([London], 1788), I, 14; at Westminster c. 1730.
[3] Trollope, *An Autobiography* (Edinburgh and London, 1883), I, 5, 13, 24.

misery of being dirty, of being uncared for and too small to know how to care for oneself; the crowded rooms, the noise in the boarding-house; the dirty-handkerchief side of life (the phrase is Orwell's) in the eternal winter; and, though Cowper would not have mentioned it, the spectre of sex. All codes of behaviour were at cross-purposes. How could one reconcile 'the extremes of Biblical injunction and common practice'? 'Be a sport' was the answer;[1] the fiat of the public schools.

This is old stuff in the twentieth century. We know all about the terrors before Arnold; if we are open-minded we admit a few of the problems in the life as it goes on in the schools today. Graham Greene has collected a whole volume of 'Essays by Divers Hands', *The Old School*, and Auden, Bates, Miss Benson, Miss Bowen, Hartley, Nicolson, Spender, and their contemporaries have contributed. Salinger writes of similar schools in America; and Orwell leaves an essay on schooldays, 'Such, Such Were the Joys', posthumously printed, which is perhaps the most penetrating autobiographical study of them all. We have now come to expect affliction rather than happiness in the life of the sensitive student at a boarding-school. But Cowper had more joy than sorrow at Westminster, far more. His criticism of the public schools is explicable without supposing that he was a victim of all he described, and was consequently miserable most of the time.[2] But would he have willingly gone back to Westminster, or sent a son there? No. 'Your boys will do admirably well without Westminster', he told his old school-fellow Bagot in 1789. 'It is a place, where—Effugere est triumphus.'[3] Cowper's criticism in 'Tirocinium' was important, for the seeds of change it sowed came to life after his death in the reforms of Arnold.

---

[1] See Rumer Godden, 'The Little Fishes', *New Yorker*, 18 Sept. 1954, p. 82.
[2] See Leslie Stephen, *D.N.B.*: Cowper.
[3] To Walter Bagot, 29 Jan. 1789: Morgan MSS. MA 86, vol. i, f. 25.

He originated a tendency for reform. The greatest authority on the public schools and British opinion writes: 'Cowper was looked back on, even late in the nineteenth century, as the father of moral criticism, as proved by the necessity that so many defenders have felt of answering his arguments.'[1]

---

[1] Mack, p. 67. After Mack's 'Prologue: 1382–1780', his first section of the book is called 'From Cowper to Arnold'.

III

THE BOYS

Boys are at best but pretty buds unblown,
Whose scent and hues are rather guess'd than known;
Each dreams that each is just what he appears,
But learns his error in maturer years,
When disposition, like a sail unfurl'd,
Shows all its rents and patches to the world.

'Tirocinium', ll. 446–51

Connections formed at school are said to be lasting, and often beneficial.... For my own part, I found such friendships, though warm enough in their commencement, surprisingly liable to extinction; and of seven or eight, whom I had selected for intimates out of about three hundred, in ten years time not one was left me.

COWPER to UNWIN, 5 October 1780

WHEN Cowper left London in 1763 and became a convert to the Evangelical group, he left also his youthful friendships—all except one or two. The decision was clearly according to his own choice and his new beliefs. Separation from the world was a primary rule of the Christian life for him and for his fellow Evangelicals. They were of the Lord's and St Paul's calling, and obeyed their command: 'Be ye not unequally yoked together with unbelievers: for what fellowship hath righteousness with unrighteousness? and what communion hath light with darkness?... Wherefore come out from among them, and be ye separate.' And had the injunction to separation not seemed so sharply drawn, Cowper would nonetheless have given up these old friends because he feared his 'enthusiasm' would irk them. As the years passed by, however, he fretted more and more that he had been forgotten by all who had formerly known him. He grew quite irritated at the loss of two who had been especially close: George Colman of Westminster School and Edward Thurlow of Mr Chapman's (where he and Cowper had first learned law together). As Cowper's enthusiasm became milder, the desire for some of the old friendships grew stronger. When the subscription list for his *Homer* was circulated (1785), he wrote to all his quondam friends still living, asking their assistance. Five years later he said: 'I cannot help considering my subscription as a sort of test of their constancy who formerly professed a kindness for me. They in whom a spark of that kindness survives will hardly fail to discover it on such an occasion, and seeing the affair in this light, I feel myself a little grieved and hurt that some names, which old friendship gave me a right to expect, are not to be found in my catalogue.'[1]

He was nevertheless overjoyed to find a considerable number of people out of his past. Among them was the Hon. Sir William Ashhurst, from whom he had purchased his chambers in the Inner Temple, and Francis Annesley, another member of the same Inn. The benevolent Annesley, eldest son of the Rev. Dr Martin Annesley of Buckleberry, Berkshire, had come to the Temple in 1753. He was a young man of learning and taste, and like Cowper, his interest was chiefly in the classics. Both were also similar in their gentle manners and quiet kindness. Annesley was devoutly religious—and an intellectual Christian—which must have been an inspiration to Cowper, then a more worldly templar, and a troubled and doubtful believer. Even as a young man Annesley was able to hold in delicate balance, his contemporaries said, the urbanities of society with Christian morality and charity.[2] For thirty-two years he was to be M.P. for Reading, and he was also in later life the hereditary Cottonian Trustee of the British Museum and the first Master of Downing College, Cambridge. He

---

[1] *Letters*, III, 486.
[2] *G.M.* LXXXII, Pt i (1812), 491–2.

37

remained through all these years a collector of rare editions of the classics, fine etchings, prints, and pictures.

There was Mathew Robert Arnott, who took Cowper's place as Clerk of the Committees in 1763, and William Buller, youngest son of John Francis Buller, M.P., of Cornwall, who was Dean of Canterbury when Cowper published his *Homer* and would later become Bishop of Exeter. He was four years younger than Cowper when they were at Westminster, but during their six years there together they may have grown to know each other well. And there were the Old Westminsters Assheton Curzon, who would later be first Viscount Curzon, and Henry Digby (brother of Edward, Baron Digby, also a school-fellow of Cowper), who would one day be first Earl Digby. In 1744 Henry and William Cowper were in the third form together, and in 1748 in the sixth.[1] Both Curzon and Digby were later M.P.'s, as were two other school-fellows, William Selwyn, and Sir Richard Hill, whose fame came not, however, in politics, but in Calvinistic Methodism—in his support of Whitefield and his attack on Oxford for expelling Methodist undergraduates. In the description of schooldays, Richard Hill's *Narrative* of his early life reads very much like Cowper's *Memoir*.[2] Both boys had transitory moments when they had 'a taste of the love of God'—moments which they longed to prolong, but which were given up for schoolboys' follies. Hill, like Cowper, had at Westminster 'several superficial repentances and resolutions'. Both tell of youthful doubts—'horrible doubts concerning the very fundamentals of religion' (Hill), 'doubt whether the gospel were true or false' (Cowper)—and each tried every means of turning his thoughts from within himself. Their autobiographies reveal remarkable parallels; they might have

---

[1] 'Westminster School Lists': Westminster MSS.
[2] Edwin Sidney, *The Life of Sir Richard Hill* (London, 1839), pp. 15–18; Cowper's *Memoir*, pp. 1–12.

been a special comfort to one another, but apparently they were acquaintances only, not intimate friends.

There were also Richard Levett, who would become a Buckinghamshire vicar, and the insolent, drunken Hon. Frederick Vane ('whom I also well remember', said Cowper in 1786).[1] He was the son of the Earl of Darlington (the patron of Christopher Smart) and brother of Anne, Smart's first love. Vane followed the Westminster tradition as an M.P. Between 1734 and 1833 the school sent 544 men into the House of Commons; it was second only to Eton (785 M.P.'s in this period), and far above the other schools (third, Harrow, with 270; fourth, Winchester, with 70). Westminster's great year was 1761, when at the general election 111 Old Westminsters entered the Lower House.[2]

There were names of others who had drifted in and out of Cowper's life from London days to the time he gathered his subscribers. Lord Dartmouth was one, of whom Cowper said he could never charge him with 'want of warmth in his friendship'. He had sat beside Cowper in the sixth form, and would become the 'one who wears a coronet, and prays' of Cowper's 'Truth'.[3] He was in later life the friend of Cowper's friend John Newton, as well as of George III, who was greatly attached to him. A pious man, Dartmouth centred his life in the Methodist cause rather than the House of Lords, where he spoke rarely. He showed no administrative capacity in his many important posts in the government at home, yet fathered Eleazar Wheelock's and America's Dartmouth College.

In the subscription-list are the Bagots, a crowd of Bagots, just as there were at school. 'All five my schoolfellows', Cowper said, 'and very amiable and valuable boys they were.'[4] And all were poetically inclined. They came from

---

[1] To Walter Bagot, 23 Jan. 1786: Morgan MSS. MA 86, vol. i, f. 7.
[2] Gerrit P. Judd, iv, *Members of Parliament: 1734–1832* (New Haven, 1955), pp. 37–9.
[3] William Legge (1731–1801), 2nd E. of Dartmouth (1750). *Letters*, ii, 438–9; ii, 17; 'Truth', l. 378.   [4] *Letters*, ii, 284.

Staffordshire, from Bagots Bromley where they had been lords of the manor since 1066. The 12,000 acres of park there remained as in the days of the Conquest: no cultivation had been carried on. Deer and a flock of wild goats roamed beneath the enormous oaks. In the house, until the twentieth century, a drum announced the meals according to ancient family custom. And when they went to school, the Bagot boys arrived preceded by a servant blowing a horn.[1]

William—second son of Sir Walter Wagstaffe Bagot, Bart., who had married Lady Barbara Legge, the aunt of William Legge, Lord Dartmouth—had been the first of the five to come to Westminster. After many years as M.P. for Staffordshire (1754–80) he was created Baron Bagot. Forty years after he had left Westminster Cowper could clearly recollect William Bagot, and Bagot's excellent reputation at the school for English and Latin compositions, and his brilliance in the House of Commons, where Cowper had heard him speak. But he was not personally known to his Lordship. With William had come his brother the witty Charles, who assumed the name of Chester in 1755. Cowper and Charles were of similar temperament: both were 'obumbrated by the boughs of Retirement' and rarely conversed with the world. When Cowper saw Charles in the 1780's, after an absence of many years, he had, to Cowper's great delight, 'now and then, the very look that he had when he was a boy; and when I see it', Cowper said, 'I seem to be a boy myself, and entirely forget for a short moment the years that have intervened since I was one. The look that I mean is...when in a laugh he shuts his eyes quite close and draws his chin into his bosom. Then we are at Westminster again.'[2] Cowper could often enjoy the

---

[1] Sophy Louisa Bagot, *Links with the Past* (London, 1901), pp. 129–30, 186, 190, 247.
[2] *Letters*, III, 202–3; and to Walter Bagot, 27 Dec. 1785, 19 March 1788, 25 Oct. 1791: Morgan MSS. MA 86, vol. I, ff. 5, 19, 38.

laughter, for the 'companionable and domestic' Charles Chester lived only four miles from Olney at Chicheley.[1]

Later there had come as a schoolboy, Richard—whom William Cowper would always remember most perfectly— with 'his light-brown short curling hair, his round plump face, and the smile that seldom deserted it'. Cowper and he had been form fellows, and they had learned to make nonsense verses together.[2] No wonder they remembered each other when one had become celebrated as a poet. The two were reunited in 1788, and Cowper found with pleasure that the face which he recalled so particularly, had during forty years changed less than that of any of his friends.[3]

After Richard there was Lewis: placid, sensitive, and pious. He would become Dean of Christ Church, Oxford, and Bishop successively of Bristol, Norwich, and St Asaph. Like his brothers he was then a poet;[4] but best of all, he became one of the few bishops of whom Cowper in later life could approve. Not only approve—he was a man after Cowper's own heart: 'at once the most holy and most agreeable of men'.[5] Cowper wrote that Lewis was possessed of 'the happiest mixture of spiritual authority, the meekness of a Christian, and the good manners of a gentleman'. A good man and peaceable, whose 'views of the Person and of the Office of Christ, of his Kingdom, of its Origin, of its progress, and of the universality of its ordain'd extent, in short of the whole End and purpose of his Mission, are to a point, my own'.[6]

[1] *Letters*, II, 391, 395; III, 270; in 1793 Cowper wrote an 'Epitaph on Mr. Chester, of Chicheley': *Poems*, p. 420.
[2] To Walter Bagot, 23 Jan. 1786: Morgan MSS. MA 86, vol. I, f. 7; and from Walter Bagot to Cowper, 17 Jan. 1786: vol. II, f. 5.
[3] *Letters*, III, 326.
[4] Some of Lewis Bagot's poems are publ. in Nichols, *Poems*, VIII, 179–85.
[5] Sophy Bagot, p. 195.
[6] *Letters*, II, 284–5, 381–2; III, 470–1; and to Walter Bagot, 27 Dec. 1785: Morgan MSS. MA 86, vol. I, f. 5.

Most important to Cowper, with the two older Bagots there came to the school Walter, Cowper's dear friend Watty. He became widely known after his death as one of Cowper's correspondents. They were 'much intimate' at Westminster, but drifted apart soon afterwards, with only two visits in the years 1750–80. Once Cowper went to visit him at Christ Church, Oxford; once Walter called on him in the Temple. Walter, like his brothers, wrote and published poetry in his youth,[1] and until his death, while he held the family livings of Blithfield and Leigh in Staffordshire, he retained his love of scholarship. He spent hours of every day in reading—especially the classics. As scholar and divine, he much prized his Polyglot Bible. 'His divinity was of the old school', his daughter said; 'untouched with enthusiasm, unperverted by party.' He was very much like Cowper, in his taste, and in his simple, amiable, gentle manners, and with a similar relish for humour. In his youth Walter had been a handsome boy and a slovenly dresser; a good rider (unlike William Cowper), a bold hunter, a superlative fly-fisher. Had he been dressed in rags, however, it was said there would still have been something in him to show the world he was a gentleman.[2]

With the Bagots Cowper had fellowship in one of the oldest and finest families in the land—with five boys who reinforced his interests in poetry and humour, in religion, in sport, and the whole life of a country gentleman. Dick Sutton was another school friend of homogeneous background and interests. He and Cowper moved through Westminster together, always in the same form. Dick was

---

[1] He contributed some Alcaic verses to the Oxford poems on the death of Frederick, Prince of Wales, in 1751.

[2] 'He is the cheerfullest creature I almost ever met with, & I am laughing with him for ever': John Johnson to Hayley, 8 June 1805: Fitzwilliam MSS. Also *Letters*, II, 391; Sophy Bagot, pp. 193–4; Joseph Welch [and C. B. Phillimore], *The List of the Queen's Scholars of St Peter's College, Westminster* (London, 1852), p. 352.

usually at the head of his class—in 1744 in the third form he was second; in 1749 in the sixth, he was first. Sutton and Cowper during the school years read through the *Iliad* and the *Odyssey* together—which should have been bond enough to keep them close. But after Dick Sutton entered Trinity College, Cambridge, in January 1750, he saw Cowper only once. This was in spite of Sutton's admission to the Middle Temple in 1754, and his transfer to the Inner Temple in 1759, where he took chambers and was called to the bar. He was probably on the continent during most of 1754–59, and soon after that he was on circuit. In June 1755 William Mason wrote to Thomas Gray describing the entourage of Sutton and two Cambridge friends at Hanover: 'With Grooms, Dogs, Tutors & all.' After 1755 the vast difference in Cowper's and Sutton's incomes, and consequently their ways of life, would also have kept them apart. The Sutton family estates were so large that when Richard died his grandson (who inherited the property) was considered one of the wealthiest men in England. He could do everything *en prince*—for example, spend upwards of £300,000 in pursuit of fox-hunting, in which he had no equal.[1]

Richard Sutton was the son of the Rt Hon. Sir Robert Sutton, K.B., sometime Ambassador to Constantinople, the Hague, and Paris. His father died in 1746 while Dick and Will Cowper were at school. Sir Robert's career had been a moderately distinguished one, as Ambassador, and as M.P. for Nottingham after 1722. But his life, and his wife's and children's lives, were marred by the scandal of the Charitable Corporation in 1732. He was one of the three directors of the company who were expelled from the House

---

[1] 'Westminster School Lists: 1744–53', ff. 86, 146: Westminster MSS.; *Letters*, II, 420–1; *Mid. Temp. Reg.* I, 347; *Inner Temp. Rec.* v, 106, 110, 112, 193, 385, 390, 421, 432; 'Chamber Book', f. 83: I.T. MSS.; William Warburton, *Letters from a Late Eminent Prelate*, ed. Richard Hurd (Kidderminster, [1809]), p. 239; Gray's *Corr.* I, 425; G.E.C. v, 162; *D.N.B.*: Sir Richard Sutton, 2nd Bt (1798–1855).

of Commons in May of that year. Sir Robert, however, does not seem to have been immediately concerned in the embezzlements of the other directors. He was guilty, Sir Paul Methuen and Henry Pelham told the House, 'of the grossest neglect in the world in suffering rogues to cheat the poor proprietors', but it was neglect only; there was no 'imputation of corruption' or 'wilful fraud'. Nevertheless the shame of the Privy Councillor Sir Robert, after the public horror and antagonism, was so great that he attempted to shoot himself.[1] And his name went down in history as a symbol of neglect:

> *Perhaps* you think the Poor might have their part?. . .
> 'God cannot love (says Blunt, with lifted eyes)
> 'The wretch he starves'—and piously denies:
> But rev'rend S[utt]on, with a softer air,
> Admits, and leaves them, Providence's care.

So wrote Pope, and even William Cowper's Uncle Ashley, in his paltry poetical way, named Sutton as the symbol of the scandal and as 'the Orphan's curse'.[2]

Pope's friend William Warburton had his living at Brand-Broughton, Lincolnshire, through the patronage of Sir Robert Sutton. Here Warburton spent the best part of his life, at leisure to study and write as much as he pleased. Here young Richard grew up, and returned each vacation from Westminster. And would come back to school, presumably, with anecdotes for his friend Cowper, about Warburton, Pope, and Sir Robert's friend Arbuthnot. There is every reason to suspect that Warburton wrote the

---

[1] John Percival, 1st E. of Egmont, *Diary*, Hist. MSS. Comm.: Egmont MSS. (1920), I, 262, 267–8; *Historical Register*, XVII (1732), 108–24, 220–32, 255–81, and especially p. 273.
[2] Pope, 'Epistle to Bathurst', ll. 101, 105–8. Pope also criticizes Sutton in 'Epilogue to the Satires. Written in 1738. Dialogue I', l. 16, and in the MS. of the *Essay on Man*, after l. 220 as publ.: Pope's *Works*, ed. Elwin and Courthope (London, 1871), II, 393. [Ashley Cowper], 'A Soliloquy' (written in 1733), *Poems and Translations* (London, 1767), p. 124.

anonymously published *An Apology for Sir Robert Sutton* (London, 1733) to defend his patron after the scandal. He had extravagantly praised Sutton in his first publication (1723), and again in the dedication to *A Critical and Philosophical Enquiry into the Causes of Prodigies and Miracles* (London, 1727).[1]

Sir Robert Sutton was a self-made man; that is, with the help of his relative Lord Lexington, and mercantile opportunities in the Levant. In that respect the families of Richard Sutton and Walter Bagot were dissimilar. There was no ancient tradition of land and wealth. Sir Robert's marriage to the Dowager Countess of Sunderland also helped him financially. John Spencer (afterwards first Earl Spencer), the grandson of the Countess of Sunderland's first husband, became her son Richard Sutton's closest friend. This same John Spencer was the son of Georgiana Carteret Spencer, who married in 1750 William, second Earl Cowper. And William Cowper of Berkhamsted also knew John Spencer, and his wife even better—'a sensible and discreet woman' —both in his youth and in his old age.[2] He dedicated his translation of the *Odyssey* to her.

Both John Spencer and Richard Sutton had lost their fathers in 1746, and Sutton's mother had died in 1749. The pattern of tragedy in the life of Richard Sutton would later be realized by his friend William Cowper. The Charitable-Corporation trouble had brought disgrace to the Suttons; the early deaths of his parents, the frequent and severe illnesses of his bashful and melancholy sister, the death of a younger brother (in 1743) who was probably insane or malformed, the perpetual alarm for an older brother who

---

[1] [Richard Hurd], *A Discourse, by Way of General Preface to...Warburton's Works* (London, 1794), p. 11; Warburton's letter to Pope, 1739: Hurd, pp. 143–6; and letter to Stukeley, 9 May 1732: Nichols, *Illustrations*, II, 14; A. W. Evans, *Warburton and the Warburtonians* (London, 1932), p. 28; see John Selby Watson, *The Life of William Warburton* (London, 1863), pp. 7–8, 17, 34; Nichols, *Anecdotes*, V, 533–42.
[2] *Letters*, I, 235; II, 71; IV, 6, 501.

had convulsive attacks[1]—all these calamities brought repeated grief to Dick Sutton. For Cowper there would come failure at the House of Lords in 1763; the suspicions at the same time about his relatives and their management of the various clerkships in the House of Lords; the early death of his mother; the death of his father while he was living in the Temple; the affecting death of his scholarly brother John. Will Cowper and Dick Sutton were more deeply related than school-fellowship could bring about, and through more than marriage-connections. They were friends through mutual experiences, and through a mutual love of literature and languages. When Sutton went up to Trinity in 1750, 'after having been long at the head of Westminster School', Warburton wrote to Richard Hurd:

> He is a perfect boy in the simplicity of his manners, but of surprising acquirements. Besides his knowledge of the ancient languages, he speaks and writes Spanish and French with great exactness, understands Italian and is now learning High-Dutch... he is the most extraordinary boy I ever knew. If you won't take my word, I will give you Dr. Nichols's who tells me he never met with his fellow.... He has an insatiable thirst after new languages. Pray check this in him. He wrote me word, the other day, he had a mind to study Arabic.[2]

Another former friend who returned at the time of the translation of Homer was Clotworthy Rowley, who, like Walter Bagot, brought a crowd of relatives with him. But these were not old friends—only Clotworthy, his 'familiar friend in the Temple'. They had been neighbours there, Cowper said, in the Inner Temple, where Rowley was admitted in 1750, and afterwards called to the bar.[3] He withdrew from the Temple in 1768, at which time he was called to the Irish bar. Then living in Dublin, he enjoyed

---

[1] Mary Granville Delany, *The Autobiography and Correspondence* (London, 1861–62), I, 4, 312–13, 344; II, 5–6, 168, 228, 447; III, 61, 91, 129, 285, 332, 438–9.
[2] *Letters from a Late Eminent Prelate*, pp. 38, 46, 55, 239.
[3] To Walter Bagot, 24 April 1788: Morgan MSS. MA 86, vol. I, f. 20; *Letters*, III, 231.

46

the patronage of a relative 'of very great property', Hercules Langford Rowley, M.P. Clotworthy himself later became M.P. for Downpatrick. He was the son of Sir William Rowley, K.B., Admiral of the Fleet, of Tendring Hall, Stoke by Nayland, Suffolk; a brother of Sir Joshua, who became Vice-Admiral of the White, and whose sons Bartholomew Samuel and Sir Charles became Vice-Admiral and Admiral respectively. Clotworthy's sons, Vice-Admiral Sir Josias, K.C.B., G.C.M.G., and Rear-Admiral Samuel Campbell Rowley, followed the distin-guished family tradition in the navy. Actually Samuel com-bined the family interests, politics and the sea, by taking his father's place as M.P. for Downpatrick while another brother William was M.P. for Kinsale. Clotworthy Rowley, unlike Sutton and Bagot of Cowper's Westminster days, was of a robust and unruly nature; he lived in accordance with the adventurous spirit of his family. Lascivious, Cowper said,[1] like many in their group in the Temple.

Rowley was an intimate friend of 'N. Wescomb, Esq; Langford', of the 'List of Subscribers' in Cowper's *Homer*. This was Nicholas Westcomb, with Rowley at Trinity Hall, Cambridge, and at the Inner Temple. He came originally from Markyate Street, Bedfordshire, and his family at that time also owned property in Berkhamsted (could he have known Cowper already in their earliest schooldays?). He, whom in youth they had called 'Cousin Westcomb', was a man who had always commanded Cowper's respect; Rowley would also feel his friend's esteem, but not until late in life.[2]

The names of two Old Westminsters, the closest of friends in youth and old age, Hastings and Impey, stood out on Cowper's list of 1791 and in the minds of all English-

---

[1] *Letters*, I, 15.
[2] Westcomb's father, William, is in 'A List of Owners of Land in Berkhamsted, Herts, 1755': B.M. Lansdowne MSS. 656, f. 22.; *Letters*, III, 486.

men of the time. In their youth both were most excellent scholars, and friendly competitors for the school's honours. Sir Elijah Impey (represented in the *Homer* by his brother Michael) was well known to Cowper at school,[1] and for Warren Hastings Cowper had even stronger affection. Great founders and symbols of British supremacy in India, and of imperial power, in 1791 they were in the midst of their monumental trial in Westminster Hall. When Hastings' trial began, Cowper, like most of his contemporaries, was outraged at what he supposed to be his and Sir Elijah's tyranny. He recommended that his cousin Lady Hesketh go to Westminster Hall,

for the sake of hearing and seeing what you will never have opportunity to see and hear hereafter,—the trial of a man who has been greater and more feared than the Mogul himself, and of his Myrmidon Sir Elijah. Whatever we are at home, we have certainly been Tyrants in the East; and if these men have, as they are charged, riotted in the miseries of the innocent, and dealt death to the guiltless with an unsparing hand, may they receive a retribution that shall make all future Governors and Judges of ours in those distant regions tremble! While I speak thus, I equally wish them acquitted. They were both my Schoolfellows, and for Hastings I had a particular value.

With what joy Cowper greeted the first signs of Hastings' vindication—in 1792, three years before the acquittal:

To Warren Hastings Esq.ʳ
By an old Schoolfellow of his at Westminster

Hastings! I knew thee young, and of a mind,
While young, humane, conversible and kind;
Nor can I well believe thee, gentle *then*,
Now grown a villain and the *worst* of men,
But rather some suspect, who have oppress'd
And worried thee, as not themselves the *Best*.[2]

---

[1] Elijah Barwell Impey, *Memoirs of Sir Elijah Impey* (London, 1846), p. 9.
[2] To Lady Hesketh, 16 Feb. 1788 and 5 May 1792: Panshanger Coll.

Here was Cowper's loyalty—proof against his own worried claims—

school-friendships are not always found,
Though fair in promise, permanent and sound.[1]

In the 'List of Subscribers' of 1791 Cowper found proof of his friends' loyalty to him. These were the old schoolmates and fellow templars, some prominent, some even famous, some unknown, who, in supporting his translation of Homer, joined nearly sixty peers and peeresses of the realm, many of them of the highest rank: Buccleuch, Buckingham, Bessborough, Barrymore, Devonshire, Fortescue, Gloucester, Guilford, Hardwicke, Montagu, Portland, Rutland, Stafford, and Uxbridge. They were among nine bishops, and the Archbishop of Canterbury; the Lord High Chancellor (Thurlow, Cowper's friend in youth) and the Speaker of the House of Commons (Addington); William Pitt, William Wilberforce, Horace Walpole, John Wesley. Among a large number of masters and fellows of Cambridge colleges (and almost none of Oxford); 'Capability' Brown and Isaac Hawkins Browne, Mrs Boscawen, Charles Burney, Joseph Cottle, Henry Dundas, and William Hayley (yet unknown to Cowper).

There was one who would certainly have had his name on this list if he had been alive: Sir William Russell, Bart, Cowper's 'favourite friend' at Westminster.[2] He was the son of Sir Francis Russell, whose family had for many generations lived at Chippenham, Cambridgeshire, and were closely related to the Cromwells.[3] Sir William's death while swimming in the Thames in 1757 was one of the severest blows that came to Cowper in his youth, falling as it did shortly after the death of his father and the breaking

---

[1] 'Tirocinium', ll. 436–7.   [2] Hayley's note: Hayley (1803), I, 13.
[3] G.E.C., *Complete Baronetage* (Exeter, 1902), II, 66. Not of 'The Chequers' (present country residence of the Prime Ministers), as Wright says, *Life* (1921), p. 15. 'Chequers' did not come into the Russell family until after the death of Sir William (1757).

WILLIAM COWPER

of his engagement of marriage to his cousin, Theodora
Cowper. In memory of Russell, Cowper wrote the verses:

Doom'd as I am in solitude to waste
The present moments, and regret the past;
Depriv'd of ev'ry joy I valued most,
My friend torn from me, and my mistress lost;
Call not this gloom I wear, this anxious mien,
The dull effect of humour, or of spleen!
Still, still I mourn, with each returning day,
Him snatch'd by fate, in early youth away,...
See me—ere yet my destin'd course half done,
Cast forth a wand'rer on a wild unknown!
See me neglected on the world's rude coast,
Each dear companion of my voyage lost![1]

Two of Cowper's best friends of Temple days were also
not among the subscribers of 1791: William Alston and
Arthur Carr.[2] And Alston at least was living at the time.
He had had the chambers above the Parliament Chamber
in the Middle Temple that adjoined Cowper's, from
November 1753 to January 1757.[3] He took the chambers
seven months before Cowper moved there, though Cowper
also came into residence in November. Alston was the son
and heir of William Alston, Esq., who had a manor and
extensive lands at Bramford, Suffolk. William the son had
come to the Temple from Pembroke College, Cambridge.
In the Temple, in their attic-chambers, the youths read
Homer together: Cowper, whose interests were usually in
literature rather than law, and Alston, sluggish and forget-

---

[1] 'On the death of Sir W. Russell': *Poems*, pp. 284–5.
[2] William Alston (1728–99) and Arthur Carr (1727–?): they seem best to fit the
'Alston' and 'Carr' of Cowper's Temple days. There is no doubt that this William
Alston was Cowper's friend, for Cowper refers in *Letters*, III, 425, to Alston's connection
with Thurlow which 'has been to him both honourable and useful'. *G.M.* LXIX, Pt i
(1799), 167: 'the Rev. William Alston, Rector of Lofthouse in Cleveland, to which he
was presented by the Lord Chancellor Thurlow.' Carr was admitted to the M.T.,
3 Feb. 1746/7 (*Mid. Temp. Reg.* I, 337); Alston, to Gray's Inn, 2 Nov. 1747 (Foster,
Gray's Inn Reg. p. 377), and to the M.T., 22 April 1751 (*Mid. Temp. Reg.* I, 343).
[3] 'Admissions to the House and to Chambers: 1737–58', ff. 302, 387: M.T. MSS.

ful of most things, especially his proper work. Alston had a 'fine classic taste' and Cowper had excelled in the classics at Westminster School. After they had read through Homer, they compared Pope's translation with the original, line by line. Cowper consequently felt himself 'better acquainted with Pope's translation...than almost any man'. The result of their co-operative comparison was 'a discovery, that there is hardly the thing in the world of which Pope was so entirely destitute, as a taste for Homer'. They were disgusted; they 'had sought the simplicity and majesty of Homer in his English representative, and had found instead of them, puerile conceits, extravagant metaphors, and the tinsel of modern embellishment in every possible position'. They were so irritated with Pope as translator that they were frequently on the point of burning his work, just as they had burnt Bertram Montfitchet's *Life and Opinions* in their friend Rowley's chambers.[1]

Alston, Rowley, Carr, and Cowper formed a clique when they all were first in the Temple.[2] Carr and Rowley were both of Irish connections. Arthur Carr was the son of the Bishop of Killaloe, and like his brothers George and Thomas and his father before him, he had gone to Trinity College, Dublin. Carr and Cowper probably drifted apart during the Inner-Temple years—when Cowper associated with the dashing, revelling literati, Colman, Thornton, Lloyd, and Churchill—but during the last, and exceedingly difficult, year there (1762–3), Carr was unbelievably kind to him.

I often think of Carr, [Cowper wrote to Rowley in 1791] and shall always think of him with affection. Should I never see him more, I shall never, I trust, be capable of forgetting his indefatigable attention to me during the last year I spent in London. Two years after I invited him to Huntingdon, where I lived at that time, but

---

[1] *Letters*, I, 15, 17; II, 410; III, 233–4; IV, 107.
[2] *Ibid.* I, 15, 17, 19; III, 425; IV, 129–30.

he pleaded some engagement, and I have neither seen him nor heard of him, except from yourself, from that hour to the present. I know by experience with what reluctance we move when we have been long fixed; but could he prevail on himself to move hither he would make me very happy; and when you write to him next you may tell him so.[1]

In 1757 their common friend Alston quit the Middle Temple in dissatisfaction with the legal profession. He began a career of travelling, then remained for several years in Rheims where he was highly esteemed. He married a young lady from Durham while living there, and shortly afterwards they left for extensive travels in France and Italy. After some time they returned to her home at Durham where Alston took orders. He became renowned in the area for his pious life and eloquent preaching, and for his learning in classical and modern literature. The studies he developed with Cowper in the Temple continued all his life; when he died he left a large number of manuscripts relating to the ancient authors. In 1788 his friend of Temple days, Lord Chancellor Thurlow—probably through William Cowper—presented him to the Rectory of Lofthouse in Cleveland.[2]

The guardian angel of all these young men, and William Cowper, was 'a man of wit and genius', Samuel Cox— 'Sam Cox, the counsel'. He was the protector of Westminster boys and recent graduates of the school in the Inner Temple, and the patron of young poets. He lived in a large house in Chancery Lane, convenient to the Temple, where he was active in the society. With William Markham,

---

[1] *Letters*, IV, 129–30. Rowley was living in Ireland in 1791, and presumably Cart had returned to his native country, so that they had opportunities of seeing each other —especially when Rowley was on circuit or engaged in Irish parliamentary proceedings. See Adelaide Collyer, 'Some Unpublished MSS. of the Poet Cowper', *Universal Rev.* VII (1890), 283, for a dream of Cowper's in 1784, in which he saw Carr and himself in a setting reminiscent of Temple days. They were in a large company of people who were in doubt and controversy concerning a future life.

[2] *G.M.* LXIX, Pt i (1799), 167; John Graves, *The History of Cleveland* (Carlisle, 1808), p. 343.

Head Master of Westminster 1753–64, and Thomas Salter, a Charterhouse master, Cox was concerned in the building of houses and making alterations in Dean's Yard, Westminster. This was done for parents who wished to send their sons to the school. Cox was the godfather of Samuel Bentham, brother of Jeremy, and persuaded Jeremy's father to send his sons to Westminster. He took vacations with William Cowper and his friends at Margate and Ramsgate, and was a friend of Maria Frances Cecilia Madan Cowper, William's especially favoured cousin. On her he wrote his 'famous song', 'When first by fond Damon Flavella was seen'; and, a frequent dabbler in poetry, he wrote other fugitive pieces.[1] William Cowper put his trust in Cox, and in his younger friends, for like most boys of his rank in English society, he was at an early age cut off from his home and parental guidance: friends and masters were *in loco parentis*, in the old university phrase. Especially for Cowper, the friendships were of the greatest importance; he did not long have any immediate family ties.

These then were the boys whom Cowper knew best at Westminster, and his closest friends during the first years in the Temple, and at the end of his stay there. In between, in his Temple days, would come an era of gay and riotous living—life with the rakes, the young 'geniuses' of the mid-century. For the most part the first friends were more dignified; they were the backbone of upper-middle and upper-class British society. Their families were like Cowper's, or even more noteworthy. They had his interests—the classics above all, and humour and light verse, the law (but not too seriously), and religion—doubts in traditional Christianity, even despair, and a few moments of shining

---

[1] Samuel Cox (1720–76): Nichols, *Poems*, VI, 311–12; *Letters*, I, 156; in list of subscribers to Christopher Smart, *Poems on Several Occasions* (London, 1752), and Robert Lloyd, *Poems* (London, 1762); John Bowring, *Memoirs of Bentham*, vol. x, *The Works of Jeremy Bentham* (Edinburgh, 1843), pp. 26–9; *G.M.* LIII, Pt i (1783), 152.

faith. They slouched in the window-seats of the 'Dames' Houses' with peers and young poets, but were not really part of either faction; they sauntered and talked in the gardens of the Inns and in the grounds of vast country estates. In small groups they went to the entertainments of the city, and during vacations they were at Bath, Margate, Southampton, and all the other watering places. They formed the essentially English, properly English, background of Cowper's *Task*, and were its readers. They were the moulders of the would-be poet of the age. In them are seen the various elements of Cowper's own personality—but in him, more complicated; the various threads more tightly drawn and more delicately woven.

IV

READING

As forth she went at early dawn
To taste the dew-besprinkled lawn,
Behind she hears the hunter's cries,
And from the deep-mouth'd thunder flies;
She starts, she stops, she pants for breath,
She hears the near advance of death,
She doubles, to mis-lead the hound,
And measures back her mazy round;
'Till fainting in the publick way,
Half dead with fear she gasping lay....
...dearest friends, alas, must part!
How shall we all lament! Adieu.
For see the hounds are just in view.
GAY, 'The Hare and many Friends'

COWPER was from childhood a scholar. By the time he had settled himself in the Temple he was master of four languages beside his own: Greek, Latin, French, and Italian. He had read continually in the literatures of these countries and in his letters he described the great pleasure he had had in reading with his friends. He read Homer with Dick Sutton at Westminster and again in the Temple with William Alston. He stretched out on a wall by the sea to read Tasso's *Jerusalem* and the *Pastor Fido* with Joseph Hill. We see the youths sprawled in fields and meadows, at the shore, in small rooms at school or in the Temple—reading together, and talking about literature. In childhood they read 'legendary tales', 'mythologic stuff', and from mother or a nurse they learned Bible stories. At school, a lot of classics and little religion—but in young manhood, philosophy prevailed.[1]

---

[1] Hayley (1803), II, 226–7; *Letters*, I, 223–4; II, 410, 420–1; III, 233; IV, 107; 'Tirocinium', ll. 181–200; Lady Hesketh to Hayley, 5 March 1801: 'I have always understood that he read a great deal while at the Temple. (tho' not much *Law* I believe) & he lived with men of the first rate understandings, & who made the best use of them...' (Add. MSS. 30803 A, f. 111).

The very first books Cowper owned, and mastered, were the *Pilgrim's Progress* and Gay's *Fables*. His Aunt Harriot Donne, wife of the Rector of Catfield in Norfolk, had given the two books to him when he was a small child. He was soon 'reckoned famous' for repeating 'The Hare and many Friends' before his family's company. Years later, when he believed himself forgotten by his friends and, like Gay's hare, often in fear and panic, he must have recalled the verses with bitter nostalgia. Just before his death, he returned to these fables, and to 'The Hare and many Friends' in particular, as one of his last amusements.[1] Cowper as a child had found in Gay what he would always love especially: a love of the humbler animals and light, moral verse. At the same time, in his 'life's happy spring', he was 'charm'd' by Bunyan's Pilgrim:

> Ingenious dreamer, in whose well-told tale
> Sweet fiction and sweet truth alike prevail;
> Whose hum'rous vein, strong sense, and simple style,
> May teach the gayest, make the gravest smile;
> Witty, and well employ'd, and, like thy Lord,
> Speaking in parables his slighted word.[2]

His tastes were thus formed in his earliest reading: what he appreciated in Gay and Bunyan, would in turn be peculiarly characteristic of his own poetry. John Gilpin and John Calvin were part of him from the beginning.

Shortly afterwards he became interested in pastoral poetry:[3]

> No bard could please me but whose lyre was tun'd
> To Nature's praises.

Heroic literature would soon pall, but not the songs

> Of Tityrus, assembling, as he sang,
> The rustic throng beneath his fav'rite beech.

---

[1] John Johnson to William Hayley, 13 Oct. 1801: Bodleian MS. Eng. misc. d. 134, f. 83; also Hayley (1803), II, 224. Cowper took the name of his favourite hare Puss from Gay's poem (see his essay on his pet hares from *G.M.* June 1784: *Poems*, pp. 652–6; and the passage in the *Task*, III, 334–51, which ends: 'I knew at least one hare that had a friend').

[2] 'Tirocinium', ll. 135–40.   [3] *Task*, IV, 704–30.

From these he turned to Milton; at the age of fourteen
Cowper read him and wondered, and forever felt the powerful music of *Paradise Lost*. He studied Cowley, 'courtly
though retir'd', and lamented his splendid wit 'entangled
in the cobwebs of the schools'.

> Thee too, enamour'd of the life I lov'd,
> Pathetic in its praise, in its pursuit
> Determin'd, and possessing it at last
> With transports such as favour'd lovers feel.

Prior was another favourite: his odes and epigrams were
perfectly in Cowper's extraordinary memory twenty years
after he had seen a volume of Prior's verse. He often read
Alma, and Butler's *Hudibras*, but unlike Johnson, never saw
in them the least resemblance to each other, except their
similar meter. He admired Prior for achieving what he
would in later life strive to find: a way of speaking in verse
the language of prose, without being prosaic. The highest
praise Cowper could give his friend Robert Lloyd was that
he had been born the sole heir of 'dear Mat Prior's easy
jingle'. Dear Mat Prior, who was able to marshal the words
of his verse 'in such an order as they might naturally take
in falling from the lips of an extemporary speaker, yet without meanness, harmoniously, elegantly, and without seeming to displace a syllable for the sake of the rhyme'.[1]

'Butler's wit, Pope's numbers, Prior's ease'—these were
Cowper's touchstones. Pope was probably always first in
his reading. The fascination of Pope had led Cowper, when
only a boy, to seek him at his lodgings. He had looked for
Pope in London, at a goldbeater's in Great Queen Street,
but he was not to be seen. Pope, as *the* poet of the preceding generation, still dominated poetry throughout
Cowper's life. His works were for Cowper's contemporaries
models of nicety in phrasing and delicacy of touch. But he

---

[1] *Letters*, I, 153, 430; II, 179–80; 'An Epistle to Robert Lloyd, Esq.': *Poems*, p. 266.

plagued them by making poetry 'a mere mechanic art'. 'And ev'ry warbler', Cowper said, consequently 'has his tune by heart.'[1]

When Cowper considered his own writings in relation to his English predecessors or contemporaries, he saw his works primarily in comparison with Pope. He was usually reacting against the Popeian ideal. If William Unwin praised him for witty letter-writing, Cowper feared he would become vain, like Pope, and 'as disgusting a letter-writer'. Pope, he believed, pointed every sentence with some conceit, and was therefore 'the most disagreeable maker of epistles' that he had ever met with, while Swift's letters were the best that could be written. As for the poets of the second half of the century, he said they served

a poem as a cook does a dead turkey, when she fastens the legs of it to a post and draws out all the sinews. For this we may thank Pope; but unless we could imitate him in the closeness and compactness of his expression, as well as in the smoothness of his numbers, we had better drop the imitation, which serves no other purpose than to emasculate and weaken all we write. Give me a manly rough line, with a deal of meaning in it, rather than a whole poem full of musical periods, that have nothing but their oily smoothness to recommend them.[2]

> Give me the line that plows its stately course
> Like a proud swan, conq'ring the stream by force.[3]

'Do you place yourself on a level with Pope? I answer, or rather *should* answer—By no means. Not as a poet. But as a Translator of Homer if I did not expect and believe that I should even surpass him, why have I meddled with this matter at all? If I confess inferiority, I reprobate my

---

[1] 'Table Talk', ll. 652–55, 764; John Johnson's notation on the second flyleaf of Cowper's copy of Pope's translation of the *Iliad* (London, 1715): 'E. Dereham | Nov[r] 14. 1798. |M[r] Cowper told me that he once passed Pope's Lodgings, when a boy, and looked for him but he was not to be seen—It was in Great Queen Street at a Goldbeater's.' The book is now in the Keynes Coll. I have not been able to discover when Pope stayed at this place, but it must have been between April 1742, when Cowper came to Westminster, and May 1744, when Pope died.

[2] *Letters*, I, 141, 196; II, 286.   [3] 'Table Talk', ll. 522–3.

own undertaking.' Cowper wrote this to Walter Bagot in
1786,[1] but his feeling was the same in his Temple days, when
he first read Pope's translation with Alston. Everything in
connection with Cowper's *Homer* was done to correct or
expose Pope. Cowper would not 'strut in buckram'; he
would not twist Homer's lines into pretty rhymes; he would
be faithful to the spirit of the original; his price would be
much more moderate; he would have as many subscribers;
if Pope captured Oxford's allegiance, he would have that of
Cambridge. And so it went. It was, sometimes, a rather
silly and childish competition, and bickering with an op-
ponent long dead. Pope had been dead for forty years when
Cowper began to write in earnest, but his rivalry was felt as
if he were still in his prime.

These were the formative writers of English for Cowper:
Bunyan, Gay, Milton, Cowley, Prior, Butler, Pope. And
Gray, chief among his contemporaries, and Churchill and
Colman and Lloyd, his friends. Cowper formed a small
library of these authors and others, in conformity with his
pocket and his principle—which was, Hayley said, the rule
of Pliny—*non multa, sed multum.*[2] He had books from his
father's library, and those he himself had collected: many
ancient writers, and Molière, Voltaire, Dryden, Thomson,
Swift.[3] He sought out Westminster-School poems, and
those by his Uncle Ashley Cowper; broadside ballads and
shilling poems and pamphlets. His books remained behind
when he left the Temple in 1763. They were sold; but
twenty-five years later he was still searching for them,
hoping that the 'bookless student' might again be furnished
with a library which was sufficient for his needs. Without

---

[1] To Bagot, 15 Jan. 1786: Morgan MSS. MA 86, vol. i, f. 6.
[2] Hayley (1803), ii, 227.
[3] From a MS. list of Cowper's books (drawn up by Sir Geoffrey Keynes) which
descended through Cowper's cousin John Johnson to Bertram Vaughan-Johnson,
whose widow sold the books to Keynes. The most interesting of these still remain
in his collection.

his books he felt he could never be a man of letters, for his book-learning by force of circumstances was that of a school-boy, only somewhat improved.[1] But Cowper was too modest. Friends lent books, and his excellent memory often-times served better than library shelves.

At Mr Chapman's his reading habits were relaxed; he spent a little time in the study of law, and much more time in conversation and the pleasures of the city. He came to the house of this attorney or solicitor early in 1750, after Westminster, and nine months at his own home in Berk-hamsted.[2] He was sent here by his father to acquire a practical legal knowledge. Chapman's house was in Greville Street, in the heart of the legal district, directly behind Furnival's Inn.[3] The man himself was pleasant and fair, but Cowper found the 'Tricks & illiberal Conduct of his fellow Clerks' disgusting, and this association contributed to his dislike of the profession even after he moved to the Temple.[4] One clerk was not of this group. He was Edward Thurlow, who came to the same place in the summer of 1751. He was twenty, and had just been sent down from Caius College, Cambridge, in his third year because of re-peated insolence and absence from chapel. Thurlow, though he participated with Cowper in gaiety at Ashley Cowper's, was undoubtedly a much more serious student of the law. In his *Education for the Bar* he recommended:

In the fourth year [of the university] to learn French, to have a cursory view of Justinian and civil law, to take up Roman History from the time of Julius Cæsar, then Tacitus. Then Selden's *Janus Anglorum*, then Wooten's *Leges Walliae*, Wilking's *Leges Saxoniae*, then Norman Statutes to the 1st of Richard I, when

---

[1] *Letters*, II, 178; III, 247, 264; IV, 151–2, 163–4.
[2] William was probably at home again that autumn, for his father had a serious 'stroke of the dead Palsy', and 'was judged to be in great danger' during Sept. and Oct. 1750: *Letters of Spencer Cowper, Dean of Durham*, ed. Edward Hughes, *Publ. Surtees Soc.* CLXV (1956), 129–33.   [3] See Appendix A, pp. 178, 180.
[4] According to Lady Hesketh in reply to a query from Hayley (letter, 1 July 1801: Add. MSS. 30803 A, f. 142).

Statute Law begins... [then] Blackstone, who will excite him to look up Bracton, Fitzherbert, Coke upon Littleton, Brook, the Register Year Books, old Reporters, Commentators, etc.[1]

If he accomplished half of this programme while at Chapman's, Thurlow would have been a very busy man. But a future Lord Chancellor would have to have this framework of the law firmly in his mind.

Cowper considered his fellow student industrious and resolute, one who would not let anything drop once it was begun. He eulogized his friend:

> Round Thurlow's head in early youth,
>   And in his sportive days,
> Fair science pour'd the light of truth,
>   And genius shed his rays.
>
> See! with united wonder cried
>   Th' experienc'd and the sage,
> Ambition in a boy supplied
>   With all the skill of age!
>
> Discernment, eloquence, and grace,
>   Proclaim him born to sway
> The balance in the highest place,
>   And bear the palm away.[2]

Sir Samuel Egerton Brydges' description of Thurlow was quite different from Cowper's. Brydges said he was more marked in youth by 'caprice, eccentricity, and audacity of mind, than by decided and leading talent.... When he was called to the Bar [22 November 1754], he was still idle and unfixed: he was a man of pleasure, and lost much of his time in social dissipation. If he read, nobody knew when he read; but in the midst of seeming inattention, and of utter neglect of the dull, technical studies of his profession, he sometimes betrayed a sleeping fire, and force of talent.'

---

[1] Quoted in Robert Gore-Browne, *Chancellor Thurlow* (London, 1953), p. 8.
[2] *Letters*, I, 150; 'On the Promotion of Edward Thurlow, Esq.': *Poems*, pp. 297–8.

61

But Brydges seems to be prejudiced here, and probably mistaken. Forty years after their days at Chapman's, Cowper recalled Thurlow's recitations of passages from *Paradise Lost* in which Thurlow was 'perfectly sensible of their music'. And Joseph Cradock wrote: 'It was generally supposed that Thurlow in early life was idle; but I always found him close at study in a morning, when I have called at the Temple; and he frequently went no farther in an evening than to Nando's, and then only in his deshabille.'[1]

Thurlow was interested in poetry, which would have delighted Cowper. For the most part, however, Thurlow was a bold, rude, vulgar man. He was sagacious in legal matters; self-confident at all times; quick in his decisions, which were delivered with a piercing glance; aloof and lonely, and extraordinarily sceptical of any religious beliefs. Long after he had left London, Cowper said: 'There are not two men upon earth more opposite upon the subject of religion than his Lordship and myself.' When he had kept the necessary terms to be called to the bar at the Middle Temple, Thurlow, like all others at that time, had no examinations to pass, he merely had to swear to repudiate the Pope.[2] Later the two Evangelicals John Thornton and John Newton (both were then friends of Cowper) gossiped about this: 'It is said to qualify he went into Church with his hat on walked up to the [Communion] Table & after receiv^g [the Sacrament] He came away without attending the Service.'[3] If not for his piety, Cowper could nevertheless remember him for his benevolence, the kind things he frequently did when they were young. Once, without any solicitation, Thurlow spent £300 to establish the penniless daughter of a friend of his father's in a millinery shop. And

---

[1] S. E. Brydges, *Autographical Memoir* (Paris, 1826), p. 7; *Letters*, IV, 109; Joseph Cradock, *Literary and Miscellaneous Memoirs* (London, 1828), I, 79.
[2] Cradock, I, 71–3; Brydges, p. 7; Gore-Browne, *passim*; *Letters*, I, 473; Sir F. D. MacKinnon, 'The Law and Lawyers', *Johnson's England*, II, 289.
[3] John Thornton to John Newton, 30 June 1778: Forster MSS.

there was none of his customary desire for an amour, because 'she was ugly to a wonder'.[1]

But when Cowper thought of Thurlow in later life, he usually thought of an unfulfilled promise. Thurlow's failure constantly rankled in Cowper. The promise had been made one day at tea with Mrs C—e, and her sister, in King Street, Bloomsbury. Cowper had said:

'Thurlow, I am nobody, and shall be always nobody, and you will be Chancellor. You shall provide for me when you are.' He smiled, and replied, 'I surely will.'—'These ladies', said I, 'are witnesses.' He still smiled, and said—'Let them be so, for I will certainly do it.' But alas! twenty-four years have passed since the day of the date thereof; and to mention it now would be to upbraid him with inattention to his plighted troth. Neither do I suppose he could easily serve such a creature as I am, if he would.[2]

It was eight more years (April 1794), and many controversies and complaints, before Cowper got his pension and won again from Edward Thurlow the friendship which had been dead since the catastrophe of 1763.[3] The reason for this long breach may have been some embarrassment on Thurlow's part after his last meeting with Cowper. He had called at Cowper's chambers in the Temple at the time of his friend's very 'darkest Despondency'. He had treated him with the utmost kindness, but could not minister to a man insane. Thirty years later, even so coarse a man as Thurlow could not recall the scene without being much affected.[4]

---

[1] *Letters*, IV, 233.   [2] *Letters*, II, 464–5.

[3] *Letters*, IV, 488. The friendship recommenced in 1791: *Letters*, IV, 108.

[4] According to Hayley's account of Cowper's statement and an interview with Lords Thurlow and Kenyon, 8 June 1792: Hayley, 'Two Memorials of Hayleys Endeavours to serve His Friend Cowper': Add. MSS. 38887, ff. 25–6. Cowper once told Samuel Greatheed Thurlow's arguments with him when he feared to appear at the House of Lords: Greatheed to Hayley, 26 Aug. 1800: Fitzwilliam MSS. Greatheed claimed that Thurlow was among the men who came for Cowper on the day when he was to be examined before the House, and found him in bed after his attempted suicide: [Greatheed], 'Memoranda respecting Cowper the Poet': John Rylands Libr. Eng. MS. 352/55, f. 3. Thurlow was probably the friend of the *Memoir*, p. 43, who told Ashley Cowper (Cowper's 'kinsman') of William's attempt.

V

THE TEMPLE

those bricky towres,
The which on Themmes brode aged backe doe ryde,
Where now the studious lawyers have their bowers,
There whylome wont the Templer Knights to byde,
Till they decayd through pride.
SPENSER, *Prothalamion*
Within the Temple Hall we were too lowd.
The Garden here is more conuenient.
I Henry VI, II, iv, 3-4

'**W**ILLIELMUS COWPER ffilius et Hæres Appa-
rens...Reverendi Johannis Cowper' was admitted
into the Honourable Society of the Middle Temple
on 29 April 1748. After his admission he had no associations
with the society until November 1753.[1] Presumably he had
left Chapman's some time during that year. In March he was
visiting in Drayton.[2] And in July he arranged for admission
to Gray's Inn[3]—probably in a desperate attempt to find
chambers anywhere in one of the Inns. He did not, however, find rooms until autumn. According to the Students'
Ledger of the Middle Temple, it seems that he took his
'complete set of chambers' there on 15 November 1753. He
had finally been successful in obtaining the rooms of John
Alexander Stainsby, who had recently migrated to the Inner
Temple.[4] Cowper made payment of his fines the following

---

[1] 'Admissions to the House and to Chambers: 1737–58', f. 185; 'Students Ledger: 1747–64', f. 146: M.T. MSS.

[2] *Early Poems*, p. 25. Probably Drayton in Norfolk, where one of the Donne family may have had a home. William Cowper was frequently at Catfield in his youth, which was the centre of the Donnes in Norfolk. See *Letters*, III, 436; IV, 4, 503; *Early Poems*, pp. 12–17.

[3] Joseph Foster, *The Register of Admissions to Gray's Inn* (London, 1889), p. 379: 17 July 1753—'William Cowper, of the Middle Temple, Gent'.

[4] Cowper's *Memoir*, p. 8; 'Students Ledger', f. 146. The notes under 'Cowper William of Great Berkhamstead Hertfordshire' are brief and rather cryptic. They seem to indicate that he took rooms which were formerly held by Edward Leeds (1695?–1758),

day and remained in residence for the Michaelmas term 1753, and the Lent and Easter terms 1754.[1] By May 1754 he had fulfilled the six years of membership which were required for call to the degree of the Utter Bar, and his name was proposed to the bench.[2] The proposal was accepted and he was called in June. At this time he purchased chambers in his own name according to the rules of the society.[3]

From 1748 to 1753 he had not kept the terms of the Middle-Temple year, nor was he present at the formal exercises which were imposed upon its members. He took no part in the ancient customs of the Temple; never argued in the moots with the other students before the benchers. He merely paid the fines at the time of his call to the bar, and satisfied the requirements of a token obedience.[4]

After his call he had additional obligations for three

---

an eminent serjeant-at-law (see *D.N.B.*), and afterwards by John Alexander Stainsby (d. 1796), both of whom had transferred to the I.T. Stainsby, admitted M.T. 16 June 1750, went to I.T. in 1753, purchasing chambers 16 May 1753 (*Inner Temp. Rec.* v, 30, 31-2, 34-6, 40, 598, n. 4).

[1] The terms 'M[ichaelmas]: 1753', 'L[ent]: 1754', 'E[aster]: 1754' are marked in the 'Students Ledger', f. 146.

[2] 'Middle Temple Book of Orders of Parliament: 1748-75', ff. 147-8: M.T. MSS.

[3] On 11 June 1754 Cowper purchased the chamber which had belonged to Thomas Herbert Noyes 'with its Appurtenances Scituate three pair of Stairs over the Parliament Chamber...for the Term of his natural Life' ('Admissions to the House and to Chambers: 1737-58', f. 319). 'Every gentleman call'd to the Barr is obliged to have a Chamber in this House in his own name' (*Master Worsley's Book* [Charles Worsley, Treasurer of the M.T., 1734], ed. Arthur R. Ingpen (London, 1910), p. 210).

[4] According to the 'Students Ledger' Cowper kept only three terms of the eight required for the call. Consequently he paid a £4. 10d. fine, and another of £14 for neglecting to appear for the six 'Vacation' Exercises and one 'Candle' Exercise which were also among the requirements. To qualify for the call, the students had to be of six-years' standing, had to perform the 'Exercises' which were 'six in Vacation, one in Term in the Hall, called the Candle Exercise (because heretofore, when there were Supper Commons, it was performed after supper, consequently by candle light), and two at New Inn (now the only Inn of Chancery belonging to this Society). The performance of which is enforced by the penalty of fforty shillings each' (*Master Worsley's Book*, p. 131). The students' year at the M.T. was divided into three parts: the Learning or Grand Vacation (twice a year, twenty-four days following the first Monday in Lent, and the same number of days beginning the Monday after Lammas Day); The Term Times; the Dead or Mean Vacation—the time between Learning Vacations and Terms (Ingpen, 'Intro.', *Master Worsley's Book*, p. 42). Payment for eight terms of commons was required, whether kept or not (*M.W.B.* p. 210).

years. He had to dine in the hall on certain occasions and perform in the exercises. On the day that these last requirements were discharged he resigned from the Middle Temple and transferred his membership to the Inner Temple.[1] In the Middle Temple his life had been one of escape and minimal participation; the inactivity had come from his shyness and boredom—his lack of interest in the law. Because of the extreme lenience in the Inns of Court, he could pay rather than perform. And at the first possible moment he left the society of one Inn for that of another. By November 1757 he had sold his old chambers[2] and had begun a life of increased leisure, free from any small struggles which he had previously experienced with the rules.

He wrote in his *Memoir*: 'I became, in a manner, complete master of myself; and took possession of a complete set of chambers in the Temple, at the age of twenty-one.' Complete master of himself he was; that is, he was totally unsupervised. His external affairs were free, but the workings of his mind were weighed down. 'I was struck,' he said, 'not long after my settlement in the Temple, with such a dejection of spirits, as none but they who have felt the same, can have the least conception of. Day and night I was upon the rack, lying down in horror, and rising up in despair.' He gave up the study of the classics, his chief interest during his last years at Westminster and at Mr Chapman's. He turned instead to the poems of George Herbert, which became his only consolation. 'I pored over him all day long.' But the depression continued for nearly a year. Not until a change of scene at Southampton was the melancholy broken.[3]

Even in this period his life was not all the blackness that

---

[1] The certificate of Cowper's admission and call to the bar was sent by the M.T. to the I.T., and remains among the papers of the latter society.

[2] On 25 Nov. 1757 he surrendered his chambers in the M.T. to 'Anthony Dickins for the Term of his natural Life' ('Admissions to the House and to Chambers', f. 401).

[3] Cowper's *Memoir*, pp. 8–11.

the *Memoir* describes. The melancholy was pervasive, but there were moments of foolery, of the dashing life of the gay blade in the Temple, and of dilettante literary efforts. The giggling at Ashley Cowper's went on—for a time at least. And there were the other activities which characterized a large part of his life from 1755 to 1763, and would be reflected in a quiet way years later at Olney. There were visits to his tailor Grainger: Cowper was all his life an elegant dresser. He dressed with restraint, yet he wanted to make 'a figure'. He walked occasionally to Covent Garden to purchase myrtles, for he had at all times the deep and truly English love of a garden. He wrote halfpenny ballads, 'two or three of which had the honour to be popular'. He wrote for the magazines; translated La Fontaine and Voltaire and Horace. He fenced, and had one of his eyes almost poked out; he went shooting. He danced all night, went to Marylebone Gardens, to the Italian operas, and to the theatre. He could and did drink a considerable amount. And so his early letters show him to be pretty much a young man of society and a member of the literati, yet more serious and with a moral sense which he regretfully did not find in his companions.[1] His gaiety and revelry were shot through with religious questionings, reflections, and meditations.

Will Cowper also sometimes studied law, a subject to which he was never particularly inclined. He continued this work year after year in order to gratify his 'most indulgent father', not because he had any hopes of success in the profession. And he wrote to his friend John Duncombe in 1758: "'Tis true enough y^t I am not fond of the Law, but I am very fond of ye money y^t it produces, and have much too great a Value for my own Interest to be Remiss in any Application to it.' However, within a few years after his

---

[1] *Letters*, I, 5–8, 14–17, 101, 282, 309, 399; III, 20 (and Wright, *Life* (1921), p. 18, n. 1); IV, 384 (and Add. MSS. 30805, f. 2); Cowper's *Memoir*, pp. 13–15.

father's death the admonition of the sundial in the Inner Temple, 'Be gone about your Business', did not have much meaning for him. He 'lost a legion of attorneys...by never doing the business' they brought him.[1] Even in the early 1760's Cowper nevertheless accomplished more than he would afterwards admit. He formed an adequate legal library (in 1770 it was valued at £20. 10s.). He acquired Martin Madan's manuscript legal case books, and these give evidence of careful reading—Cowper having made comments and additions and indexed his cousin's work.[2] While in the Temple he had a client of sorts in his boyhood friend, Dick Harcourt, and at Olney he was legal adviser to Newton and to his neighbours. He knew less of the law than a country attorney, he said, yet he thought he had as much business. The inhabitants of the town could not be persuaded that 'a head once endued with a legal periwig' could ever again be deficient in its knowledge. And he won cases, though he preferred to burlesque the solemnity of juridical proceedings.[3]

But Cowper and his friends were not in the Temple for the law alone. Since ancient times the Inns of Court had as their function not only the learning of law, but also all things to qualify young men as leaders in the affairs of the kingdom. They were the final training and testing places of gentlemen. In the Middle Ages their students were called Apprenticii nobiliores, for the Inns were the highest collegiate institution in England, to which sons of peers resorted as a matter of course. In the eighteenth century

[1] *Letters*, III, 241–2; IV, 58; David Bonnell Green, 'Three Cowper Letters', *N. & Q.* CCI (1956), 532.
[2] *Letters*, I, 111–13, 116 (and Add. MSS. 37059, f. 2); Maggs Cat., *Mercurius Britannicus*, no. 81 (July 1943), 72: from Cowper's library, Legal Case Book, 'M. Madan in Chancery Lane His Book'—entirely in his autograph, 260 pp., notes on cases, legal decisions, etc., 1752–5; there is also a 'Legal Common Place Book' which belonged to Cowper: Morgan MSS. MA 85. It bears Cowper's signature and the date, 'Feb. 12. 1757', on the first end-leaf.
[3] *Letters*, I, 99–100, 186–7, 246–7, 253; Wright, *Life* (1892), p. 251; 'Report of an Adjudged Case': *Poems*, pp. 308–9.

much of this tradition continued: sons of persons of quality came there for similar reasons. Friendship and conversation were as important to many as a knowledge of torts.[1]

The location of the Temple and its grounds and buildings were well suited to conviviality and pleasant living. Literary men sought out chambers there: Burke, Johnson, Boswell, Goldsmith, Richardson. At the boundary the Temple Bar was adorned with grisly heads of criminals, but inside the gates a colony of rooks flew about the limes and chestnuts of the gardens. The fountain of the Middle Temple, one of the sights of the city, rose to a 'vast and almost incredible altitude' of thirty feet. Walks of gravel and purbeck ran between the tall old trees, and the beds of flowers and large flowerpots along the banks of the Thames. From the open riverside the templar could see into Surrey. ''Tis certain that nothing can be finer situated than the *Temple*', wrote a contemporary critic of London.[2] In *Barnaby Rudge* Dickens expressed the feelings of many Londoners even today:

There is yet a drowsiness in its courts, and a dreamy dulness in its trees and gardens.... There is still the plash of falling water in fair Fountain Court, and there are yet nooks and corners where dun-haunted students may look down from their dusty garrets, on a vagrant ray of sunlight patching the shade of the tall houses, and seldom troubled to reflect a passing stranger's form. There is yet, in the Temple, something of a clerkly monkish atmosphere, which public officers of law have not disturbed, and even legal firms have failed to scare away. In summer time, its pumps suggest to thirsty idlers, springs cooler, and more sparkling, and deeper than other wells; and as they trace the spillings of full pitchers on the heated ground, they snuff the freshness, and, sighing, cast sad looks towards the Thames, and think of baths and boats, and saunter on, despondent.

---

[1] Ingpen, pp. 35–7; [Edward Hatton], *A New View of London* (London, 1708), II, 697.

[2] [James Ralph?], *A Critical Review of the Publick Buildings...in, and about London* (London, 1734), p. 24.

The round church of the two Temples, dedicated in 1185, had all the glory of the country's Middle Ages. The treasuries of the two societies were filled with armour, with pikes and helmets and the gold-inlaid shields of the Knights Templar. The four thousand books belonging to the Middle Temple, on law and most branches of literature, made its public library one of the most important in London. The great hall of the Middle Temple (1573) soared and arched forty-five feet above the diners; it was as grand as any in England. But commons in either Inn was much like that in the universities, and behaviour and service as slovenly as in an Oxford or Cambridge college.[1] The diners were divided into benchers, utter barristers, and students under the bar. Black gowns extending down to the feet were worn, and since the sixteenth century the students had drunk from green earthen pots and had eaten from wooden trenchers. Like the university colleges, the four Inns of Court formed four small communities, sufficient unto themselves (although the division between the two Temples was not as clearly drawn). Their members were for the most part bachelors, but a good many kept mistresses. The number of university men and the level of education generally among the lawyers was much lower than today. Their social life in hall and in chambers was less active than in the preceding centuries, but much more vigorous than is known now, for merrymaking and feasting were common throughout the year.

It is to be supposed that after 1754 Cowper saw a fair amount of this life. Members of the Temple who had chambers were obliged to keep commons for at least two weeks of every term. The chambers in the Middle Temple in Cowper's name were 'three pair of Stairs over the Parlia-

<hr>

[1] Zacharias Conrad von Uffenbach, *London in 1710*, transl. and ed. W. H. Quarrell and M. Mare (London, 1934), p. 58: 'The table had just been laid, and on it were wooden platters and green earthenware pots, into which bones are cast; there were no napkins and the table-cloth looked as if a sow had just had a litter on it. We had no desire to dine there.'

ment Chamber'.[1] His rooms most likely consisted of an outer chamber divided into three parts (shared with two others), and his own bedroom, study, and woodhouse. They faced the Middle Temple Lane and the principal gardens of the society. They were on the highest floor of the staircase at the end of the hall passage. This building adjoining the hall on the east was built in 1626. The passage through the northern third of it ran from the hall porch (in Fountain Court) past the doors to the hall (on the right) and the inner pantry and coal-house (left) and then turned to an exit in Middle Temple Lane. Here at the south-east corner of Middle Temple Hall and the end of the passage, was the Parliament Chamber and the staircase to Cowper's chambers. Directly south of the Parliament Chamber was the kitchen, and above the kitchen, the library. In one L-shaped unit were the administrative, social, and intellectual centres of the Middle Temple: the heart of the society.[2] In the garret high above the kitchen and the library were the quarters of the butlers. Up here on the 'Library Staircase', ten years after Cowper left the Middle Temple (in 1767), Goldsmith lived with the butler of the Inn, Mr Jeffs.[3]

[1] 'Admissions to the House and to Chambers: 1737–58', ff. 319, 410: M.T. MSS.

[2] The location of Cowper's rooms is by my own reckoning. Hitherto the sources for the location of these chambers and those in the I.T. were Frederick Rogers, 'Cowper in the Temple', *Cowper in London*, pp. 23–4; William Willis, *Cowper and his Connection with the Law* (Norwich, [1910?]), pp. 8–10; and Wilfrid Hooper's paper, 'Cowper and the Law', delivered 25 April 1919, which is quoted in Wright, *Life* (1921), pp. 25, 34–6, 73; and a paper, 'Cowper and the Temple', given by Hooper in 1931 (see *The Times*, 27 Nov. 1931). All of these contain errors; none have the rooms placed specifically. I am indebted to the description of the building—'the new buildings adjoining the Hall'—given in the *Middle Temple Records: Minutes of Parliament*, ed. Charles Henry Hopwood and Charles Trice Martin (London, 1904–5), II, 704, 708–9, 711, 714, 717–18, 721, 724–6, 732, 739–40, 932; III, 1020, 1102; *Master Worsley's Book*, pp. 79–81, 150–1, 154, and the maps (of Ogilby, 1677, and that of 1732) facing p. 268. Cowper's staircase in the M.T. was known in his day as that of the 'Hall Passage', or of the 'Parliament Chamber', or the first staircase in no. 2 Garden Court (the second being the 'Library Staircase'). After Hakewell's rebuilding in 1831–2, no. 2 Garden Court was called nos. 1 and 2 Plowden Buildings.

[3] Goldsmith's name does not appear in the records of the M.T. He was not a member of the Inn and therefore not a direct tenant. See James Prior, *The Life of Oliver Goldsmith* (London, 1837), II, 136.

71

We do not know why Cowper left the Middle Temple, and the society to which his grandfather Spencer Cowper, his great-uncle the Lord Chancellor, and his uncles William and Ashley Cowper had belonged. Probably he wanted more convenient and pleasant chambers. But it may be that he preferred the members of the other Inn. He was at the time a very elegant young man about town. And the Inner Temple was the more fashionable society. There is an old saying, 'The Inner Temple for the rich, the Middle for the poor'. This was especially true in Cowper's day. In 1759 the Middle Temple sent a message to the Inner suggesting that the members give an extra contribution toward the paving of Middle Temple Lane, 'there being no carriage kept by any gentleman resident within it and...[paving with granite] will be merely adopted for the conveniency of the gentlemen of the Inner Temple where many carriages are kept'.[1] In comparison with a large number of the richer society, Cowper was poor. But he perhaps had a liking for its more affluent and distinguished company.

He gained admission to the Inner Temple on 15 April 1757, but it was not until June that the formal certificate of his status was witnessed and sent by the Middle Temple. He was admitted *ad eundem gradum* at his request. On the same day, 17 June, he purchased for £250 the chambers of Mr William Henry Ashhurst up one set of stairs, on the left hand, on the second staircase in Inner Temple Lane.[2] He moved down from a garret to an airy second-floor room with a delightful view. 'Looking into Pump-court in which there are Lime-trees, they are not unpleasant', he wrote to Samuel Rose, who was eager to sublet the chambers, 'and

---

[1] *Inner Temp. Rec.* v, 594.
[2] 'Admissions Book: 1750–1831', f. 1521: I.T. MSS.; *Inner Temp. Rec.* v, 85, 88; *Letters,* I, 397; 'Chamber Book', f. 7: I.T. MSS. From the time of Cowper's death until Nov. 1803, the chambers were rented for £20 per annum. They were valued at £240 on 16 May 1800 and sold for that amount to Phillips Stephen Howell on 25 Nov. 1803. *Inner Temp. Rec.* v, 85, 415, 655, 657.

I can beside assure you on experience, that the sound of water continually pouring itself into pails and pitchers under the window, is a circumstance rather agreeable. In the country indeed, where we have purling brooks and such pretty things, a waterfall of the kind may be held rather cheap; but in the heart of London it has its value. They are also admirably well situated for business.'[1] Actually they looked into Hare Court, not Pump Court, where there was also a pump—in fact, the main pump of the Inner Temple, where the maids gathered to empty and fill and the laundresses washed—and where there were six or seven splendid limes. From his window seat, like Mr Chester in *Barnaby Rudge*, he could look down on this pastoral setting and enjoy the sights of nature which were essential to his enjoyment of life. In the court beneath the trees the nursery-maids and lovers and the idle aged strolled at intervals among the attorneys and their clients. Here was, as Boswell would say, a 'calm retirement'—for the poet of *Retirement*. The method of living in the Inner Temple, in Boswell's opinion, was 'the most agreeable in the world for a single man'. Away from the bustle of the Strand and Fleet Street was this 'pleasant academical retreat...convenient buildings, handsome walks,...the silver Thames'.[2] But the riff-raff of the city also spilled inside the gates. And among the limes and beside the splashing water of Hare Court came whores and pick-pockets and other 'nuisances in the nights', so that an extra lamp had to be installed and a special watchman employed to protect the templars in the darkness.[3] The idyllic gardens could not exclude the sinews and shabbiness

---

[1] To Rose, 20 June 1789: Hyde Coll., Four Oaks Farm, Somerville, New Jersey.

[2] *Boswell's London Journal*, ed. F. A. Pottle (New York, 1950), pp. 234, 299, 306, 316; Boswell lived in William Johnson Temple's chambers, 6 July–4 Aug. 1763. His address was 'Inner Temple N⁰ 10 opposite the Church, to the care of Mʳ Edwards Stationer London': Boswell to John Johnston, 7 July 1763: Private Papers of James Boswell, Yale Univ. Libr. MSS.

[3] *Inner Temp. Rec.* v, 72–4, 76, 149, 476.

of the world outside. The passing parade beneath Cowper's window was as various as the city itself.

It has been suggested that when Johnson was talking to Boswell on 24 May 1763 about Smart and the ways in which madness discovers itself, 'they may well have been within a few feet of Cowper, in whom, before the year was out, madness was to discover itself by his trying to commit suicide'.[1] Johnson lived at no. 1 Inner Temple Lane, up one set of stairs, from August 1760 to July 1765.[2] No. 1 (the house was destroyed in 1857) was the first house on the west side of Inner Temple Lane, coming down the lane from Fleet Street. It was a small building. Then came the first passage into Hare Court, and in this passage was no. 2 Inner Temple Lane, 'the first staircase in the passage leading into Hare Court in the Inner Temple Lane'.[3] Across the passage was a considerably larger building, the first staircase of which was no. 3 Inner Temple Lane, Cowper's address.[4] During 1760–3 Cowper and Johnson did not therefore live 'within a few feet' of each other; they were on the same side of the same lane but separated by at least three hundred feet. It does not seem likely that they ever met or knew each other.

Cowper's haphazard study of the law continued here in the Inner Temple; perhaps it was reinforced in conversation at his Uncle Ashley's—that is, when he was not chatting with his cousin, Theadora. More likely, after his father's

---

[1] Sir F. D. MacKinnon, 'Dr. Johnson and the Temple', *Cornhill*, N.S. LVII (1924), 470–1; and quoted by Hill and Powell in their edition of Boswell, *Johnson*, I, 548.

[2] Boswell, *Johnson*, III, 535.

[3] See, for example, *Inner Temp. Rec.* V, 23, 48, 111, 123, 139, 357, 415, 467. There is a little confusion in the *Records* because the chambers at no. 2 are sometimes described as above, and sometimes as 'the first staircase in the Inner Temple Lane'.

[4] *Inner Temp. Rec.* V, 415; and V, 173 (2), 360, 424—this staircase is also referred to as 'the second staircase on the right hand in the Inner Temple Lane' as it is described in the 'Chamber Book', f. 7, where Cowper's ownership of the chambers is given. Late in life Cowper identified these chambers as no. 2 Inner Temple Lane: W. B. Todd, 'Cowper's Commentary on the Life of Johnson', *T.L.S.*, 15 March 1957, p. 168. In 1809 Charles Lamb would have chambers at no. 4.

death, if he received any stimulation towards a legal career, it came from Mary Cowper and her husband, William de Grey. Mary was a favourite of her cousin. She had written the verses at Berkhamsted Church in memory of his mother. When she was only recently the bride of de Grey she had introduced William Cowper to Harriot Cowper (who became Lady Hesketh, and William Cowper's chief correspondent) on a Sunday afternoon in Norfolk Street. He was there on a holiday from Westminster School.[1] Mary's husband was a young attorney of Cambridge and the Middle Temple, fighting his way up the legal ladder. Every minute he was at work at the law. He was 'as much a man of business in his retirement [at his cottage in Taplow] as in Westminster Hall', William said. 'But by these steps he ascended the Bench.' He was an excellent example for the young man who was prone to dawdle with legal matters. Perhaps too good an example, for de Grey's drive for success was almost overpowering. In 1758 he would become King's Counsel; three years later, Solicitor-General to Queen Charlotte; then M.P. for Newport, Cornwall, and Solicitor-General to the King. In 1766 he would be Attorney-General and knighted; later M.P. for the University of Cambridge; and finally a peer—Baron Walsingham (1780). And like many eighteenth-century peers, he was by then crippled with gout.[2] It was the pattern of success.

An early stepping-stone for William de Grey was the lease of the manor of Monkenfrith at East Barnet in Hertfordshire. Here was a community of lawyers. If William Cowper did not absorb the elements of law in the Temple, he should have done so on his visits to East Barnet. Near the de Greys at Little Grove lived John Sharpe, Solicitor to the Treasury and father of the Rev. Dr Gregory Sharpe,

[1] Hayley (1803), I, 199.
[2] *Letters*, I, 224; III, 20, 241–2, 392.

75

Master of the Temple from 1763 to 1771. Their home would later be sold to Edward Willes the Solicitor-General. Another manor was occupied by William Westbrook Richardson, of the Middle Temple, barrister-at-law, who would become High Sheriff of Sussex. Richardson's place was afterwards sold to Sir William Henry Ashhurst, Judge of King's Bench, who in 1757 had sold his chambers in the Inner Temple to William Cowper. The legal world of the time was a tight little world, and Cowper when he was at East Barnet, as in the Temple, was at one of its centres.[1]

De Grey was not intimidated by his neighbours. His brilliance in the courts and his extraordinary memory were widely known. He was elegant, suave, learned, and an 'eloquent forensic speaker....His voice was musical, his temper mild yet firm, and his utterance remarkably distinct, without formality or affected precision. In this latter respect he strikingly resembled Garrick.' Gossips were prophesying his future achievements. The way of political advancement was the never-ending game of courting 'interest', and he was busy at it, and at his work in the courts.[2] If Will Cowper was not intimidated by de Grey he could acquire part of a legal education during an escape to the country. With active examples in his own family and living many years at the very source of English law, he was given every opportunity to succeed in the profession.

But what could he say of this time in the Temple, when he looked back in later years? He looked back with an Evangelical's sense of guilt,[3] which was largely justified.

[1] Monkenfrith, later Oak Hill: Daniel Lysons, *The Environs of London* (London, 1796), IV, 10; Frederick Charles Cass, *East Barnet* (Westminster, 1885-92), pp. 85-6; *V.C.H....Herts*, II, 341.

[2] Horace Twiss, *The Public and Private Life of Lord Chancellor Eldon* (London, 1844), I, 113; John Taylor, *Records of My Life* (London, 1832), I, 77-8 and II, 327-8; Edward Foss, *The Judges of England* (London, 1864), VIII, 264-6; Philip Thicknesse, *Sketches and Characters* (Bristol, 1770), p. 81; L. B. Namier, *The Structure of Politics at the Accession of George III* (London, 1929), I, 24, 36-7, 42; *The Grenville Papers*, ed. William James Smith (London, 1852-3), II, 153.

[3] See *Letters*, III, 20, 241-2; IV, 164.

'The colour of our whole life is generally such as the three or four first years in which we are our own masters, make it', he told young Samuel Rose, who was embarking on a career in law.[1]

Then it is that we may be said to shape our own destiny, and to treasure up for ourselves a series of future successes or disappointments. Had I employed my time...wisely...I had never been a poet perhaps, but I might by this time have acquired a character of more importance in society; and a situation in which my friends would have been better pleased to see me. But three years misspent in an attorney's office were almost of course followed by several more equally misspent in the Temple, and the consequence has been, as the Italian epitaph says, '*sto qui*'.

---

[1] 23 July 1789: *Letters*, III, 392.

VI

THE GENIUSES

...I was just got into the middle of the London Geniuses. They were
high-spirited and boisterous, but were very civil to me....

BOSWELL, *London Journal*

THESE words of Boswell on 24 May 1763 might well
have been written eight years earlier in a letter from
William Cowper to some old friend in Berkhamsted.
Boswell's 'Geniuses' were Bonnell Thornton, Robert Lloyd,
Charles Churchill, and John Wilkes, and a few days earlier
he had met another of their group, George Colman.[1] All
these men except Wilkes were Old Westminsters. Cowper
had known Lloyd, Colman, and Churchill at the school,
and would associate with them again, and with Thornton,
after he moved into the Temple. By the middle of the 1750's
these wits of his schooldays were drifting back to London
from the universities. Thornton had taken his B.A. at
Christ Church, Oxford, somewhat earlier (in 1747), but
Colman did not take his first degree from this college
until 1755. In the same year Robert Lloyd stood for his
B.A. at Trinity College, Cambridge. And Churchill—after
a few days in Cambridge, a Fleet marriage, and several
years in the country—was moving closer and closer to the
literary circles of the city: to Rainham (fifteen miles from
London) in 1756, and to St John's, Westminster, in 1758.[2]
This was the time of the *Connoisseur* (1754–6), in which
Thornton and Colman especially, and also Lloyd and
Cowper, were involved. But in 1755 none of these young
men was well-known, though they were all gaining reputations for cleverness and rakish living. Cowper was probably

---

[1] *London Journal*, pp. 254 and 257, n. 6.
[2] Wallace Cable Brown, *Charles Churchill* (Lawrence, Kansas, 1953), pp. 16–23.

never a flashing member of their society, yet from this time until his last year in London (1762–3), he would be identified with them, and would be a part of their escapades and literary efforts. Professor Pottle writes: 'If Boswell had not previously met Johnson, this meeting with the "Geniuses" might well have seemed to him the climax of his months in London.'[1] For Cowper, however, friendship with the 'Geniuses' did not come as the great happening of his years in the Temple, but as a gradual development in his friendships of the past decade.

In 1787 the Rev. John Newton told Miss Hannah More that the 'present Lord Chancellor [Thurlow], Mr Coleman of the Haymarket & the late Mr Bonnel Thornton, were the three persons with whom Mr Cowper was most intimate, when he resided in the Temple'.[2] Newton seems to have slighted a quiet, undistinguished friend of Cowper in selecting these three. He was Joseph Hill, not of Westminster, nor the universities, nor the Temple, but perhaps Cowper's closest friend—of these, or later, days.[3] Hill had been born near Chancery Lane, the son of an attorney who was the nephew and secretary of Sir Joseph Jekyll, Master of the Rolls. He had 'always lived in great intimacy' with William Cowper's uncle, Ashley Cowper, and his family, and soon after William left Westminster School he and young 'Sephus' or Joe Hill became friends.[4] Joe Hill had early been bred to the law; he had served as a clerk in Chancery Lane, later qualified as a solicitor and attorney, and became one of the Sixty, or Sworn Clerks in Chancery. He was, Cowper said, naturally formed for the legal

---

[1] *London Journal*, p. 266, n. 4.
[2] Newton to Hannah More, 11 May 1787: Morgan MSS.
[3] Joseph Hill (1733–1811): Wilfrid Hooper, 'Cowper's "Sephus"', *N. & Q.* 12th ser. v (1919), 258–9. (I am indebted to Hooper's article for most of my information regarding Hill.) Cowper wrote to Hill, 31 July 1769: 'I remember you with all the friendship I ever professed, which is as much as I ever entertained for any man' (*Letters*, I, 107).
[4] Hill to Hayley, 19 Feb. 1802: copy owned by Rev. W. Cowper Johnson, Norwich.

business. It was not hard to predict that he would have a crowded office.[1] Before long Hill acquired a 'flourishing and aristocratic practice, which numbered in its *clientèle* several members of the nobility'.[2] He was to become a rich man, owing to the esteem with which his wealthy clients regarded him: one client alone left him £10,000. Cowper helped Hill in his legal and financial progress by introducing him to Edward Thurlow. On his elevation to the Woolsack in 1778, Thurlow conferred on Hill one of the secretaryships in his bequest. 'I know not the income', Cowper said at that time, 'but as Mr. Hill is in good circumstances, and the gift was unasked, I dare say it is no trifle.'[3] When one recalls that these men had helped to care for their common friend Cowper during a period of lunacy, it seems an ironic appointment: Hill was made Secretary of Lunatics.

During most of his life Cowper was financially dependent on Joseph Hill. Hill not only handled Cowper's small monetary matters—paying his London bills, apportioning his income for expenses in Huntingdon, Olney, etc.—but from his own pocket made it possible for Cowper to live as a gentleman, though a very poor one. Dr Wilfrid Hooper once commented: 'Reading Cowper's letters with their incessant appeals for money, one wonders how ever he with his slender income, dependent on the favour of relatives, managed to make ends meet. The truth is that he did not manage; the "meeting" was effected by Hill out of his own means.'[4] Cowper accepted this steady aid as a normal course of events. He wrote to his friend Joe: 'The remem-

[1] *Letters*, I, 176.   [2] Hooper, 'Cowper's "Sephus"', p. 258.
[3] *Letters*, I, 148; see also I, 139, 147.
[4] Hooper, 'Cowper and the Law' (a paper read at St Andrew's Court House, London, on the occasion of the 19th annual meeting of the Cowper Soc., in 1919), quoted in Wright, *Life* (1921), p. 73. In the account of Cowper's estate, it is shown that Lady Hesketh, the administratrix, in March 1802 had to pay Joseph Hill £337, 'the Ballance of his Account of Moneys advanced to Mʳ Cowper'. (The account is publ. as an appendix to *U. & U.* p. 85.) Some conception of Cowper's indebtedness can be realized by glancing at the twenty-one letters to Hill printed in *Poems* (Bailey), pp. lxxvi–xci, where almost every letter begins with a request or thanks for £20 or £30.

brance of past years, and of the sentiments formerly ex-
changed in our evening walks, convinces me still that an
unreserved acceptance of what is graciously offered is the
handsomest way of dealing with one of your character.'[1]

Cowper's easy dependence on friends and relatives is not
one of the delightful qualities in his character. But he
should not be judged by the stringent requirements of the
self-reliant American ideal. He should be seen in the background of one of the great families of eighteenth-century
England, and of that century's world of sinecures and
patronage. Not all of Joseph Hill's money was earned. He
himself profited from the sinecures of Thurlow and others,
just as we shall see Cowper might have done but for his shy
and melancholy nature. Hill willingly gave help to his
needy friend because he believed that giving was a part of
the warmest kind of friendship, and because he wanted to
act as patron to a promising poet. All his life he was fond
of literature, and in his youth had himself 'some *flirtation at
least*, with the Muses, and wrote three or four light things
that were by no means destitute of Merit'. Hill's giving grew
also out of hours and hours of cheerful humour in their
youth. That was their primary bond of affection.[2] In 'An
Epistle to Joseph Hill, Esq.' (1784), Cowper recalled those
days in the Temple:

> Dear Joseph—five and twenty years ago—
> Alas, how time escapes!—'tis even so—
> With frequent intercourse, and always sweet,
> And always friendly, we were wont to cheat
> A tedious hour—

This was the way William repaid his benefactors—in his
own coin, which was verse and prose.

Hill was a plain man, 'close button'd to the chin', but

---

[1] *Letters*, I, 139.
[2] Lady Hesketh to Hayley, 14 Oct. 1801: Add. MSS. 30803 A, f. 169; also letter,
11 Feb. 1801 (ff. 99–100); *Letters*, I, 245–6.

a man whose language bespoke his deep knowledge of mankind. He was loved by his friends above all for his warm
heart, even though this warmth of personality could sometimes break into a hard, hot temper. When Cowper praised
his friend in public in 'An Epistle', Hill's hasty temper and
shy, retiring nature were roused. He was not pleased to
find himself exhibited, and he let Cowper know it. The
then much-more-retiring Cowper was consequently hurt.
'You may guess my Dear', he wrote to Lady Hesketh, 'that
I was mortified. In truth I could not have been mortified
more.'[1]

In the person of Hill, Cowper had a link which connected
the various elements of his early life. Hill knew the London
branch of the Cowper family; he was of the stable stock that
Cowper had associated with in his youth, though humbler
in background than most of his school friends; Hill was
working hard at the profession which Cowper was supposed
to be following; he knew the 'Geniuses' who were Cowper's
special friends during the era of his periodical publications.
He was a companion of Colman, Lloyd, Bensley, and in
fact, all the members of the Nonsense Club. Perhaps he was
a member of this group of seven Old Westminsters who
dined together every Thursday; if not, he was a guest at
their meetings.[2] For the only men certainly members were

---

[1] 'Epistle to Hill': *Poems*, p. 361; to Lady Hesketh, 23 Dec. 1785: Harvard Coll.
Libr. MS. *43M-109F. 'Epistle to Hill' was first publ. in the vol. with *The Task*
(London, 1785), pp. 285-8. Hill's strong temper was also commented on by Lady
Hesketh (to Hayley, 11 Feb. and 14 Oct. 1801) and Hayley (7 Oct. 1801): Add. MSS.
30803 A, ff. 99-100, 168-9.

[2] He was apparently not known to Bagot, Cowper's close friend at Westminster
(see Cowper's comments on Hill, *Letters*, II, 435, 457). Therefore, it is difficult to include him as 'one of a club of seven Westminster men to which I [Cowper] belonged,
who dined together every Thursday' (*Letters*, II, 317-18)—if Cowper's statement is to be
taken literally. He was nevertheless present at a meeting, and composed verses there
(*Letters*, III, 53-4). Two of Cowper's statements to Hill about the Nonsense Club further
suggest that he was not a full-fledged member. Cowper informs Hill about Gray and
the Society: 'He did not belong to our Thursday society, and was an Eton man, which
lowered him prodigiously in our esteem' (*Letters*, I, 141). And at another time: 'The
tragedies of Lloyd and Bensley are both very deep. If they are not of use to the surviving part of the society, it is their own fault' (*Letters*, I, 28). This last line would seem

Colman, Thornton, Lloyd, Bensley, and Cowper[1]—and Charles Churchill undoubtedly[2] took some part in the activities of the society.

One Old Westminster who may very well have been a member of the Nonsense Club was Chase Price. He was probably the 'Toby' and the 'C. P. Esq.' of Cowper's early poems and letters.[3] He knew the other members of the club: he subscribed to Lloyd's *Poems* in 1762 with Cowper, Colman, Churchill, Bensley (and his brothers), Thornton, and a large number of Cowper's friends from school and the Temple: Ashhurst, the Bagots, Sam Cox, Joseph Hill, Elijah Impey, Charles Morgan, Rowley, Sutton, Thurlow. Price joined his friends Wilkes, Garrick, and Churchill in the gluttony and ribaldry of the Beef-Steak Society. Here in a society celebrated for its beef and pork and wit, he outshone all others in provoking laughter. It is reported that he and the intemperate Churchill 'kept the table in a roar'.[4] Price was a rhymester, which was a requirement for the Nonsense Club, and like the members of that society, he was devoted to the theatre. He was also a member of the Inner Temple, as were Cowper and Bensley.

completely unlike Cowper—a harshness not in keeping with his character—if Hill were to be included among the members of the club. Yet John Johnson named Hill with Thornton, Lloyd, Colman, and Cowper (*Private Correspondence*, I, xxi).
  [1] Others suggested as members: (1) William de Grey (by John S. Memes, ed. *The Miscellaneous Works of William Cowper* (Edinburgh, 1834), I, 59—a very unreliable source: see Southey's *Cowper*, I, 324—accepted by Wright (*Letters*, I, 17), though only 'possibly' in *Life* (1921), p. 25; (2) Richard Cumberland—'It is possible, though not probable'—by Stanley T. Williams, *Richard Cumberland* (New Haven, 1917), pp. 13–14. The tone of Cowper's comments on Cumberland in *Letters*, III, 336, suggests that Cowper scarcely knew him, and certainly does not imply that he was a member of the club. (3) Edward Thurlow—by Memes and Eugene R. Page, *George Colman the Elder* (New York, 1935), p. 41, who bases this on Southey; but Southey nowhere suggests Thurlow, so far as I know. Only Cumberland of the three above-mentioned was at Westminster. I think it most unlikely that any one of them was a member of the club; they may, however, have attended the dinners of the society, but there is no evidence to this effect.
  [2] According to his biographer, W. C. Brown, *Charles Churchill*, pp. 63–5; Southey says he was not a member of the Nonsense Club: Southey's *Cowper*, I, 90.
  [3] See Appendix A, pp. 179–80, for considerable information about Chase Price and my reasons for identifying him with 'Toby' and 'C. P. Esq.'.
  [4] John Timbs, *Clubs and Club Life in London*, new ed. (London, 1908), p. 114.

Chase Price was most famous as the author and singer of extempore bawdy songs. In his witty compositions he tried to probe into the weaknesses of human character, to dart shafts into the foibles of virtuous men to prove his favourite maxim, that ridicule is the test of truth. Like Cowper, he knew how to seize upon the ludicrous, but Price did this maliciously—not with the kind and rollicking whimsy of Cowper. Price was a well-known patron of the courtesans of the day. And when he was not at a rowdy dinner, or with Wilkes and Mademoiselle Charpillon, or playing idly at politics, he was seeking out the great. He came from the ancient manor of the Prices, Monach-ty, near Knighton, Radnorshire, and it is said that in this Welsh village he offered his 'great friend' Rousseau a residence during his declining years.[1] As if these many interests were not enough to exhaust his passionate temperament, he was also an avid collector of art. He helped to make Mr James Christie an important dealer in art, but nearly broke him when he was unable to pay his large debt. The incident revealed the thinness of Price's moral principles, and his friend Garrick's generosity, for Garrick enabled Christie to recover from financial disaster.[2]

James Bensley is the least known of the members of the Nonsense Club. He entered Westminster School just two months before Cowper came, and was still in the school when Cowper left. He was elected with Robert Lloyd to a scholar-ship at Trinity College, Cambridge, in 1751. Although he and a friend were rusticated from the college in 1754 for 'grave irregularity and misbehaviour by insulting the Vice-

[1] [William Combe], Letters of the Late Lord Lyttelton, 8th ed. (London, 1793), I, 113–16, and The R——l Register (London, 1782), VII, 28–38; Horace Bleackley, Life of John Wilkes (London, 1917), pp. 321–2, 339; W. R. Williams, The Parliamentary History of the Principality of Wales (Brecknock, 1895), pp. 175–6; Jonathan Williams and Edwin Davies, A General History of the County of Radnor (Brecknock, 1905), pp. 86, 294–6, 306.
[2] [William Combe], The World as it Goes, 2nd ed. (London, 1779), p. 26; John Taylor, Records of My Life (London, 1832), II, 207; Joseph Farington, Diary, ed. J. Greig (London, [1922]), I, 265; W. Roberts, Memorials of Christie's (London, 1897), I, ix, 4.

Master, the Dean, and other officers of the College',[1] he went on to take a B.A. in 1755, and to become a fellow in the following year. He was admitted to the Inner Temple, but apparently he never lived among the members of that society. Bensley transferred to Lincoln's Inn in 1756, and was named of that Inn at the time of his death in 1765, when he was killed by a fall from his horse.[2] His death, which happened a few months after Lloyd had died in the Fleet, moved Cowper deeply. It brought among many thoughts of their friendship at school and in the club, the recollection that he was still in debt to his friend 'seven pounds, or nine, I forget which. If you can find out his brother', Cowper wrote to Joseph Hill, 'you will do me a great favour if you will pay him for me; but do it at your leisure.'[3] Leisure and nonchalance, as usual, were characteristic of Cowper when money and debts were concerned. The brother, Robert, he had known slightly, but he was only a boy when Cowper had left London.[4] Robert afterwards became one of the most acclaimed actors of the time, and a friend—enjoyed especially for his dry sarcastic humour—to Churchill, Lloyd, Colman, and Thornton of the old Nonsense group, and even better known in later life to William Windham and John Byng.[5]

Bonnell Thornton, a few years older than the other members of the club, was the instigator of many of its activities. In 1749 he had written *An Ode on Saint Cæcilia's Day, Adapted to the Ancient British Musick*. This was performed in 1763 with Dr Arne's music to enormous applause and amusement.[6]

---

[1] W. W. Rouse Ball, *Cambridge Papers* (London, 1919), p. 223.
[2] *London Mag.* xxxiv (1765), 266. According to a note in the Liverpool Univ. Libr. copy (Y77.2.68) of Lloyd's *Works* (1774), I, ix (apparently written by a former owner, B. N. Turner): 'Bensley died in Lincolnshire—from a mortificati[on] of a broken leg—his horse having ran [*sic*] against a Gat[e]-post with him.' Information from Mr Kenneth Povey.   [3] *Letters*, I, 28.   [4] *Letters*, II, 317–18.
[5] Taylor, *Records of My Life*, I, 431–2; II, 143–5; William Windham, *Diary*, ed. Mrs Henry Baring (London, 1866), pp. 50–1; John Byng, 5th Vct Torrington, *The Torrington Diaries*, ed. C. B. Andrews (London, 1934), I, 206.
[6] See my article, 'Dr. Arne's Music for Thornton's Burlesque Ode', *N. & Q.* ccii (1957), 71–3.

Thornton's verses were a burlesque of the odes for the St Cecilia Society—those, as he said in his Preface, of '*Johnny Dryden, Jemmy Addison, Sawney Pope, Nick Rowe,* little *Kit Smart,* &c.' and a satire on the 'Degeneracy of the present Age...in admiring that *Foreign* Musick now so much in Vogue'. As in Shakespeare's scenes of Bottom and his bumpkins, the tongs-and-bones music of the native humorous tradition was used to reinforce the literary satire. The huge crowd—Wilkes was present, and if Johnson was not, he was at least soon repeating its verses[1]—rocked with laughter at the sounds of the jew's-harp, hurdy-gurdy, salt-box, marrow-bones, and cleaver, and at the lyrics which mocked Milton's 'Nativity Ode':

> Be dumb, be dumb, ye inharmonious Sounds,
> And Musick, that th' astonish'd Ear with Discord wounds:
> No more let common Rhymes profane the Day,....

> The meaner melody we scorn,
> Which vulgar Instruments afford;
> Shrill *Flute,* sharp *Fiddle,* bellowing *Horn,*
> Rumbling *Bassoon,* or tinkling *Harpsichord.*
> In Strains more exalted the S A L T - B O X shall join,
> And Clattering, and Battering, and Clapping combine:
> With a Rap and a Tap while the hollow Side sounds,
> Up and down leaps the Flap, and with Rattling rebounds.[2]

Another of Thornton's and the Nonsense Club's satiric ventures was the burlesque of the annual exhibit of Polite Arts, in their 'Sign-Painters Exhibition' held in Thornton's chambers in Bow Street, March–June 1762.[3] Hogarth,

---

[1] *St James's Chron.* 9–11 June 1763; Boswell, *Johnson,* 1, 420. Mrs Thrale 'used to read it to Dᶜ Johnson' and was 'the *first* to shew it him': comment by Mrs Thrale in her copy of Chalmers' *British Essayists* (1817), xxx, xiv: Hyde Coll., Four Oaks Farm, Somerville, New Jersey.
[2] *An Ode on Saint Cæcilia's Day* (London, 1763), pp. 5–6.
[3] *London Register,* April 1762, pp. 345–52; Jacob Larwood [pseud. for H. D. J. van Scherichaven] and John Camden Hotten, *The History of Signboards* (London, 1866), pp. 512–26; Thornton to Mr Baldwin, printer, 3 June 1762: MS. in Yale Univ. Libr., Im/J637/+W791gh, iii, 238.

PLATE IV. BONNELL THORNTON (1724–68)

Stipple engraving, published 22 February 1794; frontispiece to the *Connoisseur* in 'Parson's Edition of Select British Classics'. Painter unknown.

under the name of Hagarty, assisted. The *London Register* praised Thornton's display of wit; he and Hogarth, the editors said, were the only men in England who could have successfully burlesqued the institution of the grand exhibition. 'There is a whimsical drollery in all his [Thornton's] plans, and a comical originality in his manner, that never fail to distinguish and recommend all his undertakings.... The Ridicule on exhibitions, if it must be accounted so, is pleasant without malevolence; and the general stroks [*sic*] on the common topics of satire are given with the most apparent good-humour.' Nevertheless a storm of controversy arose in the newspapers, and proper artists were incensed at what they considered to be mockery of their serious art.

Thornton was engaged in the publication of many light-hearted periodicals: with Smart on the *Student* and the *Midnight*, on the *Connoisseur* with Colman, on the *Drury-Lane Journal* and the *St James's Magazine*, the *Public Advertiser* and the *St James's Chronicle*.[1] His individual contributions to the magazines were considerable; according to Alexander Chalmers, 'scarce any popular topic offered of whatever kind, which did not afford to him a subject for a pamphlet, an essay, a piece of poetry, or some whimsical paragraphs for the newspapers'. But because these were anonymously published, and of a most topical interest, they do not contribute to his reputation. Colman once intended to collect Thornton's ephemera for publication, but this project was abandoned owing to the pressure of his work at the Haymarket Theatre.[2] Besides writing these many essays and verses, Thornton translated Plautus, and was considered

---

[1] According to *London Reg.* p. 345; Southey's *Cowper*, 1, 45; Gerard Edward Jensen, ed. Fielding's *The Covent-Garden Journal* (New Haven, 1915), 1, 32–3, 54–5; *Connoisseur*, publ. J. Parsons (London, 1793), III, x, and ed. Chalmers, *The British Essayists* (London, 1802), xxx, xxiii; Boswell, *London Journal*, p. 266; Herman W. Liebert, 'Whose Book? An Exercise in Detection', *Yale Univ. Libr. Gaz.* xxviii (1953–4), 71–4.
[2] Chalmers, xxx, xxiii, xxvi.

by some to be one of the finest Latin scholars of his time. Boswell found him a 'well-bred, agreeable man, lively and odd. He had about £15,000 left him by his father', Boswell said; 'was bred to physic, but was fond of writing. So he employs himself in that way.' Liveliness, in writing and in conversation, seems to have been his chief attribute; 'as a companion', said Joseph Warton, 'he was delightful'.[1]

Thornton's best friend was George Colman the Elder. And of the literati, Colman was probably also closest to Cowper. The three took their greatest pleasure in a similar kind of humour—a light playfulness and wittiness, and good-natured caricature. As a schoolboy, Colman—in spite of pressures and threats from his Uncle William Pulteney, the Earl of Bath—had spent more time in thinking about the theatre than about the law. He was as obsessed with drama as his friend Cowper was with poetry. In 1749 Colman acted in the annual Westminster production of one of Terence's comedies (he was Geta in the *Phormio*). This was the work, as always, of the King's Scholars, so Cowper could not participate, but he must have had enormous pleasure in watching the acting of his friends Colman and Lloyd, Walter Bagot, George Hobart, and Frederick Vane.[2] In 1761 Colman established himself with his five-act comedy *The Jealous Wife*; four years later he collaborated with his friend Garrick in *The Clandestine Marriage*. By 1789 he had written or adapted over forty dramatic pieces, and had been for many years manager of Covent Garden (1767–74) and the Haymarket (1777–89) theatres.

There was a period in the 1780's in which Cowper felt their friendship had become acid, especially when Colman and Thurlow had ignored the presentation copies of his

---

[1] Boswell, *London Journal*, p. 266. Joseph Warton's epitaph on Thornton in the cloisters of Westminster Abbey; trans. from Latin by Chalmers, xxx, xxix.

[2] James Mure, Henry Bull, and Charles B. Scott, eds. *Lusus Alteri Westmonasterienses* (London, 1863,) I, 83.

poems. Cowper's verses on the occasion, 'The Valediction',[1] are among his most biting. Colman he addressed as

Amusement-monger of a trifling age,
Illustrious histrionic patentee,
Terentius, once my friend, farewell to thee.

But really the friendship was always there: in 1766 Cowper could not read *The Clandestine Marriage*, not for Evangelical reasons but because of pain at the thought that he might not see Colman again. In 1785 Cowper said, 'time alone cannot efface the traces of such a friendship as I have felt for you,—no, not even time with distance to help it'. And Colman replied to his 'dear old friend and acquaintance, my dear Cowper', that he had 'never lost the remembrance of the sweet counsel we took together. I have often thought of you with a most affectionate regret, and often mentioned you in terms that went not only from the mouth, but the heart.... I am just what I was, just what you left me, the same feeling, fretful, fond, and I will say faithful, creature you once knew me.'[2]

With Robert Lloyd, Colman had written the two burlesque odes to Gray and Mason, printed in May 1760 as the 'Odes to Obscurity and Oblivion'. These were probably written as Nonsense-Club exercises.[3] They were Colman's best things, Johnson said; the first of them, the best; 'but they are both good. They exposed a very bad kind of writing.'[4] In 1763 Colman was called upon by Lloyd to assist him in his *St James's Magazine*. Lloyd was the son of Cowper's beloved 'Tappy' Lloyd, for nearly fifty years a master at Westminster School. In the year that Robert, the son, stood first in the list of Westminster scholars going to Cambridge (Trinity College), Colman held the same

[1] *Poems*, pp. 357-9. 'The Valediction' was not printed until after Cowper's death.
[2] *Letters*, I, 61; II, 419; Colman to Cowper, 22 Jan. 1785: *Poems* (Bailey), pp. lv–lvi.
[3] Colman, *Prose on Several Occasions* (London, 1787), I, xi; Gray's *Corr.* II, 674, n. 16; Southey's *Cowper*, I, 50. See Appendix A, pp. 195-7.
[4] Boswell, *Johnson*, II, 334-5.

rank among those entering Christ Church. At the University Lloyd's life was marked by irregularity in everything he did, by wildness and drinking. And the drinking continued and grew worse when he had returned to London, especially after he had left his place as an usher at Westminster. His nights, and Churchill's even more frequently, were spent in unashamed carousing.[1] In one of his amusements in verse, Boswell wrote:

> Than Robert Lloyd no stranger Blade
> Eer undertook the writing trade
> The Muses very well he knows
> But Bachus leads him by the nose
> And hence it is so wond'rous long
> For Bachus' grips are mighty strong.[2]

In contrast to thin-faced, long-nosed Robert Lloyd—but friendly and with gentle manners—was his friend Charles Churchill. Churchill was heavy-featured, with pouting, sensual lips; he was rough, blunt, and bear-like. 'The strictest friendship always subsisted between them', Wilkes said; and Lloyd was never jealous of Churchill's greater talents and success. 'He was contented to scamper round the foot of Parnassus on his little Welch pony, which seems never to have tired. He left the fury of the winged steed, and the daring heights of the sacred mountain, to the sublime genius.' He was happy for a time in the pleasures of conversation, in his classical scholarship, and his jingling verse. 'His peculiar excellence'—again from Wilkes—'was the dressing up an old thought in a new, neat, and trim manner.' Not a very large talent, but one which he carried with ease and charm. Lloyd's last days, however, were miserable. Deep in debt, he was thrown into the Fleet; there were no friends except Churchill left to help him.

---

[1] Nichols, *Anecdotes*, II, 331; John Wilkes's notes to Churchill's 'Night', *The Correspondence of the late John Wilkes*, ed. John Almon (London, 1805), III, 10–11.

[2] Among Boswell's verses written in Holland, 1763–4: Private Papers of James Boswell, Yale Univ. Libr. MSS.

PLATE V. ROBERT LLOYD (1733–64) AND
CHARLES CHURCHILL (1732–64)

Line engraving; from a contemporary periodical (?);
in the possession of the author.

Churchill paid for a servant to attend him, and gave Lloyd in addition a guinea a week. In his sufferings Lloyd became even more tenderhearted than usual, and pathetically grateful for every kindness.[1]

After Churchill died, on 4 November 1764, Lloyd wrote to Wilkes, who was in France: 'Thornton is what you believed him. I have many acquaintance, but now no friend here.'[2] Thornton and Lloyd had quarrelled, and Thornton had become his 'inveterate enemy, in the quality of his most inexorable creditor'.[3] Wilkes wrote to Colman, in a lonely, warm, sad letter after the death of Lloyd—full of love and friendship and genuine loss—that Lloyd had 'Subject of just indignation against *Thornton*: so had *Churchill*. I am a little inclin'd to revenge both their quarrels. Our dear friend wish'd I would. What is your opinion?' Colman replied: 'I leave him to your justice but commend him to your mercy. Spare him, I beseech you Good Wilkes!'[4] But in the meantime, Wilkes had found among Churchill's manuscripts a hundred lines of a violent satire against not only Thornton, but also Colman, and even Lloyd.[5]

The loves and friendships of these men were always strong and passionate: based, it would seem, on a pact of extraordinary faithfulness—financial aid, if necessary, and always moral support. If the slightest failure in the heavy demands of loyalty occurred, or if friendship seemed to

---

[1] John Wilkes, *Letters between...Grafton...Churchill and John Wilkes* ([London?], 1769), pp. 296–7, 302–4; Nichols, *Anecdotes*, II, 331.

[2] Wilkes, *Letters*, p. 304.

[3] W. Kenrick, ed. *The Poetical Works of Robert Lloyd* (London, 1774), I, xxv; see also pp. xxvi–xxvii, but Kenrick is often untrustworthy.

[4] Wilkes to Colman, 25 March 1765: Colman, *Posthumous Letters* (London, 1820), p. 87; Colman to Wilkes, June 1765: Add. MSS. 30877, f. 41.

[5] William Cooke, *Memoirs of Samuel Foote* (London, 1805), II, 147–8. John Forster, in *Historical and Biographical Essays* (London, 1858), II, 217, doubted 'the alleged desertion of poor Lloyd which is said to have suggested the satire'. Since Cooke is the primary and only real authority for this report on the 'violent satire', his word must be taken as it stands.

grow thin after years of separation (as in the case of Cowper with Colman and Thurlow), the injured member grew resentful and bitter. They were all—Cowper, Colman, Thornton, Lloyd, and Churchill—peculiarly sensitive to the fluctuations of affection, and quickly hurt. As Southey wrote, 'when Thornton is spoken of as an inexorable creditor, it may be suspected that because he had done much, more was expected from him; and that when he had gone as far or farther than his own means could well afford, he found himself like the man in the old print, who having lent his money to his friend, lost both in consequence'.[1] In the case of Churchill's satire, the whim of a day, or even of months, should not be taken as the true feeling of the man.[2] Basically, during the late 1750's and from 1760 to 1763 when Churchill had joined them, the group was bound together with deep friendship, though Cowper was particularly attached to Colman, and Colman to Thornton, and Lloyd to Churchill, and after 1762, Churchill to Wilkes.

'Half Drunk—Half Mad—and quite stripp'd of all my Money'—this, in his own words to Garrick,[3] was very frequently Charles Churchill. And his 'dictionary knows but Rogue and Whore', said Bentley. When he got rid of his two 'causes of complaint'—the wife he 'was tired of', and the clerical gown he 'was displeased with'—he began life with the bucks and bloods, in the taverns, at the stews, getting the clap, getting rid of it again, and trying out mistresses. Wilkes made some attempt, though jokingly, to speak of honour and love; but Churchill's objects were more elemental: 'My Life I hold for purposes of pleasure;

---

[1] Southey's *Cowper*, I, 104, n. 32.
[2] For the fluctuating friendships of Churchill and Garrick, see Edward H. Weatherly, 'The Personal and Literary Relations of Charles Churchill and David Garrick', *Studies in Honor of A. H. R. Fairchild*, ed. C. T. Prouty, *Univ. Missouri Stud.* XXI, no. 1 (1946), 151–60.
[3] *Private Correspondence of David Garrick* (London, 1832), II, 338; dated, perhaps autumn or winter 1761, by Weatherly, p. 157.

those forbid, it is not worth my care.'[1] But his braggadocio betrays his youth. In their correspondence, Churchill's and Wilkes's indecencies and blasphemies remain the smut of schoolboys.

Men like these were among Cowper's companions, though we do not know that he was ever especially a friend to Churchill; and though we have no record of a meeting with Wilkes, yet it seems probable that they were known to each other. Their ribald, hard-drinking, fast-living days and nights were a part of Cowper's life during the Temple years.

Friendships with these members of the Nonsense Club must have brought at least an acquaintance with more of the London literati, including Christopher Smart. Cowper subscribed to Smart's *Poems on Several Occasions* and to *A Translation of the Psalms of David*. He knew Canonbury House, Islington, where Smart lived from 1753 to 1756 and Goldsmith 1762–3.[2] Smart was a good friend of Thornton; the two collaborated on the periodicals the *Student* and the *Midnight*, and Smart dedicated his *Parables of Our Lord and Saviour Jesus Christ* to Thornton's eldest son, 'Master Bonnell George Thornton,...scarce three years of Age'. Smart's friends were remembered in his *Jubilate Agno*: 'God be gracious to Churchill, Loyd.' In April 1747 Cowper's cousin Spencer Madan (afterwards Bishop of Peterborough) had been in Smart's play—in which Smart also acted—*A Trip to Cambridge, or the Grateful Fair*.[3] There were many associations which would lead one to suppose that Cowper and Smart were known to each other.

---

[1] [Richard Bentley], *Patriotism*, 2nd ed. (London, 1765), p. 28: Canto III, l. 30; *Genuine Memoirs of Mr Charles Churchill* (London, 1765), pp. 125–7; 'Memoirs of the Reverend Mr Charles Churchill', *London Chron.* 6–8 Dec. 1764, p. 548; Churchill's letters to Wilkes in *The Correspondence of John Wilkes and Charles Churchill*, ed. E. H. Weatherly (New York, 1954), pp. 16, 19, 38, 48, 54, 71, 75.
[2] See Appendix C, p. 259.
[3] Robert Brittain, 'Intro.', *Poems by Christopher Smart* (Princeton, 1950), p. 17; [Christopher Hunter], 'The Life of Christopher Smart', in Smart's *Poems* (Reading, 1791), I, xiv.

Cowper was therefore in many ways familiar with the life of the hungry poets in the garrets and alleys of London, as well as the more elegant company of writers in the Temple; through his friends he knew the two other centres of young writers, Oxford and Cambridge. Cambridge especially, for in 1756 and thereafter his brother John was at Corpus Christi College. On visits to Cambridge Cowper must have met his brother's literary friends, and widened his own literary acquaintance. In 1761, or perhaps a little later, John Cowper acted as curate to the Rev. Francis Fawkes,[1] Vicar of Orpington with St Mary Cray, in Kent. Fawkes, a jovial man, full of humour, was the author of the extremely popular song 'The Brown Jug' and other robust comic verse. He was a friend of the Duncombes, father and son, and Dr Hawkesworth, Goldsmith, and probably of Smart, a contemporary at Cambridge, whose Tripos Verses (1740–2) he translated into English. Fawkes assisted the Duncombes (with William Cowper and others) in their translations of Horace, and translated Apollonius Rhodius, on whom John Cowper had worked for years with but little success.[2] Fawkes's translations of Anacreon and Theocritus established him among the most distinguished translators after Pope. And in 1763, with William Woty, he published one of the finest collections of contemporary verse, *The Poetical Calendar*. William Cowper, like his brother, would have found in Fawkes a man of kindred interests in humour, the classics, and the techniques of translation, which absorbed many of William's days when he was supposed to be studying law.

There was another Cambridge friend of John Cowper who was definitely a friend of William—Robert Glynn (afterwards Clobery), the leading physician of the town and

---

[1] We have no proof that Fawkes and William Cowper were personally acquainted, but it seems probable to me. See *Letters*, II, 390; H. P. Stokes, *Cowper Memorials*, pp. 17–18.   [2] Stokes, pp. 29–30, 50, 53, 98–100, 113–14.

University. He was John's doctor, and Thomas Gray's, and the associate of Gray and all the poets about Cambridge.[1] Glynn himself was a minor versifier and had won the Seatonian Prize at Cambridge; he was a 'fine old Grecian' according to Cowper, but he gained his small renown for his involvement in the Chatterton-Rowley controversy. Glynn owned many of the Rowleyan manuscripts, which he vehemently endorsed, and bequeathed to the British Museum.[2] He was known for this collection and his role of an 'original' in Cambridge. Glynn was a man of 'rough and eccentric manners', and prided himself on saying whatever came first to his mind. His astonishing ugliness was notorious; it inspired a wag of the university to write the epigram:

> This morning, quite dead, Tom was found in his bed,
> Although he was hearty last night;
> 'Tis thought, having seen Dr. Glynn in a dream,
> The poor fellow died of affright.

An excellent physician, with a wide knowledge of the field, Glynn was unremitting in his attention to his patients. But he was of the old school, his more modern contemporaries said. 'Bleeding, opium, tartarized antimony, and cathartics, were excluded from his list of remedies. It is not easy to conceive how any man could consent to deprive himself of such powerful auxiliaries in a struggle with disease.'[3] Perhaps he was so popular because he did.

[1] [David Rivers], *Literary Memoirs of Living Authors* (London, 1798), I, 214–15; Nichols, *Anecdotes*, VIII, 211–16; Henry Gunning, *Reminiscences of the University, Town, and County of Cambridge* (London, 1854), II, 98–103; Cowper to Glynn, 25 Dec. 1790: *Letters*, IV, 14–16; also I, 113, 118; Lady Hesketh to John Johnson, 8 Dec. 1790; 'Dr. Glyn...whom he [Cowper] highly respects' (Hesketh, *Letters*, pp. 15–16). Glynn was Gray's friend, and attended him in his last illness: William Mason, *Memoirs of the Life and Writings of Mr Gray* (York, 1775), p. 399.
[2] E. H. W. Meyerstein, *A Life of Thomas Chatterton* (London, 1930), *passim*; Sir Egerton Brydges, *Autobiography* (London, 1834), I, 64.
[3] Nichols, *Anecdotes*, IV, 668–9; VIII, 520; Brydges, I, 64; [Richard Gooch], *Facetiæ Cantabrigienses*, 3rd ed. (London, 1836), pp. 96, 121; R. A. Davenport, 'The Life of Robert Glynn, M.D.', Whittingham's *British Poets* (Chiswick, 1822), LVIII, 242.

During the years 1750–60, directly or indirectly, Cowper had connections with many of the leading younger poets, essayists, journalists, translators, and their patrons. He was most definitely among the Geniuses. But was he—like these men—of showy appearance, a colourful 'high-spirited and boisterous' figure who might have caught Boswell's notice? What did the Geniuses find attractive in William Cowper?

At this time he was of medium height, more strongly built than delicate; light brown hair, dark hazel eyes, his complexion ruddy[1]—florid, in fact, owing perhaps to an 'erysipelatous complaint of the face'[2] in very early life. He was still a 'florid healthy figure' at the age of sixty-one.[3] In young manhood he already had a fascinating mixture of awkwardness and dignity, melancholy and cheerfulness, gravity with sportive humour in a constantly varying countenance and personality. He dressed neatly—but was not finical—and with colour: even in old age he was most often seen in green and buff. He loathed all affectation in manners, as well as in the language he spoke and wrote.[4] Never disdaining common words or ordinary people, he was yet always a gentleman: he would be 'Sir Cowper' or 'the Esquire' of Olney.[5]

---

[1] Hayley (1803), II, 221. Hayley's description of Cowper's eyes (blue-grey) was corrected by Lady Hesketh: 'my Sist[r] [Theadora] complains that you have mistaken y[e] *Color* of our dear friends Eyes...she protests they were dark Hazel and I join her in that Decision' (to Hayley, 10 Feb. 1803: Add. MSS. 30803 B, f. 105).

[2] *Private Correspondence*, I, xv.

[3] Hayley to his wife, 25 Aug. 1792, on first meeting Cowper: Hayley's *Memoirs*, I, 434.

[4] *Ibid.*; Hayley (1803), II, 221–3; *Letters*, IV, 286; *Task*, II, 416–17.

[5] Cowper to Hill, 31 July 1769: 'Sir Cowper, for that is his title at Olney' (*Letters*, I, 106); Newton's letter, 3 Feb. 1781, is addressed to 'Sir Cowper Esq[r]': B.M.: Eg. MSS. 3662, f. 12; Samuel Teedon, *Diary*, ed. Thomas Wright (London, 1902), *passim*—Cowper is always referred to as 'the Esq[r]' by Teedon, the schoolmaster of Olney. Sir Thomas Lawrence told Farington that when he knew Cowper (at the end of his life) 'his appearance was that of a gentleman, but rather of a former fashion, what is now called "*The Old Court*"' (*Farington Diary* [London, 1923], II, 108). Lawrence's statement is corroborated in a letter from Cowper's cousin Mrs Maria Cowper to her sister, Mrs Penelope Maitland, 25 March 1786: 'I am told he dresses

He was shy: 'I am a shy animal', he said, 'and want much kindness to make me easy. Such I shall be to my dying day.' Shyness was an 'effectual and almost fatal hindrance on many...important occasions', in youth and throughout his life. Hayley, friend to both Cowper and Blake, said they were alike in tenderness of heart and in a 'too apprehensive Spirit'.[1] Yet until several years later, Cowper's nervous affections were not of any duration, but came in short, isolated depressive spells. In the long periods in between the attacks of melancholia, his 'animal sprightliness' flowed with 'great equality', so that he was never exalted in proportion to his depression. Nevertheless, his feelings were 'all of the intense kind. I never received a *little* pleasure from any thing in my life', he said; 'if I am delighted, it is in the extreme.'[2] So he was, a man of contrarieties, but these were usually so disguised, or so pleasantly revealed, as to give the semblance of a harmonious nature; that is, before insanity had severely tried his spirit.

Several elements in Cowper's character were constant in his life: humour (except in the blackest periods) and a love of retirement and domesticity:

> Domestic happiness, thou only bliss
> Of Paradise that has surviv'd the fall![3]

The same man, in his quiet way, was ambitious—but in opposition to his father's hopes, to be a poet. He said: 'I am a whimsical creature; when I write for the public I write of course with a desire to please, in other words, to acquire fame, and I labour accordingly; but when I find

---

with exactest order and neatness, *and looks like an old Nobleman'* (*Madan Family*, p. 130). Lady Hesketh told Hayley: 'in regard to my dear Cousins person I can only say when young he was genteel & Gentleman like—never handsome in my estimation at leest [*sic*], but had a very sweet quick & Intelligent Countenance' (26 April 1801: Add. MSS. 30803 A, f. 127).

[1] To Walter Bagot, 2 Aug. 1791: Morgan MSS. MA 86, vol. I, f. 35; *Letters*, IV, 416; 'Conversation', ll. 347–58: *Poems*, p. 97; Hayley to Lady Hesketh, 15 July 1802: Add. MSS. 30803 B, ff. 56–7.   [2] *Letters*, I, 188; III, 46–7.

[3] *Task*, III, 41–2; see also *Letters*, I, 107.

that I have succeeded, feel myself alarmed, and ready to shrink from the acquisition.'[1] He wrote always for publication: 'For my own part, I could no more amuse myself with writing verse, if I did not print it when written, than with the study of Tacticks for which I can never have any real occasion'; '*publication is necessary to give an edge to the poetical turn*'. 'I have (what, perhaps, you little suspect me of) in my nature an infinite share of ambition. But with it I have at the same time, as you well know, an equal share of diffidence.'[2]

Cowper was enjoyed by the literati of mid-eighteenth-century London because of a highly pleasing and interesting personality, because of poetical promise (though it did not seem as immediate or as bright as that of several of his friends), and because he was a good fellow at their gay parties and in their disreputable follies.[3] He could down four or five bottles of claret, 'without sensible effect'.[4] But he was enjoyed first of all by everyone for his conversation, at which he was a master.

Mr. Cowper was peculiarly well qualified by nature, to be an agreeable companion in a small circle. We have seen him dwell, with exquisite delight, on that delicate vein of humour, which

---

[1] *Letters*, IV, 431.

[2] To Walter Churchey, 13 Dec. 1786: Morgan MSS. MA 86, vol. I, f. 55; *Letters*, III, 36.

[3] 'A. B.' to the Editor of the *G.M.* (Nichols), 16 Jan. 1786 (vol. LVI, Pt i, pp. 4–5): 'I understand that Mr. Cowper was once a man immersed in all the gaieties of the town. If respect for his present character did not restrain me, perhaps I might have said, that he was not free from its vices. He was the companion and the delight of a convivial and jolly circle, whose society he has long renounced....' 'A. B.' was 'not a perfect stranger' either to Nichols or Cowper, and had 'a distant knowledge' of Cowper's history. Cowper read this letter, and did not deny the report of his early life; in fact, he was not at all displeased. In private conversation in later years he was probably quite realistic about the activities of the Nonsense Club, and even in his Evangelical period, he would most likely tell a vivid story of life before his conversion. He wrote to Lady Hesketh, 11 Feb. 1786: 'A letter to Mr. Urban [Nichols] in the last *Gentleman's Magazine*, of which I's book is the subject, pleases me more than any thing I have seen in the way of eulogium yet. I have no guess of the author' (*Letters*, II, 464). Nor have I.

[4] So he told Mrs Unwin. Reported by Greatheed to Hayley, 26 Aug. 1800: Fitzwilliam MSS.

gives so high a relish to the *Spectators* of Mr. Addison. Nor is it flattery to say, that he possessed the same kind of humour, in a degree not inferior to Mr. Addison himself. With a low voice, and much apparent gravity and composure, he was accustomed repeatedly to surprise his hearers with observations, which not only proved him to be possessed of knowledge and taste, but evinced an extraordinary power of being ludicrous whenever he pleased.[1]

Sir Thomas Lawrence described Cowper to Farington in almost the same way: 'Cowper's manner seemed to him to answer the description given of Addison, by Steele:—It was pleasant, with a tendency to delicate satire.'[2] It was the manner that was characteristic of so much of his verse— most noteworthy, the verse that would come later in *The Task*. But also in the *Poems*. It was the complexity of humour and satire with morality in his first book of verse that the critical Monthly Reviewers so much admired. 'Mr. Cowper's predominant turn of mind, though serious and devotional, is at the same time dryly humorous and sarcastic. Hence his very religion has a smile that is arch, and his sallies of humour an air that is religious; and yet motley as is the mixture, it is so contrived as to be neither ridiculous or disgusting.'[3]

Hayley reported that Cowper had 'uncommon talents for conversation' which was distinguished by 'mild and benevolent pleasantry, by delicate humour peculiar to himself'.[4] His peculiar kind of humour was revealed pre- eminently in his table talk; in a small group at tea or at supper he would frequently be the chief contributor. It was his way of telling a story, of course, that would convulse his audience with laughter. 'They knew that something

---

[1] Anonymous review of Greatheed's *Sermon on Cowper*: *Anti-Jacobin Rev.* VIII (1801), 271.   [2] *Farington Diary*, II, 108.
[3] Review of Cowper's *Poems*: *Monthly Rev.* LXVII (1782), 262. The reviewer was Edmund Cartwright (1743–1823), D.D., the reputed inventor of the power loom: see Benjamin Christie Nangle, *The Monthly Review: First Series* (Oxford, 1934), pp. 8, 83.
[4] Hayley (1803), II, 224–5.

delightful was coming before it came. His eye would suddenly kindle and all his face become lighted up with the fun of the story, before he opened his lips to speak. At last he began to relate some ludicrous incident,—which, although you had yourself witnessed it, you had failed to recognize as mirthful.' He was prepared at all times in conversation, as in his letters, 'to construct out of the slenderest materials an amusing incident. So ready and so graceful in fact was the poet's fancy, that he knew how to make an amusing story out of *nothing*.'[1]

It is not surprising that Thornton, Colman, and Lloyd sought his company. The appreciation of the ludicrous is common to their verse and essays and to his. Perhaps Cowper influenced them in their early compositions, which were at that time more important than his. He was undoubtedly influenced by them. Cowper's light verse resembles Lloyd's, a similar natural, playful wit; similar versification. And in structure, his longer verse—in particular when satiric—suggests Churchill's longer poems. But when Cowper finally steps forward in *The Task* and in the best of his letters, fully mature, he is distinctly himself, and has left them far behind. He is then his own master.

---

[1] Reported by John Higgins (1768–1846), a squire of Weston Underwood, and friend of Cowper, to John William Burgon, *Lives of Twelve Good Men* (London, 1888), II, 349–51; see also II, 210–11.

VII

WRITING

The Comic Spirit...is the daylight side of the night half-obscuring Cowper. GEORGE MEREDITH, *An Essay on Comedy and the Uses of the Comic Spirit*

I am glad you love Cowper. I could forgive a man for not enjoying Milton, but I would not call that man my friend, who should be offended with the 'divine chit-chat of Cowper'.
CHARLES LAMB to S. T. COLERIDGE[1]

THOUGH there is no one poem or piece of prose that is in itself unusually important, the early works of Cowper nevertheless contain passages which adumbrate almost everything he did later. His genius developed late, yet in his first writings the variety of his individual abilities is shown, and small fragments of each type of mood and verse in which he was later to excel are clearly created. The humour characteristic of 'John Gilpin' is there, and the mock-heroic of *The Task*. So is his tenderness, his particular description of nature, his mild but firm rebellion against the Augustan mode. There is at times the terror of 'The Castaway'. The poetry is largely impromptu, and lacking the real occasion for poetry it remains polite but undistinguished armchair verse. It follows in the Cowper family tradition, and seems many times to be no better than that which any well-tutored, moderately sensitive gentleman could write. And then, suddenly, there comes a line which is a foretaste of his very best poetry of twenty or thirty years later.

In one of his earliest poems Cowper tells what is, perhaps,

---

[1] Lamb to Coleridge, 5 Dec. 1796, Lamb's *Letters*, ed. E. V. Lucas (New Haven, 1935), I, 66. Coleridge originated the phrase 'divine chit-chat of Cowper': see I, 73, and Coleridge to John Thelwall, 17 Dec. 1796, Coleridge's *Letters*, ed. E. L. Griggs (Oxford, 1956), I, 279.

the basic reason for his writing poetry: to escape from depression. He told Robert Lloyd, a friend to whom he could speak without restraint, that he wrote

> ...to divert a fierce banditti
> (Sworn foes to ev'ry thing that's witty),
> That, with a black infernal train,
> Make cruel inroads in my brain,
> And daily threaten to drive thence
> My little garrison of sense:
> The fierce banditti, which I mean,
> Are gloomy thoughts led on by Spleen.[1]

The lines are typical of much of the poetry written between 1748 and 1764. They are loose and jingly. The wit which later came smoothly, is here forced. Though the tone of 'An Epistle to Robert Lloyd, Esq.' is derived from the elegant wit of a young man about town, yet the rather showy cleverness is broken by darkness and worry. The uncertainty of Cowper's life, notwithstanding some social poise, is reflected in his verse.

But the wit is important, especially as burlesque. It was part of the 'self-deception', he said, 'to which I am indebted for all the little comfort I enjoy'.[2] The first poem in the canon of his work, 'Verses Written at Bath on Finding the Heel of a Shoe' (1748), reveals him in this guise, parodying Milton.

> Fortune! I thank thee: gentle Goddess! thanks!
> Not that my muse, tho' bashful shall deny
> She would have thank'd thee rather, hadst thou cast
> A treasure in her way; for neither meed
> Of early breakfast, to dispel the fumes
> And bowel-raking pains of emptiness,
> Nor noon-tide feast, nor ev'ning's cool repast,
> Hopes she from this—presumptuous,—tho', perhaps,
> The cobbler, leather-carving artist, might![3]

---

[1] 'An Epistle to Robert Lloyd, Esq.': *Poems*, p. 267.
[2] *Letters*, I, 214.   [3] *Poems*, p. 263.

The movement and language of Milton's verse are burlesqued lightly, but at other times the same Miltonisms appear to Cowper's detriment. The influence of Milton or Pope could make him write as a poor copyist, even when he tried for a humorous effect. Sober or comical periphrasis— 'cobbler, leather-carving artist'—was not always fortunate in his poetry. Occasionally it came out as bad Homer, or bad Milton, or bad Pope. The imitative style was frequently present in Cowper's writing; many of his basic modes of expression were to remain derivative.

Another one of these was circumlocution, which Cowper used as a part of the mock-heroic scheme. The 'Verses Written at Bath' are monotonously circuitous in form. Unlike the famous cucumber passage, and other skilful Miltonic parodies in *The Task*, the humour seems cheap. A lofty poetical style is puffed out and deflated time after time. The false modesty and involved development of the simple idea appear to be unjustifiable.

In his early poetry Cowper is more successful at whimsy, in which he has no trouble with too lofty or too low a tone. Cowper needs a human foible to puncture directly (but he does it with gentleness), instead of an idea on which to generalize. Therefore he writes better light verse when he can mock the foolishness of a lover, or the uncomplicated forms of Restoration or Augustan lyric. In the songs about 'sad Phyllida' and 'hapless Celia'—trivial as they are, and clumsy in parts—Cowper's delicate burlesque comes through easily.

> No more shall hapless Celia's ears
> Be flatter'd with the cries
> Of lovers drown'd in floods of tears,
> Or murder'd by her eyes;
> No serenades to break her rest,
> Nor songs her slumbers to molest,
> With my fa, la, la.[1]

---

[1] *Poems*, p. 265.

William's sincere love poems for 'Delia', Theadora
Cowper,[1] are almost entirely conventional and uninspired.
Two or three times, however, he rises to the kind of poetry
for which he is remembered. At the close of the verses,
'On Her Endeavouring to Conceal Her Grief at Parting',
there are lines which, for the literary historian, are Cowper's
first heralding of Romantic poetry. There is a simple statement of unashamed personal emotion, as in the poetry of the
next generation, though the last two lines especially, are
constructed with a characteristically Cowperian adaptation
of earlier verse rhythm.

> Oh! then indulge thy grief, nor fear to tell
> The gentle source from whence thy sorrows flow!
> Nor think it weakness when we love to feel,
> Nor think it weakness what we feel to show.

A few years later (c. 1762) Cowper again turns from
Augustan principles to foreshadow an ideal of Romanticism:

> 'Tis woven in the world's great plan,
> And fix'd by heav'n's decree,
> That all the true delights of man
> Should spring from *Sympathy*.

In another poem he has the metre and style of 'The
Poplar-Field':

> Bid adieu, my sad heart, bid adieu to thy peace,
> Thy pleasure is past, and thy sorrows increase;
> See the shadows of ev'ning how far they extend,
> And a long night is coming, that never may end;
> For the sun is now set that enliven'd the scene,
> And an age must be past ere it rises again.[2]

Some of the quiet, pensive sounds of farewell are here, what

---

[1] *Poems*, pp. 269–83. The first poem he ever wrote to Theadora was that beginning
'This ev'ning, Delia, you and I'—so Theadora told Hayley: Hayley's *Vindication* (MS.),
f. 25.
[2] *Poems*, pp. 278, 286.

Tennyson referred to as the 'exquisite flow and even-
ness'[1] of

> The poplars are fell'd, farewell to the shade
> And the whispering sound of the cool colonnade.[2]

To write a good poem, early or late, Cowper needed the
sharper edge of circumstance. The only forceful poems, or
those which have sincerity and passion and unity, are two
written under stress. One was composed as he faced the
sudden death of a friend, Sir William Russell, and the
broken engagement with Theadora, and the other in the
fearful depression of 1763. The first was written in 1757,
and reveals already the strong personal note of tragedy that
would culminate in 'The Castaway' just before he died.

> Doom'd as I am in solitude to waste
> The present moments, and regret the past;
> Depriv'd of ev'ry joy I valued most,
> My friend torn from me, and my mistress lost;
> Call not this gloom I wear, this anxious mien,
> The dull effect of humour, or of spleen!

The alliterative pattern of the D's forms one basis of unity
for the poem. After the bitter words, 'doom'd', 'depriv'd',
'dull', 'doubt', 'destin'd', the dental sound in the last line
is turned wryly: 'All that delights the happy—palls with
me!'—with the suggestion of a final distorted pun in 'pall'.

In the same poem he uses the image of the castaway,
the most persistent metaphor in his work, and one which he
made part of himself and the symbol of his life and poetry.

> See me—ere yet my destin'd course half done,
> Cast forth a wand'rer on a wild unknown!
> See me neglected on the world's rude coast,
> Each dear companion of my voyage lost!

---

[1] Hallam Tennyson, *Alfred Lord Tennyson* (London, 1897), II, 501.
[2] *Poems*, p. 362. As first publ. in 1785, the opening line read: 'and adieu to the shade'.

The picture occurs several other times in the early poetry. In the verses beginning 'Mortals! around your destin'd heads' are these two stanzas:

> Thus the wreck'd mariner may strive
> Some desert shore to gain,
> Secure of life if he survive
> The fury of the main:
> But there, to famine doom'd a prey,
> Finds the mistaken wretch!
> He but escap'd the troubled sea,
> To perish on the beach.

The sea and the seaman imagery continue in 'Hope, like the short-liv'd ray',

> The seaman thus, his shatter'd vessel lost,
> Still vainly strives to shun the threat'ning death;
> And while he thinks to gain the friendly coast,
> And drops his feet, and feels the sands beneath:...
>
> And now the refluent wave his baffled toil defeats.[1]

In his letters he referred to the insane spell of 1763 as 'the storm'. Storms, which were at times symbols of gripping fear, could also fascinate and thrill him. 'I was always an admirer of thunderstorms,' he said, 'even before I knew whose voice I heard in them; but especially an admirer of thunder rolling over the great waters. There is something singularly majestic in the sound of it at sea, where the eye and the ear have uninterrupted opportunity of observation, and the concavity above being made spacious reflects it with more advantage...when the thunder preaches, an horizon bounded by the ocean is the only sounding-board.'[2] With this admiration and horror of the sea and the storm, he coupled his idea of the castaway—in part the conception of St Paul, who was the only one to use

---

[1] *Poems*, pp. 269, 283–5. See also the poem, possibly his, in the *Student*: Appendix B, pp. 226–9.
[2] Appendix A, p. 217; *Letters*, II, 88.

the word in the Bible. 'And every man that striveth for the mastery is temperate in all things. Now they do it to obtain a corruptible crown; but we an incorruptible. I therefore so run, not as uncertainly; so fight I, not as one that beateth the air: but I keep under my body, and bring it into subjection: lest that by any means, when I have preached to others, I myself should be a castaway.'[1] The image in Olney Hymn no. 36 (1771–2) was certainly derived from St Paul:

> Did I meet no trials here,
> No chastisement by the way;
> Might I not, with reason, fear
> I should prove a cast-away?

The castaway theme continued in 'Heu! Quam Remotus' (1774):

> Et fluctuosum ceu mare volvitur,
> Dum commovebar mille timoribus,
>   Coactus in fauces Averni
>   Totus atro perii sub amne.

In 1780 Cowper described himself as

> tempest-toss'd, and wreck'd at last,
> Come home to port no more

('To the Reverend Mr. Newton on His Return from Ramsgate'). A similar picture of him weathering the storm-driven sea comprises the last long stanza of the poem on his mother's picture (1790). Finally there is 'The Castaway' (March, 1799), almost the last verses he wrote. It ends with the ultimate unrelieved desolation.

> No voice divine the storm allay'd,
>   No light propitious shone;
> When, snatch'd from all effectual aid,
>   We perish'd, each alone:
> But I beneath a rougher sea,
> And whelm'd in deeper gulphs than he.[2]

---

[1] I Corinthians ix. 25–7. Of course it is actually the English translators who use the word.   [2] *Poems*, pp. 293, 307–8, 396, 431–2.

One stark, terrifying poem came out of the wreck of the last year in the Temple: 'Lines Written during a Period of Insanity.'

> Hatred and vengeance, my eternal portion,
> Scarce can endure delay of execution,
> Wait, with impatient readiness, to seize my
> Soul in a moment.
>
> Damn'd below Judas: more abhorr'd than he was,
> Who for a few pence sold his holy Master.
> Twice betrayed Jesus me, the last delinquent,
> Deems the profanest.
>
> Man disavows, and Deity disowns me:
> Hell might afford my miseries a shelter;
> Therefore hell keeps her ever hungry mouths all
> Bolted against me.
>
> Hard lot! encompass'd with a thousand dangers;
> Weary, faint, trembling with a thousand terrors;
> I'm called, if vanquish'd, to receive a sentence
> Worse than Abiram's.
>
> *Him* the vindictive rod of angry justice
> Sent quick and howling to the centre headlong;
> *I*, fed with judgment, in a fleshly tomb, am
> Buried above ground.[1]

These Sapphics owed something, perhaps, to the 'Sapphicks. Vpon the Passion of Christ' in Francis Davison's *A Poetical Rhapsody*:

> Hatred eternall, furious reuenging,
> Mercilesse raging, bloody persecuting,
> Slanderous speeches, odious reuilings,
> Causelesse abhorring.

Or Cowper's lines may have been indebted to Isaac Watts's efforts in a similar style, especially 'The Day of Judgment'. But beyond these models was the solace and grim damnation of the Lord God through Ezekiel: 'For thus saith the Lord God; Behold, I, even I, will both search my sheep, and seek

---

[1] *Poems*, pp. 289–90.

them out...I will seek that which was lost, and bring again that which was driven away, and will bind up that which was broken, and will strengthen that which was sick: but I will destroy the fat and the strong; I will feed them with judgment.'[1] Cowper saw himself as formerly strong, but neglectful of the mercies of God and the call of the Holy Ghost. He had experienced a horrifying fear 'that the earth would open her mouth and swallow' him as it had Korah, Dathan, and Abiram. 'For near a Twelvemonth' he had believed himself 'Sealed up under eternal wrath and yᵉ Sentence of unquenchable Vengeance.'[2]

The beat of the lines of the poem 'Written during a Period of Insanity', and the theme itself, pound vindictively to the end. The sounds which begin the first stanza, '*H*atred and *v*engeance', and that of the second, '*D*amn'd', are used again and again to weld the Sapphics together. The terror remains simple and bare and unremitting.

Except at a time of crisis, Cowper was best when he wrote in a light vein. Many of these verses have apparently been lost. His first trifle, the translation of an elegy by Tibullus, was written at the age of fourteen. And after that, there were poems on rural subjects:

> The first-born efforts of my youthful muse,
> Sportive, and jingling her poetic bells
> Ere yet her ear was mistress of their pow'rs.[3]

According to Southey, with Frederick Madan (1742–80) he wrote a 'burlesque cantata upon Spencer Madan's fiddling'.[4] In the political spirit of his father, William wrote some popular half-penny ballads, which are now not identifiable, if they are not lost. And incognito he sent

---

[1] Ezekiel xxxiv. 11, 16.
[2] Cowper's *Memoir*, pp. 51, 58; the quoted words are borrowed from Numbers xvi. 30, 32—the story of Korah, Dathan, and Abiram. Also Appendix A, p. 217.
[3] *Letters*, III, 101; *Task*, IV, 701–3.
[4] Southey to Cradock, 24 June 1836: *Selections* [from Southey's letters], ed. J. W. Warter (London, 1856), IV, 455–6.

various works to the *Gentleman's Magazine*,[1] but John Nichols, the editor, soon recognized their promise, learned the name of the correspondent, and looked forward to his contributions in either poetry or prose.[2]

A few of the poems which Cowper sent to the *Magazine* may have been reprinted in the *Annual Register*. In 1779 he wrote to William Unwin: 'I find the *Register* in all respects an entertaining medley; but especially in this, that it has brought to my view some long forgotten pieces of my own production;—I mean by the way two or three....It is at least twenty years since I saw them.'[3] This length of time, and the fact that Cowper seemed to be just beginning a long series of the *Register*, suggest the first year of its publication, 1758. Hayley could not find these verses; nor could Southey, nor Mr Povey.[4] If the poems in the *Annual Register* for 1758 which can be attributed to other authors are eliminated, one in particular remains to suggest itself as a possible candidate for one of the missing poems. It was first published in the *Gentleman's Magazine*, in the same volume as the article on chanting.[5] The poem is 'To Peace', and begins:

> Come lovely gentle peace of mind
> With all thy smiling nymphs around,
> Content and innocence combin'd,
> With wreaths of sacred olive crown'd.

---

[1] *Letters*, I, 398. At the time Hayley was preparing his *Life of Cowper* (1803), John Johnson 'exhausted' Nichols' 'repository' of the *G.M.* but was unable to determine additional works by Cowper—Johnson to Hayley, 22 April 1814: Fitzwilliam MSS. Hayley's *Memoirs*, II, 175.

[2] Walter Bagot to Cowper, 10 Feb. 1786: Morgan MSS. MA 86, vol. II, f. 6.

[3] *Letters*, III, 101. The letter is dated by Kenneth Povey, 'Some Notes on Cowper's Letters and Poems', *R.E.S.* v (1929), 3–4. Povey proves almost surely that the 'Register' to which Cowper refers is the *Annual Register*. I have searched through other journals from 1750 to 1763 with the word 'Register' in their titles, but have not found any with which Cowper might possibly have a known connection, or which have poetry that is similar to his in style. Povey suggests that in spite of the reference to 'dabbling in rhyme', which occurs in the sentence following that quoted, Cowper may be referring to prose. I do not see how the context can corroborate this supposition.

[4] *Letters*, I, 150–1, 154, 172; III, 101; Povey, *R.E.S.* v, 4–6; Hayley (1803), III, 369; Hayley's *Memoirs*, II, 152; Southey to Cradock, 3 and 29 June, 3 Oct. 1835: *Selections*, IV, 403, 406, 412.   [5] Appendix A, pp. 185–90.

Come thou, that lov'st the walk at eve,
The banks of murm'ring streams along,
That lov'st the crowded court to leave,
And hear the milk-maid's simple song.[1]

These lines bear a resemblance to Cowper's 'Ode to Peace',
probably written in 1773:

Come, peace of mind, delightful guest!
Return and make thy downy nest
   Once more in this sad heart!—[2]

Hayley writes: 'While Cowper resided in the Temple, he
seems to have been personally acquainted with the most
eminent writers of the time; and the interest, which he
probably took in their recent works, tended to increase
his powerful, tho' diffident, passion for poetry, and to train
him imperceptibly to that masterly command of language,
which time and chance led him to display, almost as a new
talent at the age of fifty. One of his first associates has
informed me, that before he quitted London, he frequently
amused himself in translation from antient and modern
poets, and devoted his composition to the service of any
friend, who requested it.' The associate was almost surely
Joseph Hill, who told Hayley about some translations or
imitations of the Fables of La Fontaine. But Hayley sought
for these in vain, and Walter Bagot, John Johnson, and
Theadora Cowper were unable to help him find them.[3]
The translations remain undiscovered.

Two translations by Cowper, of the fifth and ninth satires
of the first book of Horace, were published in 1759 in the
second volume of the Duncombes' *Works of Horace. In
English Verse.* But 'the only large Work'[4] that he was

---

[1] *G.M.* xxviii (July, 1758), 329; *Annual Register*, 1 (1758), 417–18; reprinted, *Royal
Magazine, or Gentleman's Monthly Companion*, ii (suppl. following June 1760), 371.
[2] *Poems*, p. 292.
[3] Hayley (1803), i, 18–19; Hayley's *Memoirs*, ii, 120, 152–3; Hayley's *Vindication*
(MS.), f. 31—Hayley to Theadora, 5 June 1806.
[4] Joseph Hill to Hayley, 19 Feb. 1802: copy owned by Rev. W. Cowper Johnson,
Norwich.

engaged in during these years was the translation of four
cantos of the *Henriade* (V–VIII), which he undertook at the
request of his brother John, who translated the first four
cantos and supervised the whole with Thomas Francklin
for the Smollett-Francklin edition of the works of Voltaire.[1]
Though it has recently been called 'faithful and elegant'
by Mr H. B. Evans,[2] this version of the *Henriade* is in truth
more dreary than the original. By the time that Voltaire's
imitation of Virgil had been digested by the Cowpers, and
his monotonous Alexandrines had been reduced to weak
heroic couplets, there was not much life left. Voltaire's epic
is official-sounding and polemical, and barren of epic
grandeur and imagination. It is done in good form, but it
is cold. Voltaire's *Henriade* has none of the personality that
William Cowper's work usually shows—his warmth,
whimsy, friendliness, discursiveness, delicate sense of pity,
or full realization of terror. It was singularly unsuited to
the early Romantic or the late Augustan in him. His
couplets struggle along:

> Now marching on, those dread machines appear'd.
> Which death attended, and the rebels fear'd.
> A hundred mouths pour'd forth the rapid balls,
> And iron tempests rattl'd on the walls.

Voltaire's pleas and declamations come off poorly in
translation.

> Almighty being, whose avenging arm
> Protects religion, and her sons from harm,
> How long shall justice sleep, or tyrants live,
> The perjur'd flourish, and oppression thrive?[3]

---

[1] See Appendix B, pp. 232–6.
[2] H. B. Evans, 'A Bibliography of Eighteenth-Century Translations of Voltaire',
in *Studies in French Language, Literature and History Presented to R. L. Græme Ritchie* (Cambridge, 1949), p. 52.
[3] *Henriade*, v, 1–4, 63–6, pp. 103, 106.

And when Voltaire rises to nobility and eloquence,

> Amitié, don du ciel, plaisir des grandes âmes;
> Amitié, que les rois, ces illustres ingrats,
> Sont assez malheureux pour ne connaître pas![1]

Cowper moves on stilts, far below:

> Hail heav'n-born friendship! the delight alone
> Of noble minds, and banish'd from the throne.[2]

Cowper is best when the spirit is unpretentious and still—
the spirit in which he was accustomed to write:

> The great, the boundless clemency of God,
> To sooth the ills of life's perplexing road,
> Sweet sleep, and hope, two friendly beings gave,
> Which earth's dark, gloomy confines never leave.
> When man, fatigued by labours of the day,
> Has toiled his spirits, and his strength away,
> That, nature's friend, restores her pow'rs again,
> And brings the blest forgetfulness of pain.
> This, oft deceitful, but for ever kind,
> Diffuses warmth and transport through the mind.
> From her the few, whom heaven approves, may learn
> The pleasing issue of each high concern.
> Pure as her author in the realms above
> To them she brings the tidings of his love.
>
> Immortal Louis bid the faithful pair
> Expand their downy wings, and soften Henry's care.
> Still sleep repairs to Vincenne's shady ground;
> The winds subside, and silence reigns around.
> Hope's blooming offspring, happy dreams succeed,
> And give the pleasing, though ideal meed.
> The verdant olive, and the laurel bough,
> Entwined with poppies, grace the hero's brow.[3]

Cowper's first prose writings deserve more consideration
than his early translations. His achievement here is, perhaps, more impressive than his efforts as a whole in poetry.

---

[1] *Henriade*, VIII, 322–4; *Œuvres Complètes*, ed. Louis Moland, vol. VIII (Paris, 1877), p. 211.
[2] *Henriade*, p. 191.   [3] *Henriade*, VII, 1–22, pp. 147–8.

The essays in the *Connoisseur*[1] in particular are mature and delightful: in these humorous works he is able to create a totality of effect and to maintain a consistent tone. They are, to be sure, somewhat like Johnson's description of an essay (in the *Dictionary*): 'A loose sally of the mind; an irregular indigested piece; not a regular and orderly composition.' And they follow the style of the other essays in the *Connoisseur*, which is imitative of earlier periodicals. For the most part they are light satire, ridiculing the foibles of society. Cowper's contributions are as good as any in the collection. They show the grace of his later letters and his fine sense of small, pleasantly ludicrous details. The essay on country churches is probably the best, with its amusing vignettes of the congregation, the parson, the clerk, the squire, the women in their finery. The description of the country churches themselves is in wholesome, practical contrast to the graveyard school of poets, who mope about the ruins.

The ruinous condition of some of these churches gave me great offence; and I could not help wishing, that the honest vicar,

---

[1] The number of Cowper's contributions is not absolutely certain. He himself named one (no. 119) as his (*Letters*, I, 183); he pointed out three to Hayley (nos. 119, 134, 138; Hayley (1803), II, 394), and Hayley's information was corroborated by Cowper's friend Samuel Rose (told to Alexander Chalmers: see his *British Essayists* (1802), xxx, xxxiii–xxxv). Colman and Thornton, also friends and the editors of the *Connoisseur*, credited him ('a friend, a gentleman of the *Temple*') with no. 119, and nos. 111 and 115 (concluding paper of the *Connoisseur*, no. 140 (30 Sept. 1756), p. 843 (1st ed.)) in their list of acknowledgements (only partial). The editors have marked no. 111 with Cowper's initials, 'W. C.', in editions *after the first*. No. 134 is said to be written by 'Mr. Village', the Cousin of 'Mr. Town' ('Town' was the signature used by Colman and Thornton in the *Connoisseur*, and even in their editorial correspondence —see letter from 'Town' to John Duncombe, in R. B. Peake, *Memoirs of the Colman Family* (London, 1841), I, 49). 'Village' also communicated nos. 13, 23, 41, 76, 81, 105, and 139. As Chalmers said, 'it would be too much, however, to argue that Mr. COWPER wrote all these: the character of *Mr. Village* might be common to other writers, and occasionally assumed by any correspondent whose subject it might suit'. Five papers therefore may be with relative safety attributed to Cowper: nos. 111, 115, 119, 134, 138. Southey says they are 'certainly his' (Southey's *Cowper*, I, 325). They have been accepted, for example, by Chalmers; Lionel Thomas Berguer, *The British Essayists* (London, 1823), xxx, xvi–xvii; Southey; Wright, *Life* (1921), p. 25; Page, *Colman*, pp. 26–37; Arthur Sherbo, 'Cowper's *Connoisseur* Essays', *M.L.N.* LXX (1955), 340–2.

instead of indulging his genius for improvements, by inclosing his gooseberry bushes with a *Chinese* rail, and converting half an acre of his glebe-land into a bowling-green, would have applied part of his income to the more laudable purpose of sheltering his parishioners from the weather during their attendance on divine service. It is no uncommon thing to see the parsonag[e]-house well thatched, and in exceeding good repair, while the church perhaps has no better roof than the ivy that grows over it. The noise of owls, bats, and magpies makes a principal part of the church musick in many of these ancient edifices; and the walls, like a large map, seem to be portioned out into capes, seas, and promontories by the various colours with which the damps have stained them.[1]

The slight exaggeration, with an English restraint in contrast to the American tall tale, is characteristic of Cowper's essays. In the essay on the 'delicate BILLY SUCKLING', the satire is just as typical of Cowper. There he strikes lightly at the affectations of a man who 'is the contempt of the men, the jest of the women, and the darling of his mamma. She doats on him to distraction; and is in perpetual admiration of his wit, and anxiety for his health.' Again Cowper is fundamentally a derivative writer. He is reworking the Augustan forms. The parallel constructions imply an equal comparison of unequals: juxtaposition suggests that there was a corresponding amount of time spent in wit and anxiety, and that the mamma's passion was equal to the detestation of the others. The balance of antithetical attitudes is especially unflattering, as in another sentence about Billy: 'He would rather leave the most celebrated beauty, in crossing the street, to the mercy of a drayman, than trust her with his little finger: though at the same time should his mother be so distressed, he would not scruple to bear as much of her weight as he could stand under, and to redeem her silk stockings from jeopardy would even expose his own.' In the same essay Cowper exhibits the beginnings of his

---

[1] *Connoisseur* (1756), no. 134, p. 806.

peculiar talent, the ability to catch colloquial and idio-
syncratic speech; for example, two old-maidish comments
by Billy: 'I have known him sit with his mamma's white
handkerchief round his neck through a whole visit, to
guard him from the wind of that *ugly door*, or that *terrible
chink in the wainscot*.'[1]

Cowper presumably wrote many other essays like those
in the *Connoisseur*. One or two are added in the Appendix;
most have evidently been lost. Pieces in prose and verse
were generally sent 'as soon as they were written to Coleman, Lloyd and Thornton who were always publishing,
and always glad of assistance'.[2] He was an 'occasional
contributor' to the *St James's Chronicle*, but his letters and
essays in that periodical have not been identified.[3] Henry
Baldwin, the printer, had brought this paper of wit and
literature, 'to a height of eminence unknown to any preceding Journal, nor exceeded by any of its successors'
(John Nichols), with the help of Thornton, Colman, Lloyd,
Garrick, Steevens, and Wilkes.[4] It is just possible that
Cowper also sent an essay or two to the *World*. A note in
the *Gentleman's Magazine* in 1845 made this claim. But the
attribution seems very doubtful: Cowper's name does not
appear in the standard lists of contributors, nor did Horace
Walpole and the Earl of Cork, two famous contributors,
name William Cowper in their annotated copies. However,
they were not able to list the authors of all the essays.[5]

[1] *Ibid.* no. 111, pp. 669–70.
[2] Hill to Hayley, 19 Feb. 1802.
[3] Southey's *Cowper*, I, 49; Leslie Stephen in *D.N.B.*
[4] Nichols, *Anecdotes*, VIII, 479; also Chalmers, *The British Essayists* (1802), XXX, xvii;
Wilkes, *Correspondence*, ed. Almon (London, 1805), I, xi.
[5] *G.M.* N.S. XXIV (1845), 453: 'We found in H. Walpole's copy of the World a list
of the different writers, with the numbers of the papers they contributed, which we
copied out; it agrees nearly with the printed list. The poet Cowper was a contributor.'
Walpole's copy of the *World* is now in the Pierpont Morgan Libr.: E-2.77.D.
Cowper's name does not appear in Walpole's catalogue of authors. The writer in the
G.M. may have confused William Cowper with John Gilbert Cooper, who, according
to Walpole, contributed nos. 110 and 159. The Earl of Cork's copy was sold by Parke-
Bernet, 16–17 Jan. 1950 (Cat. 1117, lot 248). Mrs Lloyd Almirall of Ridgefield,

The measure of the whole of Cowper's writing before 1764 was not large; yet in a few of the poems, essays, letters which we know are his, we can see portions of the older, greater Cowper, and sometimes these early works can stand with the letters about his hares, or the poetry of *The Task* or 'The Castaway'.

Connecticut, who bought it, has informed me that the name of William Cowper does not appear among Lord Cork's annotations, although he identifies the authors of six papers not otherwise known.

VIII

THEADORA

...her—through tedious years of doubt and pain,
Fix'd in her choice, and faithful—but in vain.
'On the Death of Sir W. Russell', ll. 9–10

So far Cowper has been seen in a world of men, which is only a partial picture. From the death of his mother when he was six (1737) until the early 1750's, when he was at Chapman the solicitor's, he was like almost any other English boy of his station. It was scarcely possible for him to know any women, except, as he said, the maids at his boarding-house.[1] But once the bonds of school life had been cut, Cowper moved quickly into the society of women. One he sought in particular: his cousin Theadora,[2] whom he loved deeply.

She was a daughter of Ashley Cowper, who was a brother of William's father. The two young lawyers, Cowper and Thurlow, spent many hours with Theadora and her older sister Harriot (who married Sir Thomas Hesketh)[3] and with her younger sister, Elizabeth Charlotte (who married Sir Archer Croft). Cowper slept at Mr Chapman's, but his days were spent in Southampton Row at Ashley's house, and here he and 'the future Lord Chancellor' were 'constantly

---

[1] *Letters*, I, 240.
[2] I have followed the spelling of her name as found in her signature to letters now in the Panshanger Coll. (Theadora to 3rd E. Cowper, 22 Dec. 1773 and 6 March 1778), and as given by Lady Hesketh (to Hayley, 30 Aug. 1801: Add. MSS. 30803 A, f. 155). She was known as 'Thea'.
[3] Lady Hesketh habitually spelled her name 'Harriot': all her letters among the Hesketh MSS. in the Lancashire Record Office (DDF.413.2) are signed in this fashion; the Hon. Mrs Penelope Madan Maitland, her cousin and especially close friend, also spelled H. Hesketh's name 'Harriot' (*Poems*, pp 659–60; *Madan Family*, pp. 124–5); in the letter of attorney given to her by Sir Thomas, 8 March 1769, she is named as 'Dame Harriott Hesketh' (Lancs. Rec. Off. MSS.).

employed from morning till night in giggling and making giggle, instead of studying law'.[1] No. 30 Southampton Row, at the north end of King Street, became Cowper's unofficial residence from 1750 to 1753. Besides the pleasant company, the location of the house itself would have been to Cowper's liking. It had even more of the spirit of flowers and trees and country than he could enjoy in the Temple gardens. It was near the quiet rural scene for which he was always looking. The homes of the row were new and the area fashionable. They overlooked the gardens and fields of the Bedford estates, and there were no houses opposite them.[2] Beyond the grounds of Bedford House, open land stretched away to Hampstead, and in the summer invigorating winds blew down from the Highgate Hills.

From July 1759 to November 1761 Thomas Gray lived in this row, 'at Mr. Jauncey's'—where Thomas Wharton had lived until Gray moved in—and his description of the prospect from Southampton Row has a Cowperian ring: 'I am now settled in my new territories commanding Bedford gardens, and all the fields as far as Highgate and Hampstead, with such a concourse of moving pictures as would astonish you; so *rus-in-urbe-ish*, that I believe I shall stay here, except little excursions and vagaries, for a year to come...here is air, and sunshine, and quiet...to comfort you.'[3] In these vast open grounds Cowper would stroll with Theadora, and with her sisters. 'Chearful & happy I was wont to stray', he said, 'Through *Ducal Bedford's* fields to *Primrose-Hill*.'[4]

---

[1] *Letters*, III, 20. See also Cowper's *Memoir*, p. 8: '...I was at liberty to spend my leisure time (which was well nigh all my time) at my uncle's in Southampton Row.'

[2] Gladys Scott Thomson, *The Russells in Bloomsbury* (London, 1940), pp. 177, 358. There was apparently no building in Southampton Row before 1722; by 1765 there were only twenty-odd houses there.

[3] Gray to Palgrave, 24 July 1759: Gray's *Corr.* II, 631; see also, I, liv–lv; II, 563–4, 632, 648.

[4] 'To My Dearest Cousin on Her Removal of Us from Silver End, to Weston': *Poems*, p. 661.

He owed the preservation of his early religious habits to Theadora's family. At Chapman's 'I might have lived and died', Cowper said, 'without hearing or seeing any thing that might remind me of a single christian duty'.[1] But Sundays were, like most other days, spent with Theadora, and so he went with her and the rest of the family to church. It was probably their parish church, St George's, Blooms-bury.[2] St George's was the recent work of Hawksmoor, with a notorious steeple of pediments and arches which supported Corinthian pillars beneath a pyramid of steps ornamented by lions and unicorns, beneath a statue of George I in Roman costume, the gift of Mr Hucks, a local brewer. It was the joke of Bloomsbury:

When Henry the Eighth left the Pope in the lurch
The Protestants made him the head of the Church;
But George's good subjects, the Bloomsbury people
Instead of the Church, made him head of the steeple.[3]

The interior was more of an inspiration to worship. And Cowper may often have worshipped at Thomas Francklin's proprietary chapel in Great Queen Street.[4] Francklin was a popular preacher, especially with the wealthy residents of Bloomsbury, and he would have had an interest in William Cowper, for he was the most loyal of Old West-minsters. By 1762 William was almost certainly known to him because William and his brother John were associated

---

[1] Cowper's *Memoir*, p. 8.
[2] According to Horwood's map; *not* St George the Martyr, Queen's Square, as Wright says: *Life* (1921), p. 17.
[3] [James Ralph?], *A Critical Review* (London, 1734), p. 99; George Clinch, *Bloomsbury and St Giles's* (London, 1890), p. 128.
[4] Thomas Francklin (1721–84). Whether in 1750–5 Francklin had a chapel in Queen Street (now Museum Street) or Great Queen Street is not certain. By 1758 he was definitely in Great Queen Street, where he also resided from 1761 until his death in 1784. In 1749 he married David Garrick and Eva Maria Violetti 'at his chapel near Russel Street, Bloomsbury [probably in Queen Street]' (*General Adv.* 23 June 1749). It seems likely that Francklin moved from one Queen Street to the other between 1749 and 1758. See Joseph Tuckett, 'Where was Garrick Married', *N. & Q.* 5th ser. VII (31 March 1877), 248–9; Sir Lawrence Gomme, *The Parish of St Giles-in-the-Fields*, Pt ii, *Survey of London* (London, 1914), V, 87–91.

with Francklin in the translation of the *Henriade* for Smollett's edition of Voltaire.

Cowper did not know these London cousins until he came to Westminster School. From that time on, Theadora and Harriot would be two of the most important people in his life, and their father, Ashley, the 'oldest and dearest of friends'. His heart, William said, 'towards me was ever truly parental'. And he was also William's chief supporter in writing: 'He was always favourable to my versifying efforts, And upon the strength of his encouragements I began in very early days to think myself somebody.'[1] Ashley himself wrote verses and collected those written by many of the members of his family:[2] his mother; William and John, his brothers; and Judith Cowper Madan (Pope's correspondent), his sister; his daughter Harriot; his cousins, Spencer, Dean of Durham, and William, the Earl, and Lady Sarah; his nephews, Henry Cowper and Martin Madan; and his nieces, Mary Cowper de Grey, Maria Frances Cecilia Madan Cowper, and Penelope Madan Maitland. In fact, Theadora said, '*all* the Cowpers were addicted to Poetry, of one kind or other—my Father and his Sister (Mrs Madan) were the best of that Generation I believe; tho' both my Uncles wrote'.[3] Ashley's literary efforts are a haphazard and hackneyed collection of moralizings, pleasantries, and scatology. He wrote frequently in bad taste and he was sometimes offensive as well as maudlin. No wonder then that in 1767 when Ashley pub-

---

[1] *Letters*, III, 50-1, 278; 'Benefactions': *Poems*, p. 658; to Lady Hesketh, 23 Dec. 1785: Harvard Coll. Libr. MS. *43M-109F—'he was always a father to myself.'

[2] See Ashley Cowper, *The Norfolk Poetical Miscellany* (London, 1744); another issue with different title-page: *The Poetical Miscellany* (London, 1754)—the authorship of many of the pieces can be determined by the MS. notes in the copy in the B.M.: 992 K. 20 and 21; 'The Family Miscellany', MS. coll. (248 ff.) of poems, letters, essays, etc.: Add. MSS. 28101—authorship of pieces is usually given; one vol. of only his own work: *Poems and Translations* (London, 1767).

[3] Quoted by Lady Hesketh in a letter to Hayley, 9 April 1802: Add. MSS. 30803 B, f. 26. See also H. P. Stokes's 'Literary History of the Cowper Family', *Cowper Memorials*, pp. 141–64.

lished his *Poems and Translations*, the Evangelical William wrote
to his Evangelical cousin Maria Frances Cecilia: 'I daresay
you condole with me upon poor A—'s Publication. Surely the
wrong side of the grand Climacteric is no season for Rhiming.
And that Holy and Blessed Name too, at which he bows the
Head upon a Sabbath, is treated with as little Reverence as
that of Mahomet; he has packed them and jumbled them together in a manner very shocking to a Christian Reader.' But
William's earlier opinion was one of pleasure in his uncle's
interest in poetry, and frequently delight in his rhyming.[1]

Theodora was learned in French, and wrote intelligent,
sensible letters. She was devoutly religious, but not of the
Evangelical group.[2] Thea, as William called her, was unusually lovely: a goddess to look at, said her perhaps
prejudiced sister.[3] She was modest, refined, and shy—very
much like William. And like him, and like her father, she
suffered from the depressions and melancholy which had
become a family disease.[4] Samuel Greatheed, friend and

---

[1] *U. & U.* p. 3. By 1785, in an effusive and exaggerated letter to Lady Hesketh,
Cowper had forgotten the unpleasant sections of Ashley's poetry: 'No man has a better
Taste than my Uncle, and my opinion of it is such that I should certainly renounce
the pen for ever, were I to hear that he wished me to do so', Harvard MS. *43M-109F.
In a coll. of miscellaneous poems in William Cowper's library there were included
two pamphlets by Ashley, *High Boys Up Go We!* (London, 1741) and *The Faction, a Tale*
(London, 1741), which in 1797 William identified as 'By Ashley Cowper, the Poets
Uncle'. (At that late date he was not reluctant to recognize himself as a poet.) The
vol. of poems is now in the Keynes Coll.
[2] Based on 5 letters from Theodora to Hayley, between 29 Aug. 1806 and 10 May
1807: quoted in Hayley's *Vindication* (MS.), ff. 35–66. Other letters from Theodora
which are known to me are those to the 3rd E. Cowper, 22 Dec. 1773 and 6 March
1778 (Panshanger Coll.), and that to Hayley (enclosed, sealed, in a letter to Lady
Hesketh, to be forwarded to Hayley), 25 Jan. [1801]: Add. MSS. 30803 A, ff. 195–6.
[3] Lady Hesketh to Hayley, 21 Feb. 1802: quoted in *Letters*, I, 3, n. 1; also Hayley
to John Johnson, 12 April 1810: Fitzwilliam MSS.
[4] *Letters*, I, 139, where William refers to Ashley's 'nervous fevers'. Lady Hesketh
told Hayley that 'tho' nobody had in general finer Spirits, or more Animation' than
her father, yet he was subject to 'a degree of low Spirits, which would sometimes hang
upon him for months together, and which were almost as affecting to see as those which
you and I Sir have witness'd with so much Pain! my dear Fathers were different indeed
in some respects, as he was always perfectly quiet and Composed, avoided Company,
and never Join'd in any Conversation, but he was not apparently actuated by those
horrors, which were permitted so cruelly to distress his Invaluable Nephew!' 25 Oct.
1801: Add. MSS. 30803 A, f. 174.

early biographer of Cowper, wrote a letter to the *Monthly Review* which said that he could not allege his reasons for regarding Cowper's 'derangement as hereditary, without indelicacy to his surviving relatives, who are mostly of a very respectable description'. Southey told his friends in conversation and in letters, that he knew insanity was 'in the Cowper blood'. And he wrote to the Reverend G. C. Gorham about a letter which Lady Hesketh had received from the Hon. Mrs Penelope Madan Maitland, her cousin and William Cowper's. Mrs Maitland's letter of 26 May 1804 was written about a subject which, she said,

has lately come to my knowledge, but on which I will form *no* Judgment, till *you direct that judgement.* A Lady asserted that (to her knowledge[)] my dear Cousin Thea was a few years back *out of her mind*: that she went away from the house she was in, (somewhere near Cambridge I think) & was absent all night, having roamed about; & was found next day & brought back. The person told all this to my eldest daughter Mrs Marsham, & assured her it was a fact: nevertheless I cannot believe it, till *you* confirm it....No one knows the sufferings of the mind of my dear cousin Thea, I verily believe: disappointed in her first affections, & enduring what she must do for her distressed Cowper. But above all, I *must* think, was *his ever entertaining* an *idea* of marrying any one but herself [William Cowper's proposed marriage with Mrs Unwin, *c.* 1773].[1]

Lady Hesketh's reply is not known, but Mrs Maitland was surely right about Theadora's insanity.[2] It was probably Thea to whom William referred when he said, 'I find that the vacancy I left at St Albans is filled up by a near relation. May the same Hand which struck off my fetters deliver her also out of the House of Bondage; and may she say when

---

[1] *Monthly Rev.* 2nd ser. LXXXI (1816), 223; Southey to John Rickman, 29 Dec. 1835: Henry E. Huntington Libr. MS. RS 690; Mrs Maitland's letter is quoted in Southey to Gorham, 23 Dec. 1835: MS. in Cowper Mus., Olney.

[2] 'She [Theadora] is still living, single, but has many years been melancholy': [Samuel Greatheed], 'Memoranda respecting Cowper the Poet': John Rylands Libr. Eng. MS. 352/55, f. 3 (n.d.; water-mark 1802; written in 1803, or shortly thereafter).

she comes forth, what I hope to be able to say from my
heart, while I have breath to utter it—It is good for me that
I was afflicted.'[1]

There is no doubt about William's love for Theadora.
The poems to Delia, his poetical name for her, reveal his
devotion. And the poem at the time of the final rupture—
'Doom'd as I am in solitude to waste' has some of the
tragic strength and sadness of 'The Castaway'. During
1752 and 1753, Theadora said, 'we saw each other *daily*'.[2]
William described and showed his beloved to his friends;
he was proud in his conquest, and truly happy in his love.[3]
She gave him a red carnelian seal ring on which was
Omphale wearing the lion's skin of Hercules. But after
a year or two of this joy, their love began to run the course of
almost any long love-affair: regrets, partings, reconcilia-
tions, and partings and sorrow again. Moreover, from the
beginning had hung over them a heavier pall than most
lovers know: their melancholy natures—which, with the
fact that they were first cousins, must have caused her
father to prohibit their marriage.[4] His 'heart was set, and
his *Peace of Mind strongly interested* in their finding happiness
independan[t of] each other'. And Theadora would not
consent to marriage without her father's approval. The

[1] To Joseph Hill, 5 Aug. 1769: *Letters*, I, 109. Theadora, like William received
benefactions from the rich Cowpers. Letters of thanks for the 3rd E. Cowper's favours
to Theadora are in the Panshanger Coll: Theadora to the Earl, 22 Dec. 1773 and
6 March 1778; Ashley Cowper to the Earl, 17 Dec. 1773.
[2] Quoted from a letter from Theadora to Lady Hesketh, in Lady Hesketh to Hayley,
13 July 1801: Add. MSS. 30803 A, f. 144.
[3] William pointed out Theadora to Walter Bagot one night at the theatre, and
according to H. F. Cary, 'Mr. Bagot was of the opinion that the malady he [Cowper]
afterwards laboured under, arose from disappointment in this affair': Cary, 'Biographical Notice of William Cowper', in *The Poetical Works of William Cowper* (London,
1839), pp. vii–viii. See Cowper to 'Toby', 21 Feb. 1754 (*Letters*, I, 5–8), where he says
that a 'small difference' between himself and Theadora is over and 'all is comfortable
and happy between us at present, and I doubt not will continue so for ever'.
[4] According to James Croft's Preface to the first publ. of the Delia poems, Ashley
'refused to accede' to the 'union of persons so nearly related': *Early Poems*, p. vi. But
according to Greatheed, William's father 'certainly did not oppose his intended
marriage': [Greatheed], 'Memoranda', f. 2.

excuse given to the world for the separation was the 'Impropriety', the '*Impossibility*' of marriage when both sides were totally without a fortune. So two or three years after their attachment began, the relationship was broken off, absolutely. They never corresponded afterwards. Still only twenty, Theodora never knew, nor would think of, another love; and all friends took care not to mention either one to the other.[1]

Little is known about Theodora. William's profound hurt after the engagement was broken caused him to keep a lifelong silence concerning her in his writings. Her few letters which exist in Hayley's copy of a correspondence between them show her dignified and quiet beside the effusive Hayley. The loneliness of her life of retirement comes sadly through the words of the letters. She was faithful to William to the end, and treasured every tiny relic which had belonged to him, every scrap of paper on which he had written. She silently aided him during his last years: the 'Anonymous' who gave him money and gifts—'the most elegant, the compactest, the most commodious desk', mounted with silver and inlaid with ivory; a snuffbox with a painting of William's three hares on its lid (by Romney); the watch which had belonged to her father.[2] Theodora preferred to remain a 'lonely Bird'—an epithet given to her by Hayley, and which she accepted. 'I have long since been a Wander[er] & a Vagabond upon the Face of the Earth', she said. 'It is a just Observation of the Truth of which I am myself an Instance that among the Evils attendant on Sorrow, it is not one of the least that by a long Continuance of it, the Mind loses the power of being

---

[1] Lady Hesketh to Hayley, 13 Sept. and 14 Oct. 1801: Add. MSS. 30803 A, ff. 162, 169–70. Greatheed said, 'There was no obsticle to her marriage with C. but his want of income for an establishment suited to their rank. The prospects only ceased at his derangement': [Greatheed], 'Memoranda', f. 3.

[2] *Letters*, II, 403, 406, 416, 455, 457–8; III, 299, 431, etc. 'Anonymous' is identified as Theodora—Lady Hesketh to John Johnson [May, 1800]: Hesketh, *Letters*, p. 105.

susceptible of Ioy—.... There are Days & Weeks that pass
when with me the Grasshopper is indeed a Burthen &
Life itself
>A Pedlar's Pack that bows The Bearer *down*

In such days I find it difficult to hold a Pen.'[1] Her quotations are from Ecclesiastes and *The Task*: the Bible and her
William filling her mind to the last. Like the preacher and
the poet, she became a symbol: of the frailty of human wishes.

Hayley was possessed with a desire to write the story of
'The Loves of William & Theodora', and if he might not,
he asked her to write it, to 'gratify an honest friendly
Desire of the faithful Hermit [Hayley] & indulge perhaps
the laudable Pride of indelible Affection'.[2] The sentence
was typical of Hayley; one can therefore imagine how he
would have described their love. But Hayley was denied
his request. Nothing was more repellent to Theadora;
nothing made her more fearful than the thought that her
love for William—desperately hidden so many years—
might be made public. Lady Hesketh and Theadora en-
treated Hayley time and again to conceal this part of
William's biography,[3] and Hayley acceded to their wishes.

After William's death Theadora refused any visits from
Hayley, or any talk with others about her cousin. She told
Hayley through her sister, 'that the slightest conversation
held...on this subject wou'd be *her Death*!' 'You', Theadora
added, 'may think this proceeds from an *affectation* of
delicacy, and feeling.' But it was true; she did continue to
suffer severely for what had been lost. Theadora, who had

---

[1] Theadora to Hayley, 10 May 1807 and 27 Aug. 1806: quoted in Hayley's
Vindication (MS.), ff. 66, 36, 38.
[2] Hayley to Theadora, 21 Sept. 1806: quoted in Hayley's *Vindication* (MS.),
ff. 48-9.
[3] For example, Lady Hesketh to Hayley, 14 Aug. 1800, 11 Feb., 26 April, 28 May,
and 13 July 1801: Add. MSS. 30803 A, ff. 43, 100, 126, 131, 145. As late as 23 Jan.
1816, John Johnson wrote to Hayley that Charles Cowper had great 'uneasiness at
any idea of publication of verses &c, &c, &c, connected with that most delicate subject',
for to Theadora 'it would be a matter of the greatest misery' (Fitzwilliam MSS.).

always shown great reserve on all subjects, never even wrote about her love for William, nor the broken engagement, to anyone except her sister Harriot. Her feelings became still more sensitive when she heard rumours of William's love for another, and read of his devotion in his poetry. It was almost unbearable that she should 'have acted a subordinate part', or 'had only prepared the way for an attachment more Solid, & more lasting'.[1]

Hayley confessed in his own *Memoirs* that he 'had heard from the Lips of Cowper, what intense affection He had preserved thro his troubled Life' for Theadora,[2] but in his life of Cowper he said only this: '...a disappointment of the heart, arising from the cruelty of fortune, threw a cloud on his juvenile spirit. Thwarted in love...the smothered flames of desire uniting with the vapours of constitutional melancholy, and the fervency of religious zeal, produced altogether that irregularity of corporeal sensation, and of mental health....'[3] The real public announcement of their love came through another friend and biographer of Cowper, Greatheed, who said that Cowper 'cherished a tender attachment to an amiable and accomplished young lady, one of his first cousins, whose hand was expected to crown his approaching establishment in life'.[4] And one of the legends of English literature and romance had begun.

Escape from the City, the Temple, and the bright world, came not only in William's visits at Theadora's house, but also in vacations, which took up most of August and September, and sometimes a large part of October.[5] Of course,

---

[1] Lady Hesketh to Hayley, 23 June, 30 Aug., 13 and 16 Sept. 1801: Add. MSS. 30803 A, ff. 137, 155, 160, 163.

[2] Hayley's *Memoirs* (MS.), VI, 39. The remark was not included in the publ. version of the *Memoirs*, ed. by John Johnson.

[3] Hayley (1803), II, 222.

[4] Greatheed, *Memoirs of...William Cowper, Esq.* (London, 1814), p. 6. Though he confessed that 'C— never named her to me': [Greatheed], 'Memoranda', f. 3.

[5] See references in *Letters*, I, 20–1, 104; Cowper's *Memoir*, pp. 22–3; *Poems*, p. 625.

when he was at school, and at first in the Temple, these would be spent at his home in Hertfordshire,[1] with perhaps short visits to Cowper cousins nearby in the same county, or to the Donnes in Norfolk. Even after his father died (1756), William seems to have gone back to his home in order to see his stepmother,[2] though he apparently did not accept her as a mother. In fact, he may have disliked her. He scarcely ever mentioned her in his letters,[3] and in 1802 Lady Hesketh told John Johnson: 'O! how I wish I cou'd furnish our Good friend Mr Hayley wth the letter dear Cowper wrote to me on the death of his mother & which made me laugh on a very Sick bed. remember she was his *Mother in Law* and *disagreable enough in all Conscience*, but the letter was Capital & to have lost it shou'd never be forgiven to H. Hesketh.'[4] Later she seemed to recall part of it, and quoted the opening from memory.

You may now dearest Coz: [Cowper had written], congratulate me on being an Independent man—if indeed a man may properly be said to be *Independent*, who has *nothing* to depend upon: my Mother:in:law is dead and has left her fortune to be divided equally between my brother & myself—a division not very unlike Splitting a hair, and which must be very agreable to my brother, who is a Cambridge man & a Logiscian and to me no less who have the honor to be Call'd a Lawyer. but pity me not dear Coz: the comforts of life [are?] so near the Ground, that we poor folks

---

[1] He was there as late as 1759: Appendix, A, p. 198.

[2] Rebecca, widow of one Marryat; she m. John Cowper, 8 Jan. 1740/1, she being then of Queen's Square, in the parish of St George the Martyr. This was near Ashley's house, and Rebecca may have met John through him. She was long a cripple (*Letters*, III, 378); 'died at Bath on the 31st of July 1762 and was buried in the Abbey at that place. Aged 61—' (note in William Cowper, the poet's, hand: Cowper family Bible, Cowper Mus., Olney). Her monument in the Abbey, Bath, gives her age at death as 63. See also Warrand, *Hertfordshire Families*, p. 146; Francis Collins, ed. *The Registers...of Charterhouse Chapel* (London, 1892), p. 39.

[3] *Letters*, I, 93, 102; III, 378, 453, where she is usually referred to as his 'mother-in-law'. According to Greatheed: 'I never heard any intimation from M$^{r.}$ C. of bad treatment from his father or stepmother, I apprehend that he was scarcely at all with her': [Greatheed], 'Memoranda', f. 2.

[4] Lady Hesketh to John Johnson, 7 Jan. 1802: Morgan MSS.

are sure to find them, while rich Rogues Jump over them & *know nothing of y^e* MATTER.[1]

Of Cowper's years in the Temple a contemporary said: 'With whatever propriety he may have been compared to the Martlet, from the natural timidity of his disposition, he could not be called "The Temple haunting Martlet", since he was seldom seen there in summer; but, with more certainty, to be found on the margin of Tewin-water, or in the shrubberies of Colne-Green [both in Hertfordshire], a mansion, whose noble owner and name-sake, was also nearly related to him.'[2] In 1752 and 1753 William Cowper stayed in Norfolk,[3] and in 1754, 1757, and perhaps 1758 he was again in Hertfordshire, with Theadora or his brother, at New Barns, the stately house of Lieutenant-Colonel Thomson, a good friend of Ashley Cowper.[4] From the extensive grounds at New Barns one could see St Albans a short distance away. And in 1764 and 1765, when William was at Dr Cotton's asylum in St Albans, Theadora may have been with her father at Thomson's house, and watching the place where her beloved was kept.[5]

William liked best to be near the sea or at the watering

---

[1] '"or *know not they exist.*" I am not sure as to the concluding sentence, but I am sure it was one or the other of those I have *mark'd.*' Lady Hesketh to Hayley, 17 Sept. [1805], Cowper Mus., Olney.

[2] *Monthly Mag.* IX, Pt i (1800), 409. Owing to a printer's error, the original reads 'Jewin-water'. It was the seat of Spencer Cowper (1725?–97)—who later became a lieut.-gen.—and his son Henry: Warrand, pp. 147–8. The other mansion (in the original, 'Cole-Green') was the seat of the Earls Cowper; rebuilt later as Panshanger; recently (since 1950) demolished. See Warrand, p. 138.

[3] At Catfield and Drayton: *Poems*, pp. xxv, 270–1.

[4] In the poem 'Written after Leaving Her at New Burns' the place name is misspelled. James Croft, who first publ. the poem, in *Early Poems*, p. 19, mistook an 'a' for a 'u' as he did in 'Cutfield' (Catfield), p. 12. The name is spelled correctly ('Newbarns') in the *text* of Ashley Cowper's poem, 'N–w B–rns', written in 1763 (*Poems and Translations*, pp. 31–3). John Cowper to Richard Gough, 3 Nov. 1757, written from St Albans: 'My Brother...has been here this Vacation.' The following year John wrote to Gough to tell him that 'I...propose sleeping my summer away in different parts of the habitable globe—at St. Alban's, at London, at Hartingfordbury, and at York'. Nichols, *Anecdotes*, VIII, 561–2.

[5] One of Ashley's ballads was written at New Barns, 16 July 1765: *Poems and Translations*, pp. 34–7.

places. As early as 1748 he had gone to Bath, and in the next
fifteen years he went to such fashionable summer towns as
Southampton, Margate, Rottingdean, Taplow, Maiden-
head, Mundesley, Weymouth, and Brighton.[1] He knew
these places, as he himself described them, of 'idleness and
luxury, music, dancing, cards, walking, riding, bathing,
eating, drinking, coffee, tea, scandal, dressing, yawning,
sleeping'.[2] He sometimes went with people who enjoyed
that kind of life. But he preferred to go to various towns
on the coast in the company of a few friends: his Uncle
Ashley, Ashley's friend Mr Quarme, and Joseph Hill. With
them William spent his time in strolling along the cliffs, the
downs, and the sand. Or simply gazing at the sea:

I think...that the most magnificent object under heaven is the
great deep; and cannot but feel an unpolite species of astonishment,
when I consider the multitudes that view it without emotion, and
even without reflection. In all its various forms, it is an object of
all others the most suited to affect us with lasting impressions of the
awful Power that created and controls it. I am the less inclined to
think this negligence excusable, because at a time of life when
I gave as little attention to religious subjects as almost any man,
I yet remember that the waves would preach to me, and that in
the midst of dissipation I had an ear to hear them. One of
Shakespeare's characters says,—'I am never merry when I hear
sweet music.' The same effect that harmony seems to have had
upon him, I have experienced from the sight and sound of the
ocean, which have often composed my thoughts into a melancholy
not unpleasing nor without its use.[3]

Melancholy was therefore sometimes part of these
vacations, or a special reason for taking them—melancholy,
both slight and deep. Such was the case when he went to

[1] Poems, p. 263; Letters, I, 223–4; II, 24, 87; IV, 439. For Mundesley and Brighton
see Connoisseur, no. 134.
[2] Letters, I, 363, 374.
[3] Lady Hesketh to Hayley, 13 Sept. 1801: Add. MSS. 30803 A, ff. 161–2. Probably
George Quarme (1716?–75), of Padstow, Cornwall; at Westminster School (c. 1729–
35); Commissioner of Taxes (1762–3), and of Excise (1766–75): Rec. Old Westm. and
Suppl. Letters, I, 358.

Southampton, to escape from his first bout of depression, which had occurred soon after he had moved into the Temple. He had previously spent much time about that resort: walking in the fields with Lady Hesketh, or sailing to Portsmouth with Sir Thomas. He went almost yearly with them, even after his engagement with Theadora was broken off, and they found his company 'chearful & pleasing'. But he never in his life spent a day in the assembly-room, and his life differed radically from the lives of those who did. 'A walk to Netley Abbey, or to Freemantle, or to Redbridge [places near Southampton], or a book by the fireside, had always more charms for me', he said, 'than any other amusement that the place afforded.' There was happiness merely in breathing the healthiest air in all England. And when he went there to rid himself of melancholy, Cowper maintained the same quiet, leisurely life. He sat and reflected while looking from Lymington at the Needles, or from Freemantle, a mile from Southampton, where he could contemplate the river, the forest, and the shrubbery.[1] One morning the air was

clear and calm; the sun shone bright upon the sea; and the country on the borders of it was the most beautiful I had ever seen. We sat down upon an eminence, at the end of the arm of the sea, which runs between Southampton and the New Forest. Here it was, that on a sudden, as if another sun had been kindled that instant in the heavens, on purpose to dispel sorrow and vexation of spirit, I felt the weight of all my misery taken off; my heart became light and joyful in a moment; I could have wept with transport had I been alone. I must needs believe that nothing less than the Almighty fiat could have filled me with such inexpressible delight; not by a gradual dawning of peace, but as it were with a flash of his life-giving countenance.[2]

Nearly a decade later when a more fearful melancholy came over him, he again sought a vacation by the sea. He

---

[1] *Letters*, II, 232, 237, 356–7, 397–8; III, 50; Lady Hesketh to Hayley, 13 Sept. 1801: Add. MSS. 30803 A, f. 162.   [2] Cowper's *Memoir*, p. 11.

went to Margate, and to nearby Ramsgate. Again he recovered his spirits: through bathing, and trips to the famous Ramsgate pier, or walks 'upon the strand at Margate, where the cliff is high and perpendicular'. One sight, in particular, he said, 'engaged my curiosity, and I went to see it—a fine piece of ruins, built by the late Lord Holland, at a great expense, which, the day after I saw it, tumbled down for nothing'.[1] Holland's follies were famous: Walpole said that the 'view might, to those who were never there, be passed for a prospect in some half-civilized island discovered by Captain Cook'. And Gray described them in his verses 'On Lord Holland[s] Seat':

> Now mouldring fanes and battlements arise,
> Arches and turrets nodding to their fall,
> Unpeopled palaces delude his eyes,
> And mimick desolation covers all.[2]

Whatever tower or fortress tumbled down in 1763—shortly after Holland had begun his building on the bleak North Foreland, without a single tree to detract from the many follies or to protect the inhabitants from the severe east winds—the collapse was probably hastened by the extraordinarily violent storm of 19 August. Rain and hail poured down upon the coastal towns of Kent. The hailstones were from two to ten inches in circumference, and the lightning appeared 'like sheets of flame'. The thunder pounded. By noon it was so dark that one could see only a few feet. The oldest inhabitants could not remember anything to equal the ferocity of the storm, and the desolation which resulted from it was inconceivable.[3]

The storm came at the beginning of Cowper's last seaside

---

[1] *Ibid.* pp. 22–3; *Letters*, I, 155–8.

[2] Walpole's *Letters*, ed. Toynbee (Oxford, 1905), XIII, 178–9; Gray, *Poems*, ed. A. L. Poole, 3rd ed. (London, 1937), p. 116.

[3] *London Chron.* XIV (20–3, 25–7 Aug., 13–15 Sept., 1–4 Oct. 1763), 181, 194, 257, 322; *G.M.* XXXIII (Sept. 1763), 444–5. An appeal was made in London for the relief of the people of Kent.

vacation. Even for one who loved the wildness of the storm and the sound of thunder rolling over the ocean, this hurricane must have been startling. It would have seemed a disturbing portent to a man faced with the strongest demands of his life. And the resulting dreadfulness of the Kent countryside, which in August looked as if it were in 'the depth of winter', must have appeared to William Cowper as a forecast of his own inevitable failure. He had begun to see in nature the emblems of his dark and lonely and despairing self. For some time at Margate, he said, 'my first reflections, when I awoke in the morning, were horrible, and full of wretchedness. I looked forward to the approaching winter, and regretted the flight of every moment, which brought it nearer; like a man borne away, by a rapid torrent, into a stormy sea, whence he sees no possibility of returning, and where he knows he cannot subsist.'[1]

---

[1] Cowper's *Memoir*, pp. 22–3.

IX

THE DEFECT

It has become the fashion to love him for his letters and his lovableness, but to be lukewarm about his poetry.

                    H. W. GARROD of Cowper—1951

There is an effeminacy about him, which shrinks from and repels common and hearty sympathy.

                    WILLIAM HAZLITT of Cowper—1818

Of course he was an invalid, and his attachment to local scenes can be discounted on that account. He had not enough vitality to seek new experiences, and never felt safe until habits had formed their cocoon round his sensitive mind. But inside the cocoon his life is genuine. He might dread the unknown, but he also loved what he knew; he felt steadily about familiar objects, and they have in his work something of the permanence they get in a sitting-room or in the kitchen garden.   E. M. FORSTER of Cowper—1932

The stocking-cap on the poet's head, the tea cup in the poet's hand had to him a look of limitation, of almost feminine restraint. Cowper's life seemed to him a sheltered one: it did no good to remind himself that Cowper had been for a good deal of his life, insane.   RANDALL JARRELL—1954

There is one curious fact revealed in these letters [from John Newton to John Thornton], which accounts for much of Cowper's morbid state of mind and fits of depression, as well as for the circumstances of his running away from his place in the House of Lords. He was a Hermaphrodite. It relates to some defect in his physical conformation; somebody found out his secret, and probably threatened its exposure.   CHARLES GREVILLE—1834[1]

For nearly a century and a half there have been comments like Hazlitt's about William Cowper. And during the past eighty years biographers have speculated about the nature of his alleged physical defect. It has been

---

[1] Garrod, 'Books and Writers', *Spectator*, CLXXXVI (1951), 690; Hazlitt, 'Lectures on the English Poets: on Thomson and Cowper', *Works*, ed. P. P. Howe (London, 1930), v, 91; Forster, 'William Cowper, an Englishman', *Spectator*, CXLVIII (1932), 75; Jarrell, *Pictures from an Institution* (New York, 1954), p. 110; *The Greville Diary*, ed. Philip Whitwell Wilson (Garden City, New York, 1927), I, 139–40.

commonly accepted that he was a man who shrank from the more vigorous aspects of human life. But just how often before the breakdown of 1763 he withdrew into his cocoon is almost impossible to determine. Were there obvious elements of effeminacy in his character, 'a look of limitation, of almost feminine restraint'?

This quality does not appear to have been at all noticeable in his youth. As a Westminster schoolboy and a rakish templar he led a full and strong, sometimes rather rough and wild, man's life. When he addressed his sweetheart in 'The Symptoms of Love', he described himself as a hunter, 'rambling alone', striding 'o'er the stubble each day with my gun'.[1] An absent-minded, love-ridden hunter, of course, but that was part of the game. Bashful in love, and in his person generally:

> His modesty was such,
> That one might say (to say the truth)
> He rather had too much.

But as he became older and acquaintanceships spread wider,

> He mended and grew perter,
> In company was more at ease,
> And dress'd a little smarter:...

> He eyed the women, and made free
> To comment on their shapes,
> So that there was, or seem'd to be,
> No fear of a relapse.[2]

His friends and companions lived the boldest possible kinds of lives. At a very early age they could match almost any gouty old roué with stories of their loves. They were lusty, and did not care who knew it; in fact, they joyfully established their reputations as rakes. Men like Churchill and Lloyd despised the silly dandies that flitted about the city, and denounced them in their poetry; Cowper, not

---

[1] 'The Symptoms of Love': *Poems*, p. 270.   [2] 'Of Himself': *Poems*, p. 269.

quite as sharp in his attacks, nevertheless frowned 'with a just disdain' at effeminates,

> whose very looks
> Reflect dishonour on the land I love.

'I cannot talk with civet in the room', he said;

> A fine puss-gentleman that's all perfume;
> The sight's enough—no need to smell a beau—
> Who thrusts his nose into a raree-show?
> His odoriferous attempts to please,
> Perhaps might prosper with a swarm of bees;
> But we that make no honey, though we sting,
> Poets, are sometimes apt to maul the thing.[1]

So he spoke later in his life, as the solid, moral country gentleman, who would not trifle with such foolishness. He did not speak self-consciously, suspiciously, or with a strange interest.

He was not of those men, in person or companionship, at any time. And whatever parts of fussiness or old-maidishness crept into his life after repeated attacks of insanity and year after year of seclusion, they do not seem to have been evident when he was a young man. After his clumsy country manners had been reformed by Theadora, he became towards women particularly, in behaviour and conversation, 'fascinating in the highest degree'.[2]

But after he had lost Theadora was he, as Hazlitt said, a coward in love, an amiable weakling? Was he 'delicate to fastidiousness, and glad to get back, after a romantic adventure with crazy Kate, a party of gypsies or a little girl on a common, to the drawing-room and the ladies again, to the sofa and the tea-kettle?'[3] Apparently not before 1763. His letters to Toby reveal a man forthright about his love affairs, and in the letter of 1758 to Clotworthy Rowley, he

---

[1] *Task*, II, 221–32; 'Conversation', ll. 283–90.
[2] See 'Of Himself' and Hayley (1803), II, 222.
[3] Hazlitt, p. 92.

is 'tortured with love' because of a beautiful girl from the West Indies, who was residing briefly in Greenwich.[1] There was also a rumour—reported by the Reverend David Simpson, who had met Cowper and who had been curate to Cowper's friend William Unwin—that '. . . Cowper's first derangement was occasioned by a love affair with the kept mistress of Lord Thurlow'.[2] After his stay in the hospital at St Albans, however, his letters are absolutely bare of any suggestion of the full love of a man for a woman. It is as if he had tightly closed the door on marital love.

Once, when he wrote 'The Lily and the Rose' *c.* 1781— the poem ends:

> The seat of empire is her cheeks,
> They [the lily and the rose] reign united there—

he said: 'I believe there is no man who has less to do with the ladies' cheeks than I have.' Cowper then quickly recalled his Temple days, a different time: 'I suppose it would be best to antedate it, and to imagine that it was written twenty years ago.' One of his exceedingly rare references to a woman's sexual attraction occurred in a letter to Rowley in 1789, and Rowley was someone who had known Cowper intimately in his youth. 'You may safely present my love to Miss Rowley', William wrote. 'A present of that sort from a man old enough to be her father can do her no harm,—at least at this distance. Were we nearer to each other, perhaps the approach might not be altogether so safe for me.'[3] Rowley, it is to be imagined, would remember a time when it would not have been safe.

For most of his life William associated with women every day—there were always one or more women hovering in the background, or sitting beside him in the parlours at

---

[1] *Letters*, I, 5–10, 14–17.
[2] Simpson to unidentified recipient, 11 June 1793: Alfred Leedes Hunt, *Evangelical By-Paths* (London, 1927), p. 89.
[3] 'The Lily and the Rose', *Poems*, pp. 312–13; *Letters*, I, 421; III, 401–2.

Olney or Weston. But his friendships were carefully non-sexual. Recently one scholar concluded that because of childhood conflicts, Cowper could not approach a woman with the normal address of a man. He believed that the unusual complexity of Cowper's attitude towards men and women was a result of latent homosexuality.[1] One bit of information which helped him reach this conclusion in his psychological study of Cowper's life and work, was the statement in the *Greville Memoirs*. As first published (1874), the decisive sentence indicated that there was 'some defect' in Cowper's 'physical conformation'. In the most authoritative edition of this work (1938) the text reads: 'He was an Hermaphrodite; somebody knew his secret, and probably threatened its exposure.'[2]

Charles Greville's source was a parcel of letters which Henry Taylor had brought to him in September 1834 to frank to Robert Southey, who was at that time writing his life of Cowper. Taylor had received the parcel from James Stephen, who was a nephew of Wilberforce, the associate of John Thornton and most of the leading Evangelicals. The contents soon became known also to James Spedding, for the five—Greville, Taylor, Southey, Stephen, and Spedding—were an especially close group in the years 1834–6.[3] The letters forwarded to Southey were from the

---

[1] H. K. Gregory, *The Prisoner and His Crimes: A Psychological Approach to William Cowper's Life and Writings*, unpublished Ph.D. dissertation (Harvard Univ., 1951), especially pp. 65, 72–4, 126–7, 209.

[2] *The Greville Memoirs*, ed. Henry Reeve (London, 1874), III, 135 (Wright, *Life* [1921], pp. 6, 42, quotes this, and adds that the defect was 'said to have been partial hermaphroditism'), and ed. Lytton Strachey and Roger Fulford (London, 1938), III, 85.

[3] *Ibid.* Southey in his 'Preface' thanks 'Mr. Stephen, of the Colonial Office, for Mr. Newton's letters to Mr. Thornton, written during his residence at Olney' (Southey's *Cowper*, I, vii). Southey to C. B., 13 March 1834: Southey's *Correspondence with Caroline Bowles*, ed. Edward Dowden (Dublin, 1881), p. 296. Spedding tells William Bodham Donne in a letter, 28 Oct. 1834, that the day previously Southey had given him 'some very strange and interesting information about Cowper....The strangest of all will not be made public': Frances M. Brookfield, *The Cambridge 'Apostles'* (London, 1906), p. 263.

Reverend John Newton, the friend of Cowper, to John Thornton, an influential Evangelical philanthropist. The secrets of the letters were hinted at when John Wood Warter and Edward Dowden in 1856 and 1881 published expurgated versions of Southey's letters. But readers were left with titillating excerpts like these: 'I have been made acquainted with something regarding Cowper much more remarkable than anything that is publicly known concerning him, or indeed than could possibly be imagined.... All I can say is, that it renders him far more an object of extraordinary compassion than he already appears to be' (Southey to Caroline Bowles, 13 March 1834). 'In these letters the mystery is revealed, and my mind is made up, after consulting with Wordsworth, that if it ever be made public, it shall not be by me. It had better be discovered hereafter by some hunter after extraordinary facts, than embodied in the Life of so truly amiable and interesting a poet' (April 1834, to the same). Warter's notes indicated that Southey had also read about a '*love* attachment' between Cowper and Mrs Unwin, 'but the details are of too private a character for publication'.[1]

Southey received the letters in batches during 1834, and returned them as soon as he had made use of them. In spite of the fact that he was determined to keep the information from the public, the news leaked out through the sensation-mongering editor of a small journal, the *Literary Times*. Somehow this man had learned the contents of the single letter which contained the reference to hermaphroditism.[2]

---

[1] *Correspondence with Bowles*, pp. 296, 299–300; see also pp. 302–3, 312–13, 319, 322, 331–9, 346, 352. Southey, *Selections from the Letters*, ed. Warter, IV, 430–1.

[2] *Bowles*, 296–300; *Selections*, IV, 374, 417–19, 536. The *Literary Times; a Journal of Literature, Science, and the Fine Arts*, 21 nos. (London, 1835–6): B.M. Cat. (The only file of this periodical which I have been able to discover was in the B.M. but was destroyed in the last war.) Southey to Charles Cradock, 3 Nov. 1835: 'He cannot have seen the letter, because he says it was written *by Cowper to one of his dearest friends*. Now, though I have not seen it, I know that it was written by *Mr. Newton* to *Mr. Thornton*. It was not sent to me with the rest of that correspondence, because it was *missing* at that time' (*Selections*, IV, 417–18).

None of the published fragments of Southey's letters actually mention Cowper's alleged hermaphroditism. But unpublished letters show Southey's knowledge and his attitude towards it. He wrote to the Reverend G. C. Gorham on 23 December 1835, about 'the only circumstance in Cowper's history which I have thought proper to withhold':

Both Mʳ Newton & Mʳˢ Unwin believed that there was a just impediment of Cowpers being joined to any person in matrimony. It was a part of his madness to fancy so,—& they both—with what appears to me marvellous credulity,—believed him: tho if the fact had been as he supposed, it was not merely unlikely, but absolutely impossible that he should ever have been sent to a public school,— or to any boarding school.—He fancied that he was an androgyne. A newspaper writer has got hold of this, & makes a great mystery of the matter, pretending to have seen a letter of Cowpers disclosing it to one of his most intimate friends, which letter, he says, I have seen. But he has seen no such letter,—for it was Mʳ Newton who stated it in a letter to Mʳ Thornton, as a fact that put an end to all scandal.—You will agree with me in thinking that all this was better withheld from the public.[1]

Southey told Henry Taylor—of all his friends, the man most concerned in this whole affair—that he had come to the conclusion 'it was part of C's madness to fancy himself in that condition. Mʳˢ U[nwin]. & Mʳ Newton might believe him,—because they could not undeceive themselves by inspection, & seem never to have questioned the probability. It is absolutely incredible that any person in that predicament should have been sent to a public school.'[2]

The rumour concerned a report of 'remarkable malformation',[3] and in discussing it one must be careful first of

---

[1] MS. Cowper Mus., Olney.
[2] Southey to Taylor, 16 Sept. 1834: Bodleian MSS. Eng. lett. d. 7, f. 304.
[3] Southey to John Wood Warter, 11 July 1834: Add. MSS. 47888. In this letter Southey writes he has concluded that the possibility of a 'remarkable mal-formation', which Newton believed to be the *cause* of Cowper's madness, 'was in reality nothing more than an imaginary *effect*'.

141

all to discriminate between hermaphroditism—where there is congenital anatomic variation in the sex organs—and abnormal psychosexual drives such as homosexuality or transvestism. The true (or glandular) hermaphrodite is exceedingly rare, but mal-development may produce an appearance of bisexual structure of the genital organs.[1] Occasionally the external opening of the urethra may be on the under surface of the penis, a condition known as hypospadias, and one biographer believes that there is a strong probability that Cowper suffered from it.[2] He pictures the fearful child, warned by his parents to keep his defect a secret. But, as Southey said, it is impossible to believe that a boy whose genitals were severely malformed would be sent to a boarding-school; and if such a boy were sent, that he could keep this condition from other boys' notice. In all likelihood Cowper for many years shared a bed with a schoolmate, in a room which probably had two or three beds. He must have bathed in public, according to school custom, as he was wont to do at Huntingdon.[3] And his school and Temple friends, who would presumably be better acquainted with his physical conformation than either Mr Newton or Mrs Unwin, gave every indication of accepting him as a normally developed male, with a man's natural abilities and desires.

The letter from John Newton to John Thornton, which contained news of the mystery, was probably written in 1774,[4] and certainly before 1790 (when Thornton died). During the summer of 1800, shortly after the death of Cowper, Newton began a memoir of the poet in which he did not speak of any 'just impediment of Cowpers being joined to any person in matrimony'; on the contrary, he

---

[1] See John M. Morris, 'Intersexuality', *Jrnl. Amer. Med. Assoc.* CLXIII (16 Feb. 1957), 538–42; Hugh Hampton Young, *Genital Abnormalities, Hermaphroditism and Related Adrenal Diseases* (Baltimore, 1937).

[2] Gregory, pp. 54–5.   [3] *Letters*, 1, 24, 28.

[4] See their correspondence in Bernard Martin, *John Newton* (London, 1950), p. 240.

wrote that Cowper's friendship with Mrs Unwin led them 'to an engagement for marriage, which was well known to me, and to most of their and my friends, and was to have taken place in a few months, but was prevented by the terrible malady which seized him about that time [January 1773]'.[1] Thoughts about the remarkable defect seem to have been forgotten, or contradicted.

From what Southey knew in 1835, and from what we know today, it would appear that if Cowper did believe he was a hermaphrodite, it was a delusion, and part of his mental disorder. At this distance in time and with the information available, any technical psychiatric diagnosis in other than the most general terms would be pretentious and misleading. His *Memoir* and correspondence, and the reports of his behaviour, suggest that his insanity was characterized chiefly by prolonged periods of depression. Cowper had the classic symptoms of the depressive phase of what is most commonly called the manic-depressive psychosis.[2] He had ideas of utter worthlessness; delusions of extreme sinfulness and guilt; he heard accusing voices; he believed that he had committed the unpardonable sin, and was hopelessly damned in the eyes of God; he repeatedly tried to kill himself.

In acute cases of depression the subject is frequently unduly concerned about supposed changes in his body, and among these delusions sexual preoccupations are notable. These may be directed towards a particular organ, and, according to Fenichel, as a rule they represent in a distorted

---

[1] Quoted from the 16 pp. fragment of Newton's memoir of Cowper in Josiah Bull, *John Newton* (London, [1868]), p. 192.

[2] For information on manic-depressive reactions I have used such works as Sigmund Freud, 'Mourning and Melancholia', in *Collected Papers* (London, 1925), IV, 152–70; 'Manic-Depressive Psychosis', *Assoc. for Research in Nerv. and Ment. Disease*, XI (1930); Otto Fenichel, *The Psychoanalytic Theory of Neuroses* (New York, 1945); Leopold Bellak, *Manic-Depressive Psychosis* (New York, 1952). An attempt to classify the case of Cowper was made in 1930 by James Hendrie Lloyd: 'The Case of William Cowper, the English Poet', *Archives of Neurology and Psychiatry*, XXIV (1930), 682–9.

manner castration-anxiety. Kraepelin says that in the depressive state the hypochondriacal delusions 'usually reach a considerable development'. The patient may believe that his genitals are shrivelled, crushed, or have disappeared.[1] A recent biographer of Cowper has written that it is 'at least conceivable that the poet might have emasculated himself if he felt guilty about sexual indulgence'.[2] The probabilities of this are almost nil. It is much more likely that Cowper's reputed hermaphroditism was a preoccupation resulting from his melancholia.

[1] See K. M. Bowman and A. F. Raymond, 'A Statistical Study of Delusions in the Manic-Depressive Psychoses', *Amer. Jrnl. Psychiat.* LXXXVIII (1931), 111–21; Aubrey J. Lewis, 'Melancholia: A Clinical Survey of Depressive States', *Jrnl. Ment. Sci.* LXXX (1934), 277–378, especially pp. 306–12: hypochondriacal delusions were found in twenty-five of the patients in this detailed study of sixty-one cases of depressive states at the Maudsley Hosp., London. See also Fenichel, pp. 262–4; Emil Kraepelin, *Manic-Depressive Insanity and Paranoia*, trans. R. M. Barclay, ed. G. M. Robertson (Edinburgh, 1921), pp. 19–20, 92–3.

[2] Maurice J. Quinlan, *William Cowper: A Critical Life* (Minneapolis, 1953), p. 43. Quinlan's suggestion is based on the case of a patient of William Heberden (one of Cowper's doctors), in which a man resembling Cowper in age and mental attitude amputated his penis and scrotum (Heberden, *Commentaries on the History and Cure of Diseases* (London, 1802), pp. 226–7, note). If Cowper had cut off his genitals, the history of this would almost certainly have been made known to Mrs Unwin and Newton by Dr Cotton, Cowper's physician at St Albans, when they later consulted him. And they would not be likely to have described such a condition as androgynous or hermaphroditic.

X

FAILURE

Cowper came to me and said: 'O that I were insane always.
I will never rest. Can you not make me truly insane? I will
never rest till I am so. O that in the bosom of God I was hid. You
retain health and yet are as mad as any of us all—over us all—
mad as a refuge from unbelief—from Bacon, Newton and Locke.'

                                                              BLAKE[1]

    Such is mans life, and such is mine
    The worst of men, and yet still thine.

      VAUGHAN, 'Misery': couplet marked by Cowper
           in his copy of *Silex Scintillans*, 1650[2]

T HE year 1763, Mr Quennell says, was a year of 'planning and renewed activity' for England after her seven-years' war with France. 'It was one of those moments, not uncommon in the history of a period, when several gifted human beings happen at the same time to reach a decisive stage, from which their subsequent courses wind away in various directions.' At the very end of the previous year, Edward Gibbon, aged twenty-five, had left the militia to begin in earnest his life as historian. On 16 May, James Boswell, only twenty-three, met Johnson. *Tristram Shandy*, the work of a middle-aged Yorkshire parson, Laurence Sterne, was one of the sensations of London, which was at the same time being politically disrupted by the activities of the patriot John Wilkes.[3] But for William Cowper the year 1763 brought depression and failure, a terribly decisive end to his early years. It brought madness;

---

[1] Blake's notes on Spurzheim's *Observations on the Deranged Manifestations of the Mind, or Insanity* (London, 1817): *The Writings of William Blake*, ed. Geoffrey Keynes (London, 1925), III, 352.

[2] See Alexander B. Grosart, 'Cowper the Poet's Copy of Henry Vaughan's Silex Scintillans', *Wales*, I (1894), 200. The book is now in the National Libr. of Wales, Aberystwyth.

[3] Peter Quennell, *Four Portraits* (London, 1945), p. 12.

and the first glance of healing light from Evangelical religion.

Cowper's friends and relations followed the country's pattern of new success. Doors were opened for them, but one after another was closed before him. In January Churchill resigned the parish of St John's, Westminster, in order to give himself completely to poetry and the life of a rake. On 5 May Clotworthy Rowley married. For the Nonsense Club the early part of June was taken up by the celebrated performance of Thornton's burlesque *Ode on St Cæcilia's Day*. A few days later William Cowper's brother John was elected Fellow of Corpus Christi College, Cambridge. During July Boswell wrote to his recent acquaintance, Bonnell Thornton, asking him to gather his friends so that he might again enjoy their company. But Thornton replied that 'Messieurs Wilkes, Churchill, and myself are to be at Aylesbury on Wednesday next, and Colman is already in the Country'. The old club was breaking up. Cowper was no longer mentioned. By autumn the activities of Churchill, Colman, and Thornton were dominated by politics rather than poetry, and John Wilkes had taken the place of older friends. Some time during the first week of August, John Cowper set off from Cambridge for a holiday in Yorkshire, and a month later his friend and William's, John Duncombe, became Vicar of St Clement's Church, West Thurrock, Essex, under the patronage of John Seare, another Berkhamsted friend.[1]

In William Cowper 'the storm was gathering all the while....Continual misery at length brought on a nervous fever', he said. 'Quiet forsook me by day, and peace by

---

[1] J. E. Smith, *St John the Evangelist, Westminster* (London, 1892), p. 105; *G.M.* xxxiii (1763), 257; *St James's Chron.* 7–9 June 1763 (performance of the ode: 10 June); Corpus Christi Coll., Camb., MSS.: 'Order Book, 1752–82'; Thornton to Boswell [?25 July 1763]: Private Papers of James Boswell, Yale Univ. Libr. MSS.; Nichols, *Anecdotes*, viii, 565; Philip Morant, *The History...of...Essex* (London, 1768), i, Pt ii, 94.

night; a finger raised against me, was more than I could stand against.' The spring went in this way, and the summer. 'The vacation being pretty far advanced', he went to Margate, where by the help of cheerful company, and a new scene, his spirits began to recover. About the beginning of October he was forced to return to his work in London. The next two months constituted the crucial period of his life; and after that—eight months of the deepest depression.[1] October, November, and December were also especially critical months for his friends, but they were leading to achievement, not despair. In October Chase Price was entertaining the militia and Tate Wilkinson at Shrewsbury, roaring out his songs, and doing amateur acting, and drinking port wine. Then at the beginning of November almost every Old Westminster was at the Westminster play. But not Cowper. His relative, de Grey, was seeking interest to gain the office of either Attorney or Solicitor-General, and for the next two months could think of little else. Just at this time Dick Sutton was chosen Recorder of the borough of St Albans. And shortly afterwards John Wilkes was wounded in a duel. During the two weeks which had preceded Wilkes's injury, spies for the Secretaries of State had found that Churchill and Thornton were with Wilkes (not Cowper) almost every day.[2] With the trouble over the duel and Wilkes's *North Briton No. 45* and the shocking *Essay on Woman*, the city could think of nothing but Wilkes for many weeks.

Cowper was left to his own desperate self. There were not many visitors nor any diversions. His devoted friend Carr

[1] Cowper's *Memoir*, pp. 19, 21–3, 60–1; also, *Letters*, I, 21.

[2] Tate Wilkinson, *Memoirs of His Own Life* (York, 1790), III, 165–73; John Wilkes, *Letters* (1769), pp. 299–300; de Grey to George Grenville, 1 Nov. 1763, seeking the offices: *The Grenville Papers*, ed. William James Smith (London, 1852–3), II, 153–60. De Grey was appointed Solicitor-Gen. 16 Dec. and rechosen M.P. for Newport, Cornwall, 28 Dec.: *St James's Chron.* 15–17 and 27–9 Dec. 1763. *Daily Adv.* 12 Nov. 1763 and *Lond. Chron.* 15–17 Nov. 1763.

was 'indefatigable' in his attention during the whole year, and a few days before Cowper was taken from London, Lady Hesketh and Sir Thomas called on him in his chambers in the Temple. He had formerly often visited them, and felt close to them; now they tried to persuade him to leave the Temple and become their 'constant Inmate'.[1] But their offer came too late.

He remained alone, except in that part of the day when he was with Ashley Cowper and engaged in frantic preparation to qualify for the position of Clerk of the Journals in the House of Lords. Ashley, the patentee of this and other deputations under the office of Clerk of the Parliaments, held the right of appointment under a grant sealed in the first year of the reign of George I.[2] Spencer Cowper had at that time purchased the office for £18,000 so that his two sons, William (d. 1740) and Ashley, could enjoy the considerable profits.[3] A century later the salary and emoluments of the Clerk of the Parliaments averaged between five and six thousand pounds a year.[4] The office-holder was the permanent head of the clerical staff of the Upper House,

[1] *Letters*, IV, 129–30; II, 384; Lady Hesketh to Hayley, 30 Aug. 1801: Add. MSS. 30803 A, f. 155.

[2] Cowper's *Memoir*, p. 17. On p. 16 Cowper writes that he was offered the position by the patentee. This has generally been presumed to have been Major William Cowper, of Hertingfordbury (see Southey's *Cowper*, I, 109; Wright, *Life* (1921), p. 40; Quinlan, *William Cowper* (1953), pp. 24–5), but a leaflet publ. by Ashley Cowper at the time of William's appointment (in 1763) says that 'Mr. *Ashley Cowper* holds it now by the same Title, under a Patent sealed in the First Year of *George* the First'. The leaflet begins: 'The Office of Clerk of the Parliaments...has been enjoyed in continual Succession by the King's Patent...' [London, 1763], 3 pp.: B.M. 748, f. 12 (4).

[3] According to the *Diary of Mary Countess Cowper*, ed. Spencer Cowper (London, 1864), p. 64, the office was purchased 25 Dec. 1714 O.S. William Cowper took office 5 Jan. 1716: *Jnls. H. of L.* xxxviii, 215.

[4] *House of Lords: Reports from the Committee*, 4 and 19 June 1824. Average receipts (1819–23): Clerk of the Journals, £982; Copying Clerk, £894; Senior Writing Clerk, £612; after 1824, C. of the P. had a salary of £4000 a year, one of the official houses, and retiring provision not exceeding £2000 a year; Clerk Assistant: £2500, official house, and retirement of £1500. According to Harry Graham, *The Mother of Parliaments* (London, 1910), pp. 246–7, note, the post of C. of the P. was 'a lucrative sinecure, worth about £7000 a year, the actual duties of the office being performed by the Clerk Assistant'. I have not been able to find any specific information concerning the incomes of these offices prior to 1819.

and had the privilege of appointing all its clerks.[1] The office itself had become a sinecure, the duties being performed by a Clerk Assistant. By a grant of May 1739, William Cowper of Hertingfordbury, grandson of Spencer (and William's son), would hold the patent in reversion after the death of his father and his Uncle Ashley.[2] But shortly after that date this younger William (d. 1769) began to receive the profits from the office—and later his brother Spencer (d. 1797)—according to a family arrangement, though Ashley held the title for over sixty years until his death in 1788.[3]

Ashley himself never attended the House of Lords; nevertheless, he supposedly had superintendency of all of its clerks and their business. He 'never interfer'd to give any Directions therein', according to official testimony before a committee of the House in November 1763, but left the supervision to Joseph Wight, his Clerk Assistant. This, in the spirit of the times, was not objected to, but the committee, meeting again in March of the following year, reprimanded Ashley Cowper for having 'perverted and misapplied' several annual sums which were paid from the Royal Bounty to minor clerks. One such sum had been 'unwarrantably' sold by William Cowper, who had preceded Ashley as Clerk of the Parliaments, and another had been given by Ashley to William de Grey, 'then nominated to the Office of Reading Clerk, and Clerk of the Committees, but who actually never executed any Office in the House'. The Lords were sufficiently annoyed to direct immediately

---

[1] 'An Act for Better Regulating the Office of Clerk of the Parliaments', 5 Geo. IV, c. 82 [21 June 1824], *The Statutes of the United Kingdom*, ed. John Raithby (London, 1824), IX, 779–80.

[2] *G.M.* LX, Pt i (1790), 216.

[3] *Letters*, III, 402; *G.M.* LVIII, Pt i (1788), 564. According to Wilfrid Hooper, who had examined the records of a Chancery suit between William (d. 1769) and Ashley Cowper, Ashley had 'agreed to hold the profits and emoluments during his tenure of the office in trust for his brother and his heirs'. Reported in Wright, *Life* (1921), p. 40, n. 1.

afterwards that 'no Reversion be hereafter granted to the Office of Clerk of the Parliaments; and that when the said Office shall become vacant, it be granted, for the future, not otherwise than so that such Clerk may be removeable from the said Office, upon the Address of this House to the Crown'. This was in spite of Ashley's printed declaration to the House, that the bounties had been 'constantly enjoyed by the Persons who from Time to Time' had been deputed to the offices of the Clerk Assistant, the Reading Clerk, the Clerk of the Journals, and the Copying Clerk.[1]

The inquiry of 1763–4 by the Lords into the state of affairs in the office of the Clerk of the Parliaments came after a long period of troubles, which had begun shortly after Spencer had received the patent. There had been continual wrangling between the minor clerks and the head clerk, because the lower members of the staff had considerable difficulty in obtaining their fees and their bounties, and were frequently in danger of losing their positions to friends of the Cowper family. The climax of these troubles came just as the already depressed and anxious William Cowper of the Temple was to receive one of his Uncle Ashley's benefits. William's patrimony was nearly spent, and he had to find some gentlemanly source of income. In April the Clerk of the Journals, Francis Macklay, had died, and William de Grey, 'for reasons relative to his own Situation', had resigned the offices of Reading Clerk and Clerk of the Committees. Ashley consequently offered William the two most valuable offices, and a friend, Mathew Robert Arnott, was suggested for Macklay's place. William

---

[1] House of Lords MSS.: 'Proceedings at Committees on Bills and Other Matters': Committee Meetings 13 Dec. 1763 and 2 March 1764; *Jnls. H. of L.* xxx, 517–19 (21 March 1764), 534 (29 March 1764); royal approval, 30 March 1764 (p. 538); printed document, 1 p., beginning, 'The Application of the Bounties by His late Majesty, as a Reward for the Services of the Clerks belonging to the Parliament-Office, having become the Subject of Inquiry, Mr. *Cowper* takes the Liberty of laying the State of that Affair before their Lordships'. Among the G. C. Carr Papers, relating to the office of C. of the P.: House of Lords Libr.

accepted at once, and then regretted his eagerness because of his 'incapacity to execute a business of so public a nature'.[1]

The duties of the Clerk of the Parliaments were divided primarily among three assistants. He sat on the lower woolsack and had a table before him. Behind him were the Clerk Assistant, who took minutes of proceedings in the House, and the Reading Clerk, whose branch of the clerical office consisted in reading the acts and papers before the peers, and in taking minutes of committee meetings. The third branch of the Clerk of the Parliaments' office was the Clerk of the Journals, whose duties were the transcription of the minutes of the House into the journals and delivering copies of these, and this officer had also 'always been considered as a private Clerk to the Clerk of the Parliaments'.[2] The business of the last office 'being exacted in private', Ashley and William agreed that it would be better suited to the latter's shy temperament, and would fall easily within the scope of his abilities.[3]

Because of the conflict with other lesser clerks, Ashley printed and sent to the House his intention to appoint William Cowper and Mathew Arnott.

In the beginning, a strong opposition...began to show itself [William wrote]. A powerful party was formed among the Lords to thwart it, in favour of an old enemy of the family, though one much indebted to its bounty; and it appeared plain, that if we succeeded at last, it would only be by fighting our ground by inches....I was bid to expect an examination at the bar of the house, touching my sufficiency for the post I had taken. Being necessarily ignorant of the nature of that business, it became

---

[1] *Jnls. H. of L.* xx–xxx (1714–64), *passim*; Cowper's *Memoir*, pp. 15–17; A. Cowper, 'The Office of Clerk of the Parliaments', pp. 2–3.

[2] A. Cowper, 'The Office...', p. 1; concerning the duties of the three branches see also Sir Fortunatus Dwarris, *A General Treatise on Statutes*, 2nd ed. (London, 1848), pp. 225–6.

[3] Cowper's *Memoir*, pp. 15, 18.

expedient that I should visit the office daily, in order to qualify myself for the strictest scrutiny. All the horrors of my fears and perplexities now returned.[1]

It was not only natural diffidence and a dread of appearing in public[2] (owing largely to the increased state of depression during the past year); any awareness of the actual state of affairs in the Clerk of the Parliaments' office would have made Cowper unusually fearful. In his *Memoir* William is on Ashley's side, yet he must have recognized that his uncle was a 'placeman'—holding a place as a price for political support, but not fulfilling its duties. The Clerkship of the Parliaments had become notorious as a sinecure.[3] The case of his relative, de Grey, who held two of the three branches of the office, but never appeared to perform his duties, could not have escaped William's notice. The pressures from 'the old enemy of the family, though one much indebted to its bounty'—William Macklay, Francis' son—came from the man in the right. The younger Macklay had been brought into the office of Clerk of the Journals by his father, who had held the position since 1736, when Ashley had sold it to him for £300. The father had collected annually the £50 from the Royal Bounty, which his predecessor had received for diligent service, though he himself had left his work on the Journals to his son, in order to exercise 'an incompatible Office in the House'—Deputy to the Reading Clerk and Clerk of the Committees.[4] The whole case of Ashley versus his clerks was a tangled mess of sinecure piling upon sinecure, with no one doing the job for which he was paid. Yet if anyone had done his work satisfactorily, it was the enemy, William Macklay. The

[1] Cowper's *Memoir*, pp. 19–20.   [2] Nichols, *Anecdotes*, III, 60–1.
[3] See Orlo C. Williams' comments on C. of the P. in contrast to the Clerk of the House [of Commons]: *The Clerical Organization of the House of Commons* (Oxford, 1954), pp. 99–100.
[4] H. of L. MSS.: Committee Meetings, 23 Nov. and 13 Dec. 1763; *Jnls. H. of L.* xxx, 519 (21 March 1764); *The Court and City Kalendar* (London, 1763), p. 22.

Lords decided in March 1764 that he was to receive the bounty so long as he continued to exercise the office. The suspicions of scandal and the guilt belonging to his family are evident in the passage of the *Memoir* in which William accuses the enemy. And these suspicions contributed, together with his fear of public speaking and examination, to the complete breakdown, which came in the first part of December. Throughout his life, William Cowper had an ambivalent attitude toward the omnipresent ulcers of 'place' and 'interest' which riddled English government in the eighteenth century. No one could take a higher moral tone against state corruption and bribery, or inveigh more violently. This was the stand of 'Expostulation', where he railed against the 'office-key, a pick-lock to a place'. Cowper would demand that the Members of Parliament be nominated and chosen in a 'disinterested manner, out of mere respect to their Honour and Integrity'. But the same man would seek out Mathew Arnott when he wanted subscribers to his *Homer*, because Arnott would for reasons of obligation to the Cowpers (his place in the House of Lords), 'not unwillingly contribute what he could to the furtherance of a work undertaken by a man who bears my name'. And for himself, William would wish for a 'sinecure' from his friend Thurlow, who became Lord Chancellor. In November and December 1763, when as at no other time he needed strength of character and purpose, this ambiguity in outlook contributed to his defeat: in the clerkship, and in his own mind.[1]

---

[1] 'Expostulation', l. 379; *U. & U.* p. 23; *Letters*, II, 399–400; also III, 123; to Joseph Hill, 6 June 1778, where he speaks of 'the sinecure he [Thurlow] promised me': *Poems* (Bailey), pp. lxxvi–lxxvii. Throughout the eighteenth century many members of the Cowper family depended upon Royal favour and court sinecures for additional income: Edward Hughes, 'Intro.', *Letters of Spencer Cowper, Dean of Durham, Publ. Surtees Soc.* CLXV (1956), ix–xii. Goldwin Smith is strong, but just in describing this ambivalence in Cowper's later life and works. 'No man', Smith says, 'was ever less qualified for the office of a censor; his judgment is at once disarmed, and a breach in his principles is at once made by the slightest personal influence.' See *Cowper*, new ed. (London, 1888), pp. 52–3.

'Oh, my good Cousin!' he had written to Lady Hesketh in August, 'if I was to open my heart to you, I could show you strange sights; nothing, I flatter myself, that would shock you, but a great deal that would make you wonder. I am of a very singular temper, and very unlike all the men that I have ever conversed with. Certainly I am not an absolute fool; but I have more weaknesses than the greatest of all the fools I can recollect at present.'[1]

The days and weeks from the end of October to 7 December form the story of the *Memoir*. It is best told there.[2] How he failed to appear at the examination before the House of Lords; how he sought madness, and it finally came to him; and how he attempted suicide again and again. He recalled that when he was about twenty years of age, his father had desired him to read a vindication of suicide.[3] He did so, and argued against it, but his father 'was silent, neither approving or disapproving'; from which William inferred that he sided with the author against his son. The recollection weighed heavily upon him. And his Uncle Ashley would not have been of help when William was filled with thoughts of self-destruction. Ashley's lack of understanding and strong denunciation of the 'cowardly' act made him singularly unfit as one of his nephew's few companions. 'What must we think of *Those* who not only break thro' all Laws of *Moral Obligation*, but even dare to act in defiance of a *Divine Command*?' Ashley had written. 'To imbrue our *Hands* in our own *Blood*, is in *us* the most daring *Impiety*—a *Sin*, of all others the most *dreadful*, as'tis the only one that cannot be *repented of*...In a Word—He that meanly quits his *Station*, or quarrels with his *Command*,

---

[1] *Letters*, I, 20–1.

[2] The most recent reprinting of the *Memoir* is that edited by Maurice J. Quinlan in *Proc. Am. Philos. Soc.* XCVII (1953), 359–82.

[3] The two MS. copies of the *Memoir* known to me (one owned by Mr Kenneth Povey, the other Mr Brian Spiller's) read '20', instead of 'eleven' as in the publ. version (*Memoir*, p. 27).

in Time of *Danger* and *Distress*, by putting an *End* to his *Being*, is no better than a rank *Coward*—a *Traitor* to Himself —and a *Rebel* against his *Maker*.'[1]

Notwithstanding this condemnation, William thought of every means of suicide: by drowning, by drinking laudanum, by stabbing, and finally by hanging. Three times he tried to hang himself by his broad scarlet garter, and failed. The garter slipped or the woodwork to which it was tied broke. In the days which followed his last attempt, the delusions of pains and burnings were upon him. There were other insane beliefs: 'I never went into the street, but I thought the people stood and laughed at me, and held me in contempt.'[2] And strongest of all was his belief that he had committed the unpardonable sin and was irrevocably damned. It was like his first, year-long depression, ten years before; but much, much more desperate.

Probably the roots of the insanity were hereditary. There is much to suggest that heredity is more conspicuous in manic-depressive insanity than in other psychoses. The loss of Theadora may well have precipitated the growing depression during the last years in the Temple. One of the experiences which most often causes acute depression is disappointment in love or the death of the love partner.[3] William himself may have recognized this. Nearly thirty years after the 'disorder of mind' of 1763, which, as he said, 'unfitted me from all society',[4] he wrote in a review of a young man's poems:

We should have supposed this young gentleman, a boy, had he not assured us himself,

---

[1] Ashley Cowper, 'On Suicide', *The Norfolk Poetical Miscellany*, II, 268–70. Ashley's essay reflects the great interest in the eighteenth century in the ethics of suicide. See Lester G. Crocker, 'The Discussion of Suicide in the Eighteenth Century', *Jnl. Hist. Ideas*, XIII (1952), 42–72.
[2] Cowper's *Memoir*, p. 49.
[3] Fenichel, pp. 390–1; Freud, 'Mourning and Melancholia', *C.P.* IV, 153, 161.
[4] To Hayley, 6 April 1792: Panshanger Coll.

'That love gently knocks at his heart,
And whispers—that he is a man!'

But this is not the worst of the business, for in the last stanza of his poems he expresses himself thus:

'Let us, whom youth, whom health, with joy inspires,
Learn this great lesson from Eliza's fate,
To finish life before that life expires,
Nor wait for seasons that may prove too late.'

The line distinguished by italics is a very alarming one, especially considering that it is written by a lover mourning the death of his mistress. His tutor should watch him narrowly, and his bed-maker should every night take care to secure his garters.[1]

The wry humour belies Cowper's true feelings. The reference to garters is painfully close to his own experience.

Cowper would from this time on know well what he called 'nervous fevers'. 'Other distempers only batter the walls', he said, 'but *they* creep silently into the citadel, and put the garrison to the sword.' His mind would frequently take a 'melancholy cast', like some pools he had seen, 'which, though filled with a black and putrid water, will nevertheless, in a bright day, reflect the sunbeams from the surface'. This, he fully understood,

of all maladies that man infest,
Claims most compassion, and receives the least.[2]

However, he had still to learn the meaning of safety, escape, and failure. It came to him over fifteen years later, in a quiet strength and calmness growing out of despair. He saw it in the uncomplicated forms of nature, which usually brought health to his despondent soul. The record is subdued, as it should be, but as Professor Kenneth MacLean

[1] *Analytical Rev.* vi (Feb. 1790), 194; see Appendix C, p. 251.
[2] *Letters*, i, 139, 165–6; iii, 462; 'Retirement', ll. 301–2.

says, 'what is particularly remarkable about this record is its mark, often painful, of sincerity and simple truth. Nothing has been faked. This is human terror. This is terror in a garden.'[1]

> Safety consists not in escape
> From dangers of a frightful shape;
> An earthquake may be bid to spare
> The man that's strangled by a hair.
> Fate steals along with silent tread,
> Found oft'nest in what least we dread,
> Frowns in the storm with angry brow,
> But in the sunshine strikes the blow.[2]

A temporary escape from depression, and temporary exultation, would come to Cowper through conversion to the Evangelical religion.

---

[1] Kenneth MacLean, 'William Cowper', in *The Age of Johnson: Essays Presented to Chauncey Brewster Tinker* (New Haven, 1949), p. 267.
[2] 'A fable', *Poems*, p. 303.

XI

THE SAINTS

...that maniacal Calvinist and coddled poet.
                                   BYRON of COWPER
I have found what I have been looking for all my life, a poet
whom I can read on a Sunday, and whose *whole* writings I can
recommend to my young and my female friends, without restric-
tion or exception.   HANNAH MORE of COWPER[1]

I T occurred to Cowper, during a fairly calm moment in
his despair, that his cousin, Martin Madan, might be
able to help him. Cowper had become preoccupied with
thoughts about the unpardonable sin and damnation. His
depression now centred almost exclusively on religious
problems. Madan, trained like Cowper at Westminster
School and in the law, had been converted by John Wesley
from a deep-drinking all-night reveller at the Poetical Club[2]
to one of the most dramatic Methodist preachers in London.
He spoke to huge gatherings, like one 'baptized with the
Holy Ghost and with fire, fervent in spirit'.[3] William had
previously found the Evangelical Madan irksome,[4] but now
he came as a comforter. He had a 'fine voice and something gracefull and pathetick in his manner'; he could also
speak with fury to wrest the despondent from their terrors:
'Like Boanerges, a son of Thunder, he proclaimed the law
from the flaming mountain; and from the summit of Zion's
hill he appeared a Barnabas, a son of consolation. ...his
countenance was majestic, open, and engaging, and his looks

---

[1] Byron to John Murray, 20 May 1820: *Works: Letters and Journals*, ed. Coleridge
and Prothero (London, 1901), v, 25; Hannah More to Mrs Bouverie, 13 March
[1785?], *Memorials...of Admiral Lord Gambier*, ed. Lady Georgiana Chatterton (London,
1861), I, 154.
[2] *Madan Family*, p. 105.
[3] According to the Rev. James Hervey in [A. C. H. Seymour's] *The Life and Times
of Selina Countess of Huntingdon* (London, 1844), I, 431.
[4] Cowper's *Memoir*, p. 54; *Letters*, I, 63.

commanding veneration...his language plain, nervous, pleasing, and memorable; and his arguments strong, bold, rational, and conclusive: his doctrines were drawn from the sacred fountain: he was mighty in the Scriptures.'[1]

He was a man of confidence and action—and of faith. He had the attributes which Cowper needed. Madan came into Cowper's life 'as a burning and a shining light, and as one of those "who, having turned many to righteousness, shall shine hereafter as the stars for ever and ever"'. He spoke to William of original sin and the corruption of every man born into the world. Cowper perceived something like hope dawning in his heart, for the doctrine set him more on a level with the rest of mankind, and made his condition appear less desperate. Madan then told of Christ's atonement and justification for the sins of the world, and Cowper burst into tears at the thought of mercy and forgiveness. But he could not take hold of faith in Christ, though he earnestly desired it; as the days passed the old torments returned, and his momentary joy was wiped away.

Satan plied me closely with horrible visions and more horrible voices.... Then did the pains of hell get hold on me, and, before daybreak, the very sorrows of death encompassed me. A numbness seized upon the extremities of my body, and life seemed to retreat before it; my hands and feet became cold and stiff; a cold sweat stood upon my forehead; my heart seemed at every pulse to beat its last, and my soul to cling to my lips, as if on the very brink of departure. No convicted criminal ever feared death more, or was more assured of dying.... At every stroke, my thoughts and expressions became more wild and incoherent; all that remained clear was the sense of sin, and the expectation of punishment.[2]

His brother John had come and had found William alone in his chambers in this demented state. It was clear to

---

[1] *Madan Family*, p. 110; Seymour, 1, 167.
[2] *Letters*, 1, 63; *Memoir*, pp. 55, 58–9.

John that immediate medical attention was necessary. Therefore he and his relatives arranged for William to go to St Albans, where a house for the insane was kept by Dr Nathaniel Cotton, with whom William was known to have a slight acquaintance. It was not only his skill as a physician which recommended Cotton to their choice, but also 'his well-known humanity, and sweetness of temper'. When his depression cleared, William found him to be a pious and sensible man, truly a philosopher according to Cowper's description of the character: 'every tittle of his knowledge in natural subjects being connected in his mind with the firm belief of an Omnipotent agent'. He was especially admired because he had been the friend of the late Dr Philip Doddridge, whose *Practical Discourses on Regeneration* and *Rise and Progress of Religion in the Soul* were read by Cowper with great pleasure during his stay at St Albans. 'Next to the Word itself', said Cowper, his books 'are my daily bread'.[1]

Cotton had received his training under Boerhaave at Leyden. At Dunstable, Bedfordshire, and at St Albans he had acquired considerable fame for his humanitarian attention to the insane. His hospital for their care in St Albans had first been on a small scale, but before William Cowper came to him he had moved to a spacious place called 'The College' or the 'Collegium Insanorum'. It was on Dagnall Street,[2] not far from the great abbey. The doctor lived with his family in St Peter's Street, where he quietly passed most of his life, visiting his patients, and writing poetry and prose. The editors of the *Gentleman's Magazine* reported that 'he was just such a man as his works speak him to be, pious, mild, good-tempered, against whom the breath of Slander never ventured a whisper, but whose

---

[1] *Memoir*, pp. 59–60; Cowper's 'Hope', ll. 205–6: '...COTTON, whose humanity sheds rays | That make superior skill his second praise.' *Letters*, II, 242; see also I, 30; *N. & Q.* cx (1904), 3.
[2] After 1825 called College Street. The building was demolished in 1910.

company was much courted and highly relished by all his acquaintance, being most amiable and engaging in his manners, and bearing the character of a skilful and experienced Physician'.[1]

In a time when conditions in private madhouses had become such a scandal that a committee of the House of Commons had decided that the intervention of the legislature was necessary,[2] Cowper was fortunate in being able to go to a place where the physician was both well trained and kind. Dr Cotton would permit only a few patients: never more than ten and usually only three or four.[3] In this environment Cowper gradually prospered. By May 1764, after five months, he was able to enter into conversation with the Doctor, and to laugh and tell stories. But the sentence of doom had not actually been lifted from his spirit. On 25 July when John Cowper visited his brother, he still found him frighteningly reserved. During that day, however, William became a little more cheerful. Something seemed to whisper to him at every moment: 'Still there is mercy.' And from that time on the depression began to break; the old terror fluctuated with hope, and hope was winning control. Happiness had returned, and soon it almost overwhelmed him. One day he opened the Bible to discover the verse in Romans: 'Whom God hath set forth to be a propitiation through faith in his blood, to declare his righteousness for the remission of sins that are past, through the forbearance of God.'[4]

Immediately [he said], I received strength to believe it, and the full beams of the Sun of Righteousness shone upon me. I saw the sufficiency of the atonement he had made, my pardon sealed

---

[1] *G.M.* LXXVII, Pt i (1807), 500.
[2] See reports in *G.M.* XXXIII (1763), 25-6, 126-7; Daniel Hack Tuke, *Chapters in the History of the Insane in the British Isles* (London, 1882), p. 92.
[3] *Hertfordshire County Records: Calendar to the Sessions Books* (Hertford, 1935), vol. VIII, ed. William Le Hardy, pp. xxx, 234, 244, 254, 273, etc.; *Hertford County Records...Session Rolls* (Hertford, 1905), vol. II, ed. W. J. Hardy, pp. 134, 138, 139, 143, 147-53.
[4] Cowper's *Memoir*, pp. 61, 63-4, 67; see also *Letters*, I, 32-5.

in his blood, and all the fulness and completeness of his justification. In a moment I believed, and received the gospel.... Unless the Almighty arm had been under me, I think I should have died with gratitude and joy. My eyes filled with tears, and my voice choaked with transport.... To rejoice day and night was all my employment. Too happy to sleep much, I thought it was but lost time that was spent in slumber.... My physician, ever watchful and apprehensive for my welfare, was now alarmed, lest the sudden transition from despair to joy, should terminate in a fatal frenzy.[1]

The frenzy relaxed into peace, and in a short time Dr Cotton was convinced that his patient had recovered. Cowper nevertheless remained at 'The College' for a year, and he had 'much sweet communion' with his physician. The Gospel was the theme of their conversation. After some months William asked his brother to find rooms for him near Cambridge, where John lived, for William was determined to sever his connections with London. As a result of this decision he quit his position as Commissioner of Bankrupts (which brought him about £60 a year), and because he now felt his ignorance of the law would not permit him to take the customary oath. Consequently, he was reduced to an income scarcely sufficient for the barest existence.[2]

In June 1765 John Cowper succeeded in obtaining rooms for his brother at Huntingdon, sixteen miles from Cambridge. There he would be close enough for the two to see each other once or twice a week, which they did, but far enough away for John not to be bothered excessively by his untoward brother. 'On the [1]7th of June, 1765,' he said,

---

[1] *Memoir*, pp 67-9.

[2] *Ibid*. pp. 70-1. As a Commissioner of Bankrupts Cowper had extensive powers. He could 'convey a copyhold estate without a surrender to the lord...convey an estate-tail, and bar all the remainders without a fine or recovery...break open outer doors to seize the bankrupt's property...seize or assign all the debts due to the bankrupt...', etc. Edward Christian, *The Origin, Progress, and Present Practice of the Bankrupt Law* (London, 1818), II, 8, see also I, 14; and Edward Green, *The Spirit of the Bankrupt Laws*, 4th ed. (London, 1780), pp. 300-11.

'having spent more than eighteen months at St. Alban's, partly in bondage, and partly in the liberty wherewith Christ had made me free, I took my leave of the place at four in the morning, and set out for Cambridge.'[1]

He was accompanied by a servant, Sam Roberts, who had watched over him at Dr Cotton's, and waited on him 'with so much patience and gentleness', that he could not bear to leave him behind. With them came also a boy, Dick Coleman, who like Sam, remained with Cowper during most of his life. Dick was about seven, 'the son of a drunken cobbler at St. Albans, who would probably have starved him to death', William said, 'or have poisoned him with gin, if Providence had not thrown him in my way to rescue him'.[2]

After a few days in Cambridge the three settled in Huntingdon (22 June), in a sixteenth-century house on the west side of High Street, north of the George Hotel.[3] For Cowper the chief attraction of the town was the retirement it permitted him. He had always been fond of seclusion, and from now on he would absolutely avoid any noisy or crowded scene—any sense of the city. The 'strange and uncommon incidents' of his life, as he referred to them (sometimes, more frankly, the 'insanity'), had rendered him incapable of receiving pleasure from the excitement which he had enjoyed when he lived in the Temple.[4] He wrote a hymn, 'Retirement', to celebrate the pleasantness he found in the new place:

> Far from the world, O LORD, I flee,
> From strife and tumult far;
> From scenes, where Satan wages still
> His most successful war.

---

[1] William Cowper's *Adelphi*, reprinted in Stokes, *Cowper Memorials*, p. 69; *Memoir*, p. 73. The correct date is given in *Letters*, I, 23.

[2] *Letters*, I, 83. See also Cowper's comments in a letter, 8 July 1792: 'There is one Richard Coleman in the world, whom I have educated from an infant, and who is utterly good for nothing' (*Letters*, IV, 250).

[3] *V.C.H....Huntingdon* (London, 1932), II, 128.

[4] *Letters*, I, 107; *N. & Q.* cx, 3.

The calm retreat, the silent shade,
With pray'r and praise agree;
And seem by thy sweet bounty made,
For those who follow thee.

Through this calm retreat flowed the same river which he would watch for years at Olney, the River Ouse: 'the most agreeable circumstance in this part of the world', he said. 'It is a noble stream to bathe in, and I shall make that use of it three times a week.' He studied the play of light upon its waters and saw mirrored his own character:

> The Ouse, dividing the well-water'd land,
> Now glitters in the sun, and now retires,
> As bashful, yet impatient to be seen.[1]

The land about the town lay flat and open. The fields were divided by the river, which also separated Huntingdon from the town of Godmanchester. In each place there were about two thousand inhabitants. There was not a show of much business in the towns, William Cobbett said,

but, Huntingdon is a very clean and nice place, contains many elegant houses, and the environs are beautiful. Above and below the bridge, under which the Ouse passes, are the most beautiful, and by far the most beautiful, meadows that I ever saw in my life. ...Here are no reeds, here is no sedge, no unevenness of any sort. Here are *bowling-greens* of hundreds of acres in extent, with a river winding through them, full to the brink. *One* of these meadows is the *race-course*; and so pretty a spot, so level, so smooth, so green, and of such an extent I never saw, and never expected to see. From the bridge you look across the valleys, first to the West and then to the East; the valleys terminate at the foot of rising ground, well set with trees, from amongst which church spires raise their heads here-and-there. I think it would be very difficult to find a more delightful spot than this in the world. To my fancy (and every one to his taste) the prospect from this bridge far surpasses

---

[1] *Letters*, I, 24; *Task*, I, 323–5.

that from Richmond-Hill.—All that I have yet seen of Huntingdon I like exceedingly. It is one of those pretty, clean, unstenched, unconfined places that tend to lengthen life and make it happy.[1]

John Cowper had chosen the town wisely; he had fulfilled his brother's requirements:

> Scenes must be beautiful, which daily view'd,
> Please daily, and whose novelty survives
> Long knowledge and the scrutiny of years.[2]

The town boasted a 'card-assembly, and a dancing-assembly, and a horse-race, and a club, and a bowling-green', Cowper said; none of which he would see. The races brought the fashionable world to the town at the end of July or the beginning of August, and then there were balls and large social events given by the country gentry. But Cowper did not attend. Instead he tried unsuccessfully to manage his household; tried weakly to buy groceries in proper proportions, and if possible, to economize as well. He took walks—his favourite pastime during all his life— along the banks of the Ouse to the village of Hartford and the forest of Sapley. As in the Temple, he spent much time in reading, even more hours of every day, but now the reading matter was Evangelical literature and 'The Word' itself. His meditations when walking, or alone in his room, were taken up with recollections of what had happened at St Albans—of the horrors before and the joys afterwards— and with many anxious thoughts about taking Holy Orders. After some time, however, he abandoned the idea of a clerical profession, because his dread of public speaking seemed an insuperable obstacle. In spite of his shyness, in less than three months he was on very good terms with five families, besides two or three 'odd scrambling fellows' like himself. And he could say that if he had had the choice of

---

[1] William Cobbett, *Rural Rides*, ed. G. D. H. and Margaret Cole (London, 1930), I, 76-7.
[2] *Task*, I, 177-9.

all England in which to settle, he could not have chosen better for himself, and most likely would not have chosen so well. He was contented.[1]

His greatest problem was one of finances. 'Upon the whole, my dear Rowley', he had written in 1762, 'there is a degree of poverty that has no disgrace belonging to it; that degree of it, I mean, in which a man enjoys clean linen and good company; and if I never sink below this degree of it, I care not if I never rise above it.' But he *did* care: he cared about his tailor, his food, his quarters, and his servants. His income was reported to be but £20 a year, and it could pay only a small share of his expenses. The rest came from his relatives and friends, and for the most part from Joseph Hill. 'I was born to subsist at the expense of my friends', he said, without sorrow or shame. They enabled him to live comfortably, as his connections demanded, and as they themselves wished.[2] But he might have aided by small measures of economy. This he could not do. Throughout his life he indulged in many unnecessary expenses—which he deemed necessary for a gentleman. And, in truth, they were rarely beyond the standards of the simplest *gentle* folk.

While in Huntingdon, Cowper lived in such a way that the most stringent demands of the Evangelicals would have been satisfied. He was enthusiastic about every point of doctrine, and in daily life he wore gracefully the utmost piety. He carried into effect the Evangelical ideal: he made dogma life. Yet he was foolish and sometimes reckless in his financial arrangements. In his first three months he 'contrived to spend the income of a twelvemonth'. There were many unpaid bills for most expensive care at one of the finest private hospitals and from one of the best physicians; a personal servant; a ward, who had taken

[1] *Letters*, I, 26–7, 32, 45–6, 51–2, 81, 103; *N. & Q.* cx, 3.
[2] *Letters*, I, 19; Mrs Maria Cowper to Mrs Penelope Maitland, 27 Jan. 1790: *Madan Family*, p. 130; *U. & U.* p. 52; *Letters*, II, 380.

Cowper's fancy; a horse, so that he could more easily visit his brother at Cambridge: no wonder that his relations finally became irritated. And one, at least, threatened to withdraw his contribution towards William's support.[1]

On 11 November 1765, about five months after he had come to Huntingdon, Cowper moved up High Street to a much newer house a little north of St Mary's Church. This was the home of the Reverend Morley Unwin, who had been from 1746 to 1762 master of the Huntingdon school (Cromwell's school). He had remained as lecturer in the town and had 'a few select Pupils to board'.[2] William had met the Unwins after he had been in the town two months. He told Lady Hesketh and Joseph Hill that

the race of the Unwins, consisting of father and mother, son and daughter, [are] the most comfortable social folks you ever knew. The son is about twenty-one years of age, one of the most unreserved and amiable young men I ever conversed with....The father ['a man of learning and good sense, and as simple as parson Adams'] is a clergyman, and the son is designed for orders.... [Mrs Unwin] has a very uncommon understanding, has read much to excellent purpose, and is more polite than a duchess.... [and the daughter is] quite of a piece with the rest of the family.

Mrs Unwin had a special relish for humour, and would laugh on the slightest provocation. She was fond of English poetry and fine clothes, and enjoyed the company of the principal families of a town noted for its society. She was considered to be 'a sensible and accomplished though far from a handsome woman'. Most remarkable were the serenity and sweetness of her manners. Of the Unwin family, she in particular made Cowper feel immediately like a near relation, and he found in her what seemed to

---

[1] *Letters*, II, 380, 429–30.
[2] *V.C.H....Huntingdon*, II, 110, 126. He was 'lecturer' (a preacher chosen and supported by the parish—or in this case, the Mason's Company—to give afternoon or evening lectures) from 1734 to 1767; Unwin received £60 a year for preaching each Sunday afternoon. Greatheed to Hayley, 4 Oct. 1800: Fitzwilliam MSS.

him a perfect combination of piety with a gentle, cheerful, intelligent character.[1]

Mrs Unwin—it has often been said by Cowper's friends and relatives as well as by himself—was like a mother to him. The closeness of their relationship, and the fact that she was more than twenty years younger than her husband, while only seven years older than Cowper, created gossip in the town. This was intensified after the death of Mr Unwin: 'black and shocking Aspersions...Things which our Soul abhors are imputed to us', Cowper told a relative. She, who was 'more polite than a duchess', was a draper's daughter from Ely. In 1742, at eighteen, she had married Mr Unwin and had gone to live in Grimston in Norfolk. 'That place seems however to have been as barbarous as its Name, and M[rs] U. who was already deeply read in the legendary lore of a Country Library found the farmers Wives and daughters so much beneath her own mental Standard, that to gratify her M[r] U. repaired to Huntingdon....'[2]

The day that Cowper went to live with the Unwins marked the end of his early life of flux and continual in-security. He found their home, he said, 'a place of rest prepared for me by God's own hand, where he has blessed me with a thousand mercies, and instances of his fatherly protection'. Mrs Unwin, and then the children, were soon completely in agreement with Cowper's religious opinions, which were more Evangelical than theirs had been. He and they grew in that devout and strict faith. When Cowper

...came to board in the family, a sudden and obvious revolution took place....When any one visited them...[he] spoke little, often reclined in his Chair, with his eyes nearly closed; but if an

---

[1] *Letters*, I, 45, 49, 53; Lady Hesketh's letters to Theadora, quoted by Croft in his 'Anecdotes': *Early Poems*, pp. 57–9; Greatheed to Hayley, 4 Oct. 1800.

[2] Lady Hesketh to Hayley, 23 June and 13 Sept. 1801: Add. MSS. 30803 A, ff. 138, 162; Hayley to Lady Hesketh, 27 Sept. 1801: *ibid.* f. 163; Greatheed to Hayley, 4 Oct. 1800; *U. & U.* pp. 6, 11; William Benham, 'Introductory Memoir', *The Poetical Works of William Cowper* (London, 1870), p. xxxiii.

Idea was started that excited his attention, he delivered a few sentences, which were certain to be received as an Oracular decision of any question that had been agitated. He visited nobody, which everybody lamented, as he was universally thought to be capable of any pursuit and attainment, although not then known to be a Poet. Mrs U. soon became a stranger everywhere but at home, and with her company dismissed her amusements.... [She] became a Franche Religieuse, and the attachment natural between the Convert and the Converter, together with the Aversions discovered by Mrs U. rendered...[them] almost inseparable. They walked much, and avoided meeting, as well as visiting, any of their neighbours.

Sometimes, however, Cowper would accompany Martin Madan when he was on a preaching tour in the neighbourhood. On 16 November 1766 William heard his first 'Gospell Sermon', one given by Madan at Kettering in Northamptonshire. Such sermons were not preached by the Reverend Mr Unwin. He continued to believe in a more traditional Anglican way, to the time of his sudden death on 2 July 1767.[1]

By the death of Mr Unwin a door had been opened, Cowper said, for the family 'to seek an Abode under the Sound of the Gospel. Mrs. Unwin has determined to do so, thinking it her indespensible Duty.' And as for himself: 'my soul within me is sick of the spiritless unedifying Ministry at Huntingdon. It is a matter of the utmost Indifference to us where we settle, provided it be within the Sound of the glad Tidings of Salvation.' Four days after Mr Unwin's death Cowper met the Reverend John Newton of Olney, who became eager for them to settle in his parish. On 3 August they visited the town, and by the 27th a house

---

[1] Cowper's *Memoir*, p. 83; Seymour, *Countess of Huntingdon*, II, 141–2; Greatheed to Hayley, 4 Oct. 1800; 'The Diary of the Revd Abraham Maddock, 1765–1771': Add. MSS. 40653, f. 32. [Sunday, 16 Nov. 1766] 'This Day Mr Madan came & brought Mr Cooper, of Huntingdon, a Relation of his, who was converted by reading Mr Herveys works, and who never had heard a Gospell Sermon untill this day— Mr Madan preach'd on Joh: VIII. 36. If the Son therefore shall make you free, ye shall be free indeed.' *U. & U.* pp 4–5.

there had been decided upon. On 14 September the Unwin family and William Cowper were transplanted, to a place 'abounding with Palm Trees and Wells of living water'.[1] Spiritually it might seem like Eden; physically, its people and buildings and its riverside were often mean, cold, bleak.

William Cowper was now almost thirty-six years old. He would remain at Olney for nineteen years, the heart of his life as a man and as a poet. His friendship with the Unwins and with Newton, and the removal to Olney, brought Cowper to the beginning of the great plateau of his career. When he left that place in November 1786 he had published the two volumes of poetry which are central to the canon of his work. He was famous.

The middle years constituted his era of pietism. After Newton left Olney in 1780, Cowper's religious thoughts mellowed and deepened and grew broader. In Huntingdon his Evangelicalism was fervent, but it could not long remain so intense. He felt the spiritual passion slipping from him, and he tried in every way to recapture its burning presence. He bolstered himself with Evangelical tracts and books; he entered into doctrinal correspondences. But the old fire had been consumed. He cried out: 'Oh that the ardour of my first love had continued!'[2]

Like his friends among 'the Saints'—those who preached renunciation of the world and set a goal of extreme holiness in everyday life—he had difficulty in forming a realistic synthesis of the natural and the spiritual man. His problem and the problem for all of the Evangelicals was how to maintain a devotion which was constantly intense but solemn. In the Evangelical meditations, narratives, and

---

[1] *U. & U.* pp. 5–6, 8, 11; the notebook kept by Newton, quoted in Josiah Bull, 'The Early Years of the Poet Cowper at Olney', *Sunday at Home*, XIII (1866), 347–9; John Newton, *Letters*, ed. Josiah Bull (London, [1869]), pp. 151–3; Newton to the E. of Dartmouth, 5 and 16 Sept., and 24 Oct. 1767: *Hist. MSS. Comm., 15th Report*, Append., Pt i (Dartmouth MSS.), pp. 183–4; and Newton to 'William Cooper, Esqre', 18 Aug. 1767: B.M. Eg. MSS. 3662, f. 2.   [2] Cowper's *Memoir*, p. 69.

diaries there are again and again cries against that which Samuel Johnson called the 'vacillation and vagrancy of mind'. Mrs John Thornton, wife of the leading Evangelical philanthropist, bemoaned 'this poor Machine...tho I endeavourd to say let it live or Dye, be Sick or well with a Sincere Submission at the Sacred table, yet so intimate is the Connection between Soul & body, that the latter wofully obstructs the Aspirations of the former, toward Heaven'. John Newton lamented his 'sadly cold & wandring' thoughts, though he had an outward liberty of speech when preaching the sermon or administering the sacrament.[1] They all sought to hold the body in permanent submission in order to be free for unvarying keenness of worship. All were bewildered when rigourism did not achieve the full and holy life.[2]

Good and evil were seen purely as black and white abstractions. Cowper and his friends were not prepared for a grey world. Earnestness, renunciation, discipline, separation, created little sympathy for mankind as a whole, for anyone, in fact, who was less serious than a 'Saint'. There was almost a note of pride in Cowper's statement to Newton: 'You may look round the Christian world, and find few, I believe, of our [his and Mrs Unwin's] station, who have so little intercourse as we with the world that is not Christian.'[3]

The Evangelical's 'profound desire for holiness' was achieved by a 'combination of ordered piety and ordered discipline'.[4] Cowper described a day at Huntingdon with the Unwins:

We breakfast commonly between eight and nine; till eleven, we read either the Scripture, or the sermons of some faithful

[1] Johnson, prayer for 20 April 1778, *Johnsonian Miscellanies*, ed. G. B. Hill (Oxford, 1897), I, 86; meditation by Mrs John Thornton, 6 Nov. 1763: Forster MSS.; 'Diary of John Newton, 1756–1772', f. 415, and *passim*: Morgan MSS.
[2] See, for example, L. E. Eliott-Binns, *The Early Evangelicals* (London, 1953), pp. 432–48; M. G. Jones, *Hannah More* (Cambridge, 1952), ch. IV.
[3] *Letters*, III, 100.   [4] Jones, p. 87.

preacher of those holy mysteries; at eleven we attend divine service, which is performed here twice every day; and from twelve to three we separate and amuse ourselves as we please. During that interval I either read in my own apartment, or walk, or ride, or work in the garden. We seldom sit an hour after dinner, but, if the weather permits, adjourn to the garden, where with Mrs. Unwin and her son I have generally the pleasure of religious conversation till tea-time. If it rains, or is too windy for walking, we either converse within doors, or sing some hymns of Martin's [Martin Madan's] collection, and by the help of Mrs. Unwin's harpsichord make up a tolerable concert, in which our hearts, I hope, are the best and most musical performers. After tea we sally forth to walk in good earnest. Mrs. Unwin is a good walker, and we have generally travelled about four miles before we see home again. When the days are short, we make this excursion in the former part of the day, between church-time and dinner. At night we read and converse, as before, till supper, and commonly finish the evening either with hymns or a sermon; and last of all, the family are called to prayers.[1]

Miss Jones has best summed up the religious party to which Cowper belonged: 'For over two hundred years the Anglican Church of the Reformation settlement had taught the doctrines of the Trinity, the fall of man, his redemption through Jesus Christ and the obligation of holiness.... What was new...was the deep and abiding consciousness of the reality of God which filled the minds and hearts of the Evangelicals, and the supreme importance which they attached to conversion—the spiritual encounter between God and man, when God in his own good time brought the individual into direct personal contact with himself.' Religion, for the Evangelical, 'demanded the undivided allegiance of the individual'; it was based on 'a conception of religion as *the* essential of life...a matter of unceasing practice in living the Christian life....'[2]

Even after the first weeks of white-hot enthusiasm,

<hr>

[1] *Letters*, I, 80-1.   [2] Jones, pp. 88-9, 97.

Cowper had the eagerness of spirit natural to persons newly converted, which forced these ideas upon friends, relatives, and casual acquaintances. Looking back after many years, he saw his impatience and excess:

Forgetting that I had not *those* blessings at my command, which it is God's peculiar prerogative to impart—spiritual light and affections, I required, in effect, of all with whom I conversed that they should see with my eyes; and stood amazed that the Gospel, which with me was all in all, should meet with opposition, or should occasion disgust in any....Good is intended, but harm is done too often by the zeal with which I was at that time animated. ...I do not now, neither have I for a long time, made it my practice to force the subject of evangelical truth on any....If a man asks my opinion, or calls for an account of my faith, he shall have it; otherwise I trouble him not. Pulpits for preaching, and the parlour, the garden, and the walk abroad for friendly and agreeable conversation.[1]

As a consequence of his conversion, Cowper's patterns of writing were radically changed. If his speech followed his letters in tone and style, and it undoubtedly did, then he talked in the conventional phraseology of the Evangelicals. Even a serious and devotional Quaker could object to the speech of someone like Miss Hannah More. Though the tone of her voice was 'soft and pleasing', her language was 'tinctured with a party slang offensive to good taste'.[2] Cowper's letters from Huntingdon are filled with a similar jargon, a heavy-handed, worn-out forcing of the 'spiritual, as well as the ordinary import'[3] of a word, and the use of sanctimonious phrases to create a spirit of religiosity about all affairs. In everything he wrote he twisted powerful Biblical metaphors to describe circumstances in the lives

---

[1] *Letters*, III, 5–6.
[2] According to Sarah Hoare, dau. of Samuel Hoare, the Quaker banker: quoted in Vct Templewood, *The Unbroken Thread* (London, 1949), p. 62. Lady Hesketh told Theadora about 'the little puritanical words' which fell from Mrs Unwin's lips from time to time (*Early Poems*, p. 57).
[3] Cowper to Martin Madan, 24 June 1765: *N. & Q.* CX, 2.

of eighteenth-century Christians. The result did not create impassioned expression or suggest fervid emotion. It was just the opposite: the language was an inadequate realization of the feelings and caused many to be suspicious about their source and power. The style seemed intellectually lazy; the old clichés were hollow. The rhetoric was a lie to the actual sincerity.

The same language is in Cowper's *Memoir*, written in 1766 or 1767, some time after he had moved into the Unwins' home but before Mr Unwin had died. By September 1767 Cowper had sent his 'Narrative' (the *Memoir*) to Martin Madan and was in turn reading the report of Madan's conversion.[1] It had become the custom for one recently converted to write the story of his newly found faith. Such memoirs were at times written for public edification (John Newton's *Authentic Narrative* in 1764), but usually they were not to be trusted, as Cowper said, 'in the Hands of an unenlighten'd Person'.[2] The theme was the amazing grace of God, who had saved a miserable wretch. The typical memoir served as a confessional, and there was always an interest in a memorable story—in stirring, almost gothic details.[3]

In Cowper's brief *Memoir* there are at least forty-five verses or phrases from the Bible. A large number of these are from the Old Testament, because he and most Evangelicals were like the Puritans in their Hebraic interest. Isaiah is frequently referred to, as are Jeremiah and Job, and the Pentateuch and the Psalms. In addition to the direct references there are many words which have a Scriptural ring—words which were part of the Evangelical speech and writing. The voices which come to Cowper

---

[1] *U. & U.* p. 16.   [2] *U. & U.* p. 29.

[3] Newton to Cowper, 14 July 1767, after he had just met Cowper: 'My heart seemed to have much to say to you, and a longing desire to hear more of your memorable story' (*Sunday at Home*, XIII, 348).

sound like Biblical injunctions: '*Consider and live*'; and his own speech echoes King James's translators: 'Bless you, for praising him whom my soul loveth!' Chapters vii, xvi, and xxx of the book of Job are used as a general background to the *Memoir*, and at times Cowper is so permeated with the Scriptures that he creates his own verse out of several from that book or others in the Bible. 'O Lord, thou didst vex me with all thy storms, all thy billows went over me; thou didst run upon me like a giant in the night season, thou didst scare me with visions in the night season.'[1] The sentence contains allusions to four or five verses in Job, one in Jonah, and one in the Psalms.[2] But the power of the original lines in Job has faded. Bunyan could fit verses from the English Bible into the similar rhetorical patterns of his own seventeenth-century style. When the language of the Authorized Version, however, was pushed into a framework of eighteenth-century prose, or when it was used in a nineteenth-century speech of one of the characters in *Jane Eyre* or *The Heart of Midlothian*, the narrative was strained, and the words of the speaker sounded mannered and outworn.

Cowper had moved from the conventions of clever society to those where seriousness was the most important quality in a man and his writings. But he would leave the dry usages of that world also. He emerged from it slowly, with a poised grasp of the rich tradition of the English Bible and Church, and of its moral and devotional literature. He would remain for years in Evangelical retirement, but he would rise above the dangers of an extremely narrow religious position, and the deadening seclusion.

[1] *Memoir*, pp. 35, 48, 76.
[2] Job xix. 2, 'How long will ye vex my soul...?'; Jonah ii. 3, 'all thy billows and thy waves passed over me'; Psalm xlii. 7, 'all thy waves and thy billows are gone over me'; Job xvi. 14, 'he runneth upon me like a giant'; Psalm xxii. 2, 'O my God, I cry in the daytime, but thou hearest not; and in the night season, and am not silent'; Job xxx. 17, 'My bones are pierced in me in the night season'; Job vii. 14–15, 'Then thou scarest me with dreams, and terrifiest me through visions: So that my soul chooseth strangling, and death rather than my life'.

He had withdrawn from society for protection against the ravaging insanity within himself. His courage did not come in action with or against an aggressive society. He was brave, rather, in weathering and sometimes fighting more subtle and terrifying foes. These were the enemies which crept over the walls around his small garden-world. Nevertheless, through all his trials Cowper maintained his amiable character, except when depression crushed him to silence. He was gentle and kind and sweet tempered; and out of this sweetness there would come forth strength.

A

UNCOLLECTED LETTERS AND
ESSAYS: 1750–67

[I]

THIS is the earliest surviving Cowper letter. It was known to Hayley and Lady Hesketh, and to John Johnson, but in accordance with Lady Hesketh's wishes was not included in Hayley's or Johnson's editions of the letters. Hayley had been 'much pleased with its humorous and innocent vivacity', and had thought of printing it, but acceded to her unexpected request, for it was 'only a point of feminine delicacy and taste'.[1] Lady Hesketh's surprisingly finical taste in this matter shows her reluctance to present to the world any intimate knowledge of Cowper's early life. The protective Harriot was especially unwilling that the world should know anything which might concern her sister Theadora and Cowper's love for her. The obliging Hayley easily submitted.

It seems likely that Cowper had not been at Mr Chapman's very long. He sends his close friend Walter Bagot his new address. On 29 April 1748, while still at Westminster School, he was admitted to the Society of the Middle Temple.[2] His name appears in the school lists until 1749. He is then in the sixth form: Richard Sutton, an especially good friend, was first in the form; Cowper, third; Morgan (named in this letter), sixteenth; and Bagot, eighteenth. Morgan and Bagot are there in 1750, Morgan in the sixth form and Bagot among the 'Alumni'.[3] Cowper probably left Westminster, as was customary, when the school was dispersed for the Whitsuntide holidays, after the Election ceremonies (for the scholarships to Christ Church, Oxford, and Trinity, Cambridge).[4] In 1749 the Election took place on 8 May. He writes in his *Memoir*: 'At the age of eighteen...I was taken from

---

[1] Hayley's *Memoirs*, II, 56; Hayley to Lady Hesketh, 11 Sept. (with the part of the letter to Bagot which Hayley intended to publish), and from Lady Hesketh in return, 17 Sept. 1805: Cowper Mus., Olney. [2] *Mid. Temp. Reg.* I, 339.
[3] 'Westminster School Lists: 1744–53', ff. 76, 78, 86: Westminster MSS.
[4] Tanner, *Westminster School* (1951), pp. 105–7; *Rec. Old Westm.* I, v.

Westminster; and having spent about nine months at home, was sent to acquire the practice of the law with an attorney' (p. 8). He became eighteen in November 1749, and probably returned to London from Berkhamsted sometime in February 1750. It was long enough before this letter for him to have had time to write twice to his, and Bagot's, friend, 'Toby'.

The date of the letter from Chapman's[1] must therefore be 1750, not 1749.[2] The home of this attorney was where he lived three years, and where his fellow-student was Edward (later Lord Chancellor) Thurlow.

The letter is of particular interest because it gives some additional information about Toby. We learn that he is an Old Westminster who has left the school and is now at Oxford. He lives (or has lived), at least part of the time, in Wales. From the two letters to Toby which have been published (*Letters*, I, 5–11) we know that he is the recipient and collector of Cowper's poetry (he receives a poem with each letter), that he knows Theadora, and that he is a 'libertine'. 'I know not any Reason you have to Despair of succeedg. in your Addresses to a Virtuous Woman', Cowper writes in 1754. 'I wish you was once fairly taken in, for an affair

---

[1] The letter to Lady Hesketh, 17 April 1786, also gives the name of the attorney: 'I did actually live three years with Mr. Chapman, a solicitor.' Chapman probably held both qualifications, which was not uncommon in the eighteenth century. Officers of the Common Law Courts were attorneys, and those of the Court of Chancery, solicitors. (See Sir F. D. MacKinnon, 'The Law and the Lawyers', *Johnson's England*, II, 287, n. 3.) No more than this was known about the man until 1870 when William Benham identified Chapman as a solicitor, 'of Ely Place, Holborn'—without any indication of his source (Benham, ed., *Poetical Works of William Cowper*, 'Globe Ed.' (London, 1870), p. xxvi). This identification of Cowper's residence during 1750–3 has been followed by all biographers since that time, and by Mr Robert Gore-Browne, the biographer of Thurlow (*Chancellor Thurlow* (London, 1953), p. 7). But Ely Place was not created until after the Bishop of Ely's House was taken down in 1775 (H. B. Wheatley and P. Cunningham, *London Past and Present* (London, 1891), II, 13–14). Grevile (or Greville) Street, according to this letter, was the location of Mr Chapman's residence. The street is just above Holborn and runs between Brooke Street and Leather Lane, directly behind Furnival's Inn. Cowper's room may have overlooked the gardens of the Inn. More than this is not known about Chapman. The name is too common and appears with too great a frequency in the parish registers of this area and in the registers of the Inns of Court, to identify the man with any certainty.

[2] The postmark supports the internal evidence, but does not prove it. 12 March 1749 N.S. was a Sunday, and in 1750 N.S., a Monday. Without the internal evidence it would seem possible for Cowper to have written the letter on Sunday and posted it on Monday. 'T' in the postmark must stand for 'Temple', the only one of the six offices of the Penny Post with the initial T: John Chamberlayne, *Magnae Britanniae Notitia*, 37th ed. (London, 1748), II, iii, 70.

of that sort would undoubtedly complete your Reformation; nothing else can....I look upon you as one of the very best Species of Libertines otherwise I should not Subscribe myself your Affectionate Friend.'[1]

There is one other friend at this time whom we know to have received poems in letters from Will Cowper. He is 'C. P. Esq.' Two poems addressed to him were preserved in Theadora's collection of William's youthful verse.[2] Only one man in the list of Old Westminsters seems qualified to be 'C. P.' He is Chase Price (1731–77) who was in the sixth form with Cowper, Morgan, and Bagot in 1749, the last boy (twentieth place) in the form.[3] He went down from the school in 1749 when Cowper did; matriculated at Christ Church, Oxford, 24 May 1749; was of Knighton, Radnorshire, Wales. He was a writer of verse in a very casual way and an enthusiastic patron of the theatre.[4] He was admitted to the Inner Temple in 1750 or 1751, and afterwards called to the bar with Cowper's friend Nicholas Westcomb (1757).[5] Price was one of the most celebrated and ribald wits of his time; William Combe said he 'was, undoubtedly, the *Falstaff* of the present age'. Philip Thicknesse claimed that he did not know among all his acquaintances a more agreeable companion than Chase Price. Price knew Rockingham well, and was an even more famous voluptuary than his friend John Wilkes. He was among the 'Geniuses' of the town—especially Wilkes, Churchill, Thornton, and Lloyd—whom Boswell met in 1763.[6] From the second letter printed in this

---

[1] Letter of 21 Feb. 1754, written from the Temple: the collection of Mr Arthur A. Houghton, Jr.

[2] 'In a letter to C. P. Esq.', and 'In a Letter to the Same', *Early Poems*, pp. 4–5.

[3] 'Westminster School Lists', f. 87.

[4] Jonathan Williams and Edwin Davies, *A General History of the County of Radnor* (Brecknock, 1905), pp. 86, 224. Price wrote *The Torpedo, A Poem to the Electrical Eel. Addressed to Mr. John Hunter, Surgeon: and Dedicated to the Right Honourable Lord Cholmondeley* (London, 1777); 'A New Edition, with Large Additions' (1777) [both Yale Univ. Libr. Cat.]; 4th ed. (1777) [B.M. Cat.]. The poem was published anonymously in the year of Price's death. The authorship is attributed to Price according to a note on the title-page of the copy in the Yale Medical Libr.: Historical Libr.: 'by the late Chase Price'. It is an exceptionally lewd poem—an account of contemporary adulteries in English society. See also Tate Wilkinson, *Memoirs of his Own Life* (York, 1790), II, 175–6; III, 165–73.

[5] *Inner Temp. Rec.* v, 9, 83, 171; *Letters*, III, 486; Cowper's *Homer* (Subscribers).

[6] [William Combe], *The World As It Goes*, 2nd ed. (London, 1779), p. 27, n.; [Combe], *Letters of the Late Lord Lyttelton*, 8th ed. (London, 1793), I, 113; [Philip Thicknesse], *Sketches and Characters* (Bristol, 1770), p. 93; George Thomas Keppel,

12-2

Appendix it is now clear that 'Toby' (from Toby jug and conse-quently a fat, jolly tippler?) and 'C. P.' were the same man.[1] He was almost surely the 'Falstaff' of the mid-eighteenth century, Chase Price.

The letter which follows is the typical production of a schoolboy. Cowper's allusions to the school, 'a nasty, stinking abominable Prison', and to 'old Argus', the watchful 'Dog', are not to be taken very seriously. They represent the schoolboy affectation of never speaking well of a school within the society or the family.

*   *   *

Monday. 12 March 1750. Walter Bagot.
Address: To Walter Bagot Esq[r] at the College in Little Deans Yard Westminster
Postmark: PENY POST PAYD T[EMPLE] MO[NDAY]
Pierpont Morgan Library: MA 86, vol. I, f. 2.

Grevile Street March 12th 1749

Dear Watty

In order to Vindicate M[r] Morgans[2] Veracity & my own honour, I send you this. Does not this Sound well? I think there is some-thing Theatrical in it; & the same Spirit kept up through a Tragedy might make a great Figure upon y[e] English Stage.

Odd Enough! two friends corresponding by Letter at the Distance of a Mile & a half. An Indifferent person, would think we were afraid of seeing each other. No Rivers to interpose their

6th E. of Albemarle, *Memoirs of...Rockingham* (London, 1852), II, 235–7; Horace Bleackley, *Life of John Wilkes* (London, 1917), pp. 321–2, 339; *Boswell's London Journal, 1762–1763*, ed F. A. Pottle (New York, 1950), pp. 266, 270; *Boswell on the Grand Tour: Germany and Switzerland, 1764*, ed. Pottle (New York, 1953), p. 162; Boswell to Andrew Erskine, 7 July 1763: Private Papers of James Boswell, Yale Univ. Libr. MSS.
[1] To Toby, 1 April 1752. When the letters to Toby were first published—[Samuel Davey], 'The Literature of Letter Writing', *Archivist*, v (June 1892), 20–1—the editor wrote: 'We have not been able to trace the correspondent (Toby) to whom the letters are addressed.' Wright was the first to give an attribution: 'probably Clotworthy Rowley', *Letters*, I, xxii, 5; and all biographers and editors since that time have followed him. Rowley did not attend Westminster, and was probably unknown to Cowper until after he had taken rooms in the Temple (1754).
[2] Almost surely, Charles Morgan, s. of Charles, of Llandovery, Carmarthen, Gent.; admitted to Westminster in 1746, aged 13; left 1750; matriculated 30 June 1750, Christ Church, Oxon., aged 17; B.A. 1754, M.A. 1757; subscriber to Smart's *Poems on Several Occasions* (London, 1752), and Robert Lloyd's *Poems* (London, 1762)—as 'Rev. Mr. Morgan, Stud. of Christ Church, Oxon.'. Cowper had probably seen Morgan and had told him that he planned to write to Bagot.

Streams impassable; the Distance so Inconsiderable; ye Weather fine, and both desirous of a Meeting: Why then says that Indifferent person, what a Devil should hinder you? why don't you meet? why thou Leaden-headed Puppy, says I, I'll tell thee why. This same Mr Bagot is confined within ye musty Walls of a nasty, stinking abominable Prison; and I myself am an humble Servant to old Father Antick the Law;[1] and Consequently have but very little time to myself. But Methinks, says he, you might find an hour or two some Evening, and that would be a little Satisfaction— well thought on, faith[2] Sir says I—& now Watty what say you to this honest Fellows proposal? will you appoint a time, I'll meet you at any place you shall name?[3] Can you impose upon old Argus?[4] Or is ye Dog more watchfull with 2 Eyes than his Grandfather was with a Hundred?

Morgan wanted me to come & shake Hands with you through the Door; but that was so like Pyramus & Thisbe that I could not bear ye Thoughts of it.

Let me know in your Answer where Toby is, when you heared from him & how I may direct to him. I writ to him at Oxford & I hear he is in Whales; & though I have writ to him twice, would you think it! I have not heared from him once since I have been at Chapman's.

I am Dear Watty, (thinking this long Enough for ye Penny post) yours sincerely

William Cowper

Direct to me at Mr Chapmans in Grevile Street near Holbourn

---

[1] *I Henry IV*, i, ii, 69.

[2] He probably intended to write 'faithful'.

[3] Cowper wrote to Lady Hesketh, 30 Nov. 1785: 'In the course, as I suppose of more than twenty years after we left school, I saw him but twice;—once when I called on him at Oxford, and once when he called on me in the Temple' (*Letters*, ii 391). After 1783 Cowper and Bagot visited several times and corresponded frequently.

[4] Hayley wrote to John Johnson, 24 May 1805: 'ask your kind host [at Blithfield, Walter Bagot], *what* was the *prison* and *who* the *Argus*...I guess the prison to be the college at Westminster, and Argus, the schoolmaster; but I may be wrong in my conjecture' (Hayley's *Memoirs*, ii, 152–3). Hayley's conjecture seems right. 'Argus' was probably the Second or Under Master (later Master of the King's Scholars) for Bagot was a Scholar. The Under Master at this time was Pierson Lloyd. In the eighteenth century Westminster does not appear to have had a school porter, other than one of the King's Scholars during the day. Sergeaunt, *Annals of Westminster School*, pp. 149, 152–3; letter from Mr L. E. Tanner, 30 Aug. 1956.

[II]

Wednesday. 1 April 1752. 'Toby' [Chase Price?].
Sotheby, Wilkinson and Hodge Cat., 29 April 1897, lot 283. Extract
from catalogue.

In return for your very agreeable favour I shall only present
you with a few lines which entered into my Pate as I was walking
in the fields this morning before breakfast and think of what
compliment I should coin that might be worthy your acceptance. . . .

> Trust me, the meed of Praise dealt thriftily
> From the nice scale of Judgment Honours more
> Than does the lavish and oerbearing Tide
> Of profuse Courtesy—not all the gems
> Of India's richest soil, at random spread
> Oer the gay vesture of some glittering dame
> Give such bewitching Graces to the person
> As the scant lustre of a few, with choice
> And comely guise of ornament bestow'd.[1]

. . .The very thing you say of Happiness I said tother day of
Content, which is only another name for ye same thing[.] it will
help to fill up this so I will send it you.

> Oh ask not where contentment may abide
> In whose still mansion those true joys abound.
> That pour sweet balm o'er fortune's fest'ring wound
> Whether she chuse sequester'd to reside
> In the lone Hamlet on some mountain wide
> Whose rough top with brown oaks or pine trees crowned
> Casts a dim shade a settled gloom around—
> Or whether she amidst the glittering tide
> Of Courtiers pouring from the thick throng'd gate
> Of Majesty be seen, she nor assumes
> The high-swoln Damp of haughty miened State
> Nor constant to the low roofed cottage comes

---

[1] These lines were first printed in *Early Poems*, p. 5. The title there: IN A LETTER
TO THE SAME [C. P. ESQ.]. | *IN IMITATION OF SHAKESPEARE*. Variations
other than spelling and punctuation: [l. 7] bewitching Graces: alluring vantage
[l. 9] bestow'd.: disposed.

On honest minds alone she designs to wait
There closes still her downy feathered Plumes
Nor wandering thence shifts her serene abode
Pleased to possess the noblest work of God.[1]

...An admirable thing is just published by Mason of Cambridge, which you shall read when you come to town. He calls it Elfrida, a Dramatick Poem.[2] It is written upon the Greek plan, like 'Samson Agonistes' & 'Cosmus' [*sic*]. I do not find that it is much known in the world as yet, I picked it up accidently at Brown's Coffee House[3] and having read it there, recommended it to 2 or 3 who may be called sound & staunch Judges of all works of genius, I need not tell you how they approved of it, after having told you that it met with my Sov'reign approbation....

[IIa]

MAGGS Catalogue 486 (1926), lot 2068, describes a letter from William Cowper 'to his solicitor, 2pp., 4to. East Barnet, 6th March, 1753. On personal matters, mentioning his state of health'. This letter was purchased from Maggs by Professor Richard L. Purdy of Yale University, and it remains in his collection. I have examined the manuscript of this letter and have concluded that it is not in the autograph of William Cowper the poet, nor does it reveal any reference to known events in his life at this time. It was probably written by his cousin William Cowper (1721?–69) the Major, of Hertingfordbury, Hertfordshire, from the home of his sister, Mary Cowper de Grey, at East Barnet in the same county (see above, pp. 75–6).

[III–V]

THE three extracts which follow are from letters to John Duncombe, a miscellaneous writer and frequent contributor to the

---

[1] To the best of my knowledge, the lines have not been reprinted. The last line is a borrowing from Pope, *Essay on Man*, IV, 248: 'An honest Man's the noblest work of God.'

[2] Publ. March 1752: see John W. Draper, *William Mason* (New York, 1924), p. 342; Philip Gaskell, *The First Editions of William Mason* (Cambridge, 1951), p. 3.

[3] Located in 'Mitre court, leading to the temple. Chiefly frequented by gentlemen of the law. Tea, coffee, and other refreshments': [John Feltham], *The Picture of London for 1803* (London, [1803]), p. 353.

Gentleman's Magazine, where he succeeded Dr John Hawkesworth (1715?–73) in the 'Review of Books'.[1] Duncombe's connections with the Cowper family are discussed in chapter I. These letters are written at the time of his publication of *The Works of Horace in English Verse. By Several Hands. Collected and Published by Mr. Duncombe*, vol. I (London, 1757), vol. II (London, 1759), to which Cowper contributed two translations (in the second volume). The letters presumably are in part concerned with this work.

*   *   *

Thursday. 16 June 1757. John Duncombe.
Alfred Henry Huth, *The Huth Library* (London, 1880), v, 1684. Extract from book.

For my own part, I believe, no man ever quitted his native place with less Regrett than myself.[2]

[IV]

Saturday. 31 December 1757. John Duncombe.
Collector [catalogue of Walter R. Benjamin, Autographs: 18 East 77th Street, New York], LXIV (April 1951), lot W 727. Extract from catalogue.[3]

...As to your long story of gingerbread and Faggots,[4] I understand but half of it. I know I promised you some Gingerbread with Sweetmeats, which promise I have not yet perform'd, but are

---

[1] Nichols, *Anecdotes*, VIII, 277.

[2] This comment should be compared with his remarks ten years later in a letter to Mrs Madan: 'From his Orchard [the Rev. James Moody's, at Dunton, about twelve miles from Berkhamsted] I could see some Hills within a small Distance of my Native Place, which formerly I have often visited. The Sight of them affected me much...' (15 Oct. 1767: *U. & U.* p. 17).

[3] Miss Mary A. Benjamin, director of the firm, informs me that she is unable to establish the present ownership of the MS.

[4] See Richard Bradley, *Dictionaire Oeconomique: or, The Family Dictionary* (London, 1725), vol. I, s.v. *Faggots of Oranges:* 'Orange-Peels turn'd or par'd very thin, in order to be preserv'd, more especially those of sweet *Oranges*...commonly call'd *Faggots*.' This meaning of 'Faggots' is suggested by the parallel word 'Sweetmeats', often preserved or candied fruit. There may be a figurative significance to these words and 'Gingerbread', which at times implies something showy and unsubstantial; or may be a term of burlesque or ironic praise; or in the phrase, 'cake and gingerbread', something easy and pleasant (*O.E.D.*). Cowper's promise of 'some Gingerbread with Sweetmeats' therefore probably refers to a light essay or poem which he was supposed to write for Duncombe, like the 'Narration' which Duncombe has sent to him.

you sure therefore yt. I will never perform it?[1] You are too hasty in reproaching me with Breach of promise; I would rather marry a Pastry cook's Daughter, on purpose to supply you with ginger-bread.... You have split my Brain with your confounded Faggot-sticks, & I can make neither Head nor Tail of ye whole story: But it is like ye rest of your Narrations, the chief Perfection of which is that they are absolutely unintelligible... I would re-commend it to you, now you have made yourself almost a Master of ye Paradise lost, to read the Iliad & ye Odyssey in their original Languages.... God bless you Old boy....

I am sorry I have no Frank, but you may charge ye Postage to one of your Clients.

[v]

Saturday. 22 July 1758. John Duncombe.
Sotheby, Wilkinson and Hodge Cat., 8–9 July 1878, lot 65 [from the collection of George Manners]. Extract from catalogue.

You are descended from Job, as you are plagued with more than half his sufferings.

[vi]

THIS letter to the *Gentleman's Magazine* may possibly be Cowper's. It bears his customary signature, 'W. C.',[2] and it includes a paragraph which has parallels with the description of singing in country churches in *Connoisseur*, no. 134:

The good old practice of psalm-singing is, indeed, wonderfully improved in many country churches since the days of *Sternhold* and *Hopkins*; and there is scarce a parish-clerk, who has so little taste as not to pick his staves out of the New Version. This has occasioned great complaints in some places, where the clerk has been forced to bawl by himself, because the rest of the congregation cannot find the psalm at the end of their prayer-books; while others are highly disgusted at the innovation, and stick as obstinately to the Old Version as to the Old

---

[1] These two sentences were poorly transcribed in Parke-Bernet Cat. 1190 (30 Oct.–2 Nov. 1950), lot 276 [MS. from the collection of Oliver R. Barrett].

[2] See, for example, his contributions to the *St James's Mag.* (Appendix A, p. 211), and his references in the *Letters* concerning contributions to the *G.M.* where he especially considered 'W. C.' as 'my signature'. In 1785 he was irritated when someone in that magazine appropriated the signature, and decided therefore 'in future to insert an asterisk between my two initials by way of discrimination' (*Letters*, II, 304–5; III, 138).

APPENDIX A

Stile. The tunes themselves have also been new-set to jiggish measures; and the sober drawl, which used to accompany the two first staves of the hundredth psalm with the *gloria patri*, is now split into as many quavers as an *Italian* air.[1]

W. C.'s letter is an answer to '*Some few Queries offer'd to the Publick concerning the present Method of chaunting in Choirs; which Queries may be answer'd, or not answer'd, just as People think proper*', sent to the *Gentleman's Magazine* by 'H—s W—m' of Worcester, on 27 July 1758.[2]

*   *   *

Sunday. 17 September 1758. 'Mr Urban'.
Gentleman's Magazine, xxvııı (September 1758), 422–4.

Sept. 17, 1758.

Mr URBAN,

Having observed in your last Magazine the Queries relating to Chaunting in Choirs, to be answered or unanswered, as people should think proper; I here trouble you with the following hasty Answers to such of them as I thought proper to be answered, and leave it to you to insert, or not insert them in your next, as you shall think proper.

Yours, &c.   W. C.

Ans. to Qu. 1, 2, *and* 3.[3]—It has been generally thought that St *Ambrose* (who was a native of *Arles*) first introduced the antiphonant method of chaunting, or one side of the choir alternately responding to the other, into the church of *Milan*, about the latter end of the 4th century; (for he died archbishop of that province *A. D.* 397.)[4] Some indeed are of opinion that *this* church, as well as *others*, had musical offices *before* St *Ambrose*'s time, whose office

---

[1] *Connoisseur*, no. 134 (19 Aug. 1756), pp. 807–8 (1st ed.).
[2] *G.M.* xxvııı (Aug. 1758), 355–6.
[3] 'Q. Who was the first author or contriver of a chaunt? Q. What was his name, or where did he live, or where did he die? Q. Was he of *Italian, French, Dutch*, or *English* extraction, or what extraction was he of?'
[4] St Ambrose (340?–97), born at Trier or Trèves, but in the past Arles and Lyons were also suggested (*Catholic Encyclopedia*). St Paulinus, Ambrose's biographer, said that the beginning of antiphonal music took place during the persecution of Ambrose by the Empress Justina: 'Hoc in tempore primum antiphonæ, hymni, ac vigilæ in ecclesia Mediolanensi celebrari cœperunt' (*Patrologia Latina*, xıv, 31). 'W. C.'s' comments on Ambrosian music have been substantiated for the most part by twentieth-century scholarship.

186

however (which was afterwards called *the Ambrosian rite*) having been long established in the church of *Milan* was continued there, even *after* St *Gregory* the great introduced into other churches of the west, the *Gregorian* chaunt, or *Roman* song, now commonly called the *plain song*, and still in use in the church of *Rome*; wherein all the choir and people sing in unison. Our plain chaunts of the psalms are somewhat different from this last, but whether invented by the same St *Gregory*, or whether a nearer imitation of the *Ambrosian* song I leave others to determine.[1] However this be, I think any one that duly considers our present method, (*viz.* the stopping the music as directed by the points at the middle and end of each verse, and singing the notes immediately preceding those stops in such a time as that all the choir may chime in together, the rest having been sung in a swifter time to one and the same note—) must own it to be a well contrived method; as it is equally guarded from the inconveniences of two extreams, *viz.* the not giving the people sufficient time to consider what they say or sing, (which is too frequently the case when the psalms are read parochially;) and on the other hand, the drawling them out to such an immoderate length of time and in such a manner, as to tire devotion instead of animating and improving it. We may add also, that in our way of chaunting all begin and end the verse together, without that confusion which cannot be avoided in a large church where singing is not used, and where the people cannot so well hear, or join in time with each other.

The 4th, 5th, and all the subsequent quæries to the 16th inclusive, are I think so trifling, as to require no answer, or at least none but what is included in the above.

In answer to his 17th quæry, *viz. whether those who have any ears for musick, or those who are real friends to church musick, are under any particular obligations to the author of such a contrivance?*[2] I can only say, that although I don't pretend to understand musick (however pleased when I hear it) yet, on the authority of those that do understand it, I may venture to answer in the affirmative.

---

[1] The chants in the Anglican Church are derived mainly from the Gregorian plainsong (*Grove's Dict.* II, 172–4).

[2] '*such a contrivance*': referring to the preceding query: 'Whether the first chaunt was composed either in a flat key or a sharp key, or whether it was quite destitute both of flats and sharps, or whether it was compos'd in a *natural* key?'

I must own I don't understand the meaning of the 18th quæry,[1] so must leave it to be answered by those who are better able to cast up what the quærist calls *the sum-total of harmony*.

The 19th quæry[2] I think may be answered in the affirmative: It is true that chaunting may not always do justice to the words of the psalms, because they were not composed for this musick, nor every verse of a psalm for the *same* musick: and yet a return of the same musick for each verse is necessary, unless you will have the whole psalter set to musick by an able master, which I believe no lover of chaunting will oppose: but even then, however careful the composer may be to make the sound to echo to the sense, it can't be expected that the musick will express the emphasis that would be proper to every word when well read *without* musick. We may observe also that such a composition as this must be confined to the members of the choir, the common people being unable to join therein, as they may do in our present method of chaunting.

The latter part of this 19th quæry may (as requiring much the same answer) be joined with the 20th or last, *viz. Whether chaunting the psalms be a proper, natural, or affecting method of singing them? And whether such a constant repetition of the same sounds for a considerable time together, can animate our devotions, or answer the original end and design of church musick?*

Answer. I am well assured, as well by my own experience, as by that of others, that it can and does animate our devotions, how often soever the same sounds are repeated; and if it has this effect on those who are unskilled in musick, and have neither voice to produce, nor ear to distinguish true harmony, much more must it affect those who can better judge of and enjoy its beauties and perfections.—The psalms were made to be sung, and the spirit and meaning of the original is certainly much better preserved in prose than in verse; especially if the former be a sufficiently[3] close translation, without a too servile regard to the *Hebrew* idiom; and the latter made by such as understood not the

---

[1] 'Whether in case all the harmony was carefully extracted out of all the chaunts that ever were compos'd, or will be compos'd, what would or will be the sum total of such harmony?'

[2] 'Whether the best chaunt that ever was compos'd can do the least justice to any single verse in the whole compass of the psalms?...'

[3] The original has a printer's error: 'snfficiently.'

original text: And if they are best sung in prose, why not in our present way of chaunting, till the quærist or some otherperson of taste furnish us with a better?

After all, I believe there are many persons who have an aversion (whether natural or acquired) not only to this, but all other kinds of church-musick; except perhaps the drawling or bleating thro' a few lines chosen by an ignorant parish-clerk, out of *Hopkins* and *Sternhold*'s version, and that without any regard to its connection with what goes before or follows: Let such go to some parochial church, where the inimitable beauties of *David*'s psalms are disguised by the most monstrous dresses, and *Sternhold out-Sternholded* by the formal lay-elders who are his greatest admirers: There they may in a doleful snuffling tone sing an edifying stave, by which we are instructed that he that goes to glean upon the *land*, can't there fill his lap with grass grown on the *house-top*; (*Psal.* cxxix. 8. *Hopk.* and *St.*)[1] In this he may hear of *Kedar*'s *black* tents putting *Isaac*'s *sect to shame.* (*Ps.* cxx. 5. same version.)[2] Of the *stock of travellers* and *Jacob the Israelite!* (*Ps.* xxiv. 6.)[3] and many other such, equally agreeable to the psalmists original meaning, and to common sense. —But it may be asked, what a bad translation of the psalms has to do with the musick? 'Tis granted it has not, unless they are so fitly

---

[1] Thomas Sternhold and John Hopkins, *The Whole Book of Psalms, Collected into English Meter* (Oxford, 1679), p. 87: Psalm cxxix. 5–7:

> They that hate me shall be asham'd,
>   and turned back also:
> And made as grass upon the house,
>   which with'reth e're it grow:
> Whereof the mower cannot find
>   enough to fill his hand:
> Nor can he fill his lap, that goeth
>   to glean upon the land.

[2] *Ibid.* p. 85: Psalm cxx. 5:

> Alas! too long I slack,
> Within these tents so black,
>   Which Kedars are by name,
> By whom the flock elect,
> And all of Isaac's sect
>   Are put to open shame.

[3] *Ibid.* p. 19: Psalm xxiv. 6:

> This is the brood of travellers,
>   in seeking of his grace:
> As Jacob did the Israelite,
>   in that time of his race.

adapted to each other as to be equally bad, in which case we cannot expect them to be good helps to devotion? And I have therefore often wondered that they should have been so long continued in our parish churches without any public authority, but a bare permission only.

There are other well-meaning people who dislike cathedral service because they cannot understand it when they hear it; that is, for want of being accustomed to it, for a little use would soon render it intelligible to them; and notwithstanding the constant repetition of the same sounds, those who are truly devout, will, instead of being tired with such repetitions be better pleased with, and find their devotions more and more warmed and enlivened thereby: For we may make the same observation in this respect, as the pious *Nelson*[1] has done in answer to the objection against frequently receiving the Holy Eucharist, as if it deadened devotion and diminished that respect which men ought to have for it; *this* (says he) *is founded upon the experience men have that their familiarity and intimate converse with men and things in this world, is apt to diminish their value and respect for them; not considering that it is quite the contrary in spiritual things, the frequent use whereof is the likeliest means to encrease our veneration and respect towards them.*[2] So that tho' too much familiarity with the same things breeds contempt, in the common course of worldly concerns, yet an habitual devotion will be found by those who will seriously and in good earnest make trial thereof, to be no more diminished by the repetition of the same sounds than of the Lord's prayer or the chorus in the 136th psalm,[3] both which are equally liable to the same objection.

[VII, VIII]

THE two letters to 'Jack' which follow were probably addressed to John Duncombe, for the style of the first letter in particular, and many of the references ('you never could write or Speak good

---

[1] Robert Nelson (1656–1715), religious writer. His *Companion for the Festivals and Fasts of the Church of England* (London, 1704), 21st ed. (1757), had an 'unrivalled popularity as a popular manual of Anglican theology' (*D.N.B.*).

[2] [Robert Nelson], *The Great Duty of Frequenting the Christian Sacrifice*, 10th ed. (London, 1734), pp. 69–70; 1st ed. (1707), 13th ed. (1756). This is enlarged from the chapter on vigils (dealing with Holy Communion) in the *Companion*.

[3] 'For his mercy endureth for ever': repeated at the end of each of the twenty-six verses of Psalm cxxxvi.

English'; 'your Clerk'—cf. 'your Clients'; 'old Boy'), are reminiscent of letter III (31 December 1757) to Duncombe. Although
a letter from Cowper to him on 21 November 1758 (about two
months before the first letter printed here) begins 'My dear John',
in the message Duncombe is called 'old Jack'. And in that letter
Cowper asks him to 'Make my Compliments to Mrs Essington',
who is also mentioned in a letter below. Duncombe's address in
November 1758[1] was: 'The Post House, Great Berkamstead,
Hartfordshire.'

The Jack of the following letters must have been from the
neighbourhood of Berkhamsted. The two letters have several
references to prominent families of that town, the Essingtons and
the Harcourts, and the Cowpers of Hertingfordbury, part of the
great county family.

There is a slight possibility that Jack may have been John
Seare[2] of 'The Grove', near Tring, a mile or two from Berkham-
sted. The Seares shared with the Gore family the manor of
Marsworth, Buckinghamshire, just over the Hertfordshire border.[3]
The Gores were of 'Tring Park', the most splendid seat near
Berkhamsted. Mentmere, the manor adjoining Marsworth, was
owned by Richard Bard Harcourt, mentioned in the letter.[4] John
Seare had been at Westminster during William Cowper's last two
years. In this time he may very well have met Cowper's cousin
Martin Madan, a young bachelor of the Inner Temple, only
recently called to the bar. Seare and Duncombe were friends:

---

[1] David Bonnell Green, 'Three Cowper Letters', N. & Q. CCI (1956), 532.

[2] John Seare (1733?–92), s. of Michael, who was of an ancient Hertfordshire and
Buckinghamshire family; admitted to Westminster School, Jan. 1747/8, to Christ
Church, Oxon., 11 June 1752; m. Mary, dau. and heiress of Caleb Grantham of
'High-House', the manor at West Thurrock, Essex (1756); Sheriff of Herts (1766–7):
G.M. XXVI (1756), 548 and LXII, Pt ii (1792), 675; Duncan Warrand, Hertfordshire
Families (London, 1907), p. 284; Philip Morant, The History...of...Essex (London,
1768), I, Pt ii, 91–5; George Lipscomb, The History...of Buckingham (London, 1847),
III, 411, 416.

[3] John Duncombe used the Gores and 'Tring Park' as an illustration in the 2nd ed.
of Horace (London, 1767), I, 38. The house, which had been built from designs of Sir
Christopher Wren, was owned by the Gore family from 1705 to 1786. Charles Gore
(d. 1810), as well as William Cowper, was named a beneficiary in the will of Sir Thomas
Hesketh who m. Harriot Cowper, William's cousin: abstract of Sir Thomas's will in
the Hesketh Papers: Lancashire Rec. Off. MSS. DDF. 413. 2. 'Tring Park' later
became the seat of the Rothschilds (1872), who in 1885 became the Barons Rothschild
of Tring.

[4] V.C.H....Buckingham, III, 398.

they had both come from families which had been for many years owners of property in the Berkhamsted–Tring area. In 1763 Seare presented Duncombe to the vicarage of West Thurrock, Essex, which he held until 1769.[1]

* * *

Thursday. 11 January 1759. 'Jack' [John Duncombe?].
Henry E. Huntington Library: HM 12585.[2]

My Dear Jack—

I am glad you can prevail ̧with yourself now & then to Stick a Pen in your Old Claw, and tell me you are in the Land of the Living. If your Face and Person are as little altered as your Stile, you must needs be as well worth seeing as ever, and I heartily wish I could have Ocular Proof of it. Dick[3] says you never could write or Speak good English in your Life, which is so true, yᵗ it were vain to denie it, but your Language has always been more Entertaining than yᵉ best English I ever met with. I shall be sorry to receive a Letter from you in more Elegant phrase than usual, and immediately conclude yᵗ being too much Indisposed to write yourself, you have made Roley Poley,[4] or your Clerk or some such Scholar, your Amanuensis. I met Dick Harcourt[5] in Hyde Park yesterday, he looked well & was in high Spirits, so perhaps he has swallowed the grape shot[6] you speak of with Success. Martin Madan's Wife

---

[1] Morant, I, Pt ii, 94; Andrew Kippis, *Biographia Britannica* (London, 1793), v, 510.
[2] A large part of this letter was printed in Adrian H. Joline, *Meditations of an Autograph Collector* (New York, 1902), pp. 121–2.
[3] See below, n. 5. [4] I have not been able to identify 'Roley Poley'.
[5] Richard Bard Harcourt (1724?–1815), s. of Henry, of Pendley, Herts; at Eton four years; admitted Caius Coll., Camb. (1742), Lincoln's Inn (1744); m. Rachel Nesbitt at Aldbury, Herts (1756); held manors of Pendley, Bunstreux, Hastoe, and Wigginton in Herts: Lipscomb, IV, 591; *G.M.* LXXXV, Pt i (1815), 186; *Hertford County Records: Sessions Books*, ed. William Le Hardy (Hertford, 1931 and 1935), VII, 435; VIII, 573, 589; *Hertfordshire Parish Records: Marriages*, ed. W. P. W. Phillimore (London, 1907), I, 122; *Letters*, I, 99–100: 'You [Hill] are a better counsellor than I was, but I think you have much such a client in me as I had in Dick Harcourt.' At Berkhamsted Cowper 'was haunted by the younger Harcourt' (part of letter to Hill, 29 June 1785: *Poems* (Bailey), p. xxix). This was probably John (1728?–48), who attended Merton and Wadham Colls. A much younger brother, Henry (1740?–1800?), attended Peterhouse, Camb., and was later Rector of Warbleton and Crowhurst, Sussex. There were eleven sisters, four of whom died young (Lipscomb, IV, 591).
[6] The reference to 'grape shot', that is, small cast iron balls, strongly connected together so as to form a charge for cannon (*O.E.D.*), probably had a personal or

is just brought to bed of another Son, his Family now consists of 2 Sons and as many Daughters[1]—The girls are both likely to be handsome; I have never seen ye Boys, but they say That which is just born, has a Foot much longer than yours already, so he is likely to be a Proper Man.—I am going to spend 2 or 3 days at the Park,[2] if ye Bankrupts[3] will give me leave; Will Cowper always enquires after you, when he has an Opportunity, and so does every Will Cowper I know. They are Whimsical Fellows, or they would not do it.

I had been Informed before your Letter told me so y^t Mrs Essington[4] had been out of Order, & was sorry to hear it. Upon your account, as well as her own I heartily wish she may recover, for I look upon her as one of the few Comforts you have, and as a Friend you can't well afford to part with. Though you don't mention Madam Harcourt,[5] I will—How should I know whether she is well or Ill unless you tell me? Farewell old Boy! shall I never

---

contemporary signification which I do not know. Mr Kenneth Povey has suggested to me that it may be a humorous name for one of those remedies with numerous constituents, aimed at everything in the hope of hitting something.

[1] Martin Madan (1725–90), m. Jane Hale (1723?–91), dau. of Sir Bernard Hale, chief baron of the Irish Exchequer; their children living at the date of this letter were (1) Martin (1756–1809), (2) Ann Judith (d. 1829), (3) Maria (d. 1829), and (4) William (1759–69), the s. just born to Mrs Madan at the time of the letter. See *Madan Family*, pp. 104–21.

[2] The residence at Hertingfordbury, Herts, of William Cowper (1721?–69) who m. Maria Frances Cecilia Madan (1726–97).

[3] Cowper was a Commissioner of Bankrupts, which brought him £60 year: Wright, *Life* (1921), p. 36. He probably began work in this office shortly after the death of his father (1756), who was the patentee for making out commissions of bankruptcy. Cowper's name appears in the list of sixty Commissioners of Bankruptcy appointed by the Lord Keeper of the Great Seal (Lord Chancellor), from 1758 to 1765 (*Court and City Register*).

[4] Mary Essington, probably the widow of either Thomas or John Essington (see N. Salmon, *The History of Hertfordshire* (London, 1728), p. 125; the Church Accounts, St Peter's, Berkhamsted [1584–1748]: Add. MSS. 18773, f. 304); she was in 'A List of Owners of Land in Berkhamsted, Herts, 1755' (B.M. Lansdowne MSS. 656, f. 6), as the owner of 'Broadoak ffarm, Meadow by Ravens Lane, Land at ffriday street, Land by Cross of the oak'; on 7 Aug. 1733 O.S. she had been godmother to Theodora Judith Cowper, William's sister (Cowper family Bible, Cowper Mus., Olney).

[5] Sarah Frances Bard Harcourt (d. 1764), widow of Henry (d. 1743), and mother of Richard ('Dick') Bard Harcourt. She was the dau. and heiress of Sir John Bard, Bt, and Lady Persiana (dau. of Henry, E. of Bellmont, and sister to the Princess Rupert): Cussans, III, 35; Lipscomb, IV, 591. In 1755 she owned the house occupied by 'Mrs. Duncombe' in Berkhamsted and herself lived in Egerton House (B.M. Lansdowne MSS. 656, ff. 10, 12). On 17 Dec. 1737 O.S. she had been godmother to William Cowper's brother John (Cowper family Bible).

see your Belly peeping from under your Waistcoat again, and your left Foot shaking itself upon your right Knee? You Date your Letter yᵉ 9ᵗʰ of May, no doubt intending to persuade me yᵗ April is past, that so I may forget to make a Fool of you—But look well to yourself, for I have a Cap & Bells yᵗ will just fit you.

Yʳˢ Dear Jack, with the Old Wish of a Happy New Year

Wᵐ Cowper

Temple
Jan. 11. 1759.—

[VIII]

Tuesday. 12 June 1759. 'Jack' [John Duncombe?].
Henry E. Huntington Library: HM 6559.

Dear Jack,

I have a great respect for your Virtues, notwithstanding yᵗ in your Letter to my Brother[1] you talk Bawdy like an Old Midwife.[2] You wonder I am not a more Punctual Correspondent; how the Devil should I be so, or what Subject can I possibly find to Entertain you upon? If I had a share in the Cabinet Councils of every Court in Europe, you would have no Pleasure in a Political Epistle; if I was a greater Philosopher than Sir Isaac Newton, you would think me a Fool if I should write to you upon yᵉ Subject of yᵉ Centripetal & Centrifugal Powers, the Solar System, and the Eccentrick Orbits of the Comets; and as great a Lawyer as I am, I dare not Indulge myself in the Pedantry of my Profession, lest you should not understand me, or I should not understand myself—In short I am afraid to tell you any thing but yᵗ I am yʳ most Obedᵗ & Afftte ħble Servᵗ

Wᵐ C.

June 12.
1759.

---

[1] John Cowper (1737–70).
[2] If 'Jack' is John Duncombe, then this youthful comment is in contrast to Cowper's statement in 1789 that J. D. was of 'unblemished morals', and to John Nichols' many descriptions of the 'sweetness' of his character. *Letters*, III, 377; Nichols, *Anecdotes*, VIII, 271–8.

[IX]

THE following was a contribution to the Nonsense Club in the form of a letter which suggests that it had been sent from Berkhamsted—it may or may not have been actually sent. Cowper is playing with a picture of himself as Madge the barn owl, the country boy, in the 'wood' (Berkhamsted was noted for its surrounding woods), without the liquor (one must see him also as the Rector's son) and the various stimulations of the gay society of club life in London. There are indirect references to the heavy drinking of the Nonsense-Club members, who could easily spare a 'shower or two' for him from themselves, well-soaked in wine. Cowper also plays the part of the fool. The several threads of humour are brought together when he says that his (that is, Madge the owl's) 'ivy-bush is sadly out of repair'. He is undoubtedly referring to the old phrase, 'to look like an owl in an ivy-bush', common in the language and literature of sixteenth- and seventeenth-century England.[1] According to Giovanni Torriano's definition (1666), the phrase means to be 'a ridiculous object and spectacle to all the World'.[2] In Swift: '"How did the fool look?" [Colonel Atwit] "Look? Egad he look'd for all the world like an owl in an ivy-bush."'[3] It was still a proverbial saying in North Lincolnshire in 1900.[4] The ivy-bush seems to have suggested the bush of the even more familiar proverb, 'Good wine needs no bush': the bush being the traditional sign of a tavern and hence coming to stand for the tavern itself.

This letter was reprinted in Southey's *Cowper*, xv, 291–2. I have decided to give it here, though it is not really 'uncollected', because it has generally been ignored by biographers and by editors of the letters, with which it might well be included. I add it also to give an example of the kind of writing done at meetings of the Nonsense Club, and to strengthen my description of Cowper's life in the Temple.

*   *   *

---

[1] See Morris Palmer Tilley, *A Dictionary of the Proverbs in England in the Sixteenth and Seventeenth Centuries* (Ann Arbor, 1950), p. 517.

[2] Torriano, *The Proverbial Phrases* (London, 1666), p. 40 (s.v. *civetta*).

[3] Swift, *Polite Conversation* (Dialogue I), *Works*, ed. Temple Scott (London, 1907), xi, 263.   [4] *N. & Q.* 9th ser. vi (1900), 328, 396–7.

Undated. Written 'when Cowper was a young man in the Temple,
as a contribution to the "Nonsense Club"' (John Johnson).
Private Correspondence of William Cowper, Esq., ed. John Johnson, 2 vols.
(London, 1824), I, xxi–xxiv.

LETTER FROM AN OWL TO A BIRD OF PARADISE.

Sir,

I have lately been under some uneasiness at your silence, and
began to fear that our friends in Paradise were not so well as
I could wish; but I was told yesterday that the pigeon you employed as a carrier, after having been long pursued by a hawk,
found it necessary to drop your letter, in order to facilitate her
escape. I send you this by the claws of a distant relation of mine,
an eagle, who lives on the top of a neighbouring mountain. The
nights being short at this time of the year, my epistle will probably
be so too; and it strains my eyes not a little to write, when it is not
as dark as pitch. I am likewise much distressed for ink: the black-
berry juice which I had bottled up having been all exhausted,
I am forced to dip my beak in the blood of a mouse, which I have
just caught; and it is so very savoury, that I think in my heart
I swallow more than I expend in writing. A monkey who lately
arrived in these parts, is teaching me and my eldest daughter to
dance. The motion was a little uneasy to us at first, as he taught
us to stretch our wings wide, and to turn out our toes; but it is
easier now. I, in particular, am a tolerable proficient in a horn-
pipe, and can foot it very nimbly with a switch tucked under my
left wing, considering my years and infirmities. As you are
constantly gazing at the sun, it is no wonder that you complain
of a weakness in your eyes; how should it be otherwise, when mine
are none of the strongest, though I always draw the curtains over
them as soon as he rises, in order to shut out as much of his light
as possible? We have had a miserable dry season, and my ivy-bush
is sadly out of repair. I shall be obliged to you if you will favour
me with a shower or two, which you can easily do, by driving a few
clouds together over the wood, and beating them about with your
wings till they fall to pieces. I send you some of the largest berries
the bush has produced, for your children to play withal. A neighbouring physician, who is a goat of great experience, says they will
cure the worms; so if they should chance to swallow them, you
need not be frightened. I have lately had a violent fit of the

pip,[1] which festered my rump to a prodigious degree. I have shed almost every feather in my tail, and must not hope for a new pair of breeches till next spring; so shall think myself happy if I escape the chin-cough,[2] which is generally very rife in moulting season.

I am, dear Sir, &c. &c.

MADGE.[3]

P.S.—I hear my character as first minister[4] is a good deal censured; but 'Let them censure; what care I!'

[x–xii]

THE next three letters concern the letting or selling of a house in Red Lion Square, London. William Cowper and his brother must have inherited it, most likely through the death of their father in 1756. Its connection with the Cowper family is not known to me. The people mentioned in the letters are probably unidentifiable, including the mysterious woman who is benefiting from Tar Water. Perhaps the 'Limner', Mr Fry, of the first letter is Thomas Frye (1710–62), portrait painter and engraver in mezzotint. He may have been looking for a house, because he had given up his position as manager of the china factory at Bow, moved to Wales and then took a house in Hatton Garden (London) about this time (D.N.B.).

*   *   *

[1] Probably diarrhoea. Pip is usually considered to be a disease in poultry occurring in the mouth and throat, often causing a scale on the tip of the tongue; Cowper uses the word in this way in 'Conversation', l. 356: 'Faint as a chicken's note that has the pip' (*Poems*, p. 97). The *O.E.D.* gives no authority for making it a disease affecting the rump, but there is a tradition of applying the word to various diseases in human beings, usually humorously, and often suggesting venereal disease.

[2] Chincough, now more commonly called whooping cough. The word was also used in connection with animals for a humorous effect by Addison (*Tatler*, no. 121): '...Cupid, her lady's lap-dog, was dangerously ill...."[he] has always been phthisical, and as he lies under something like a chin-cough, we are afraid it will end in a consumption."'

[3] It may have been the practice in the Nonsense Club or among Cowper's friends to take names of birds or animals. His letter to Hill, 10 Oct. 1755, is signed '*stalking Horse*' (*Poems*, p. 625). This letter from Madge may have also been addressed to Hill. Hill had the MS. in 1802, when it was sent to Hayley. Hill to Hayley, 19 Feb. 1802: copy owned by Rev. W. Cowper Johnson, Norwich.

[4] First Minister: in the latter part of the eighteenth century, the common designation for the Premier or Prime Minister (*see O.E.D.* s.v. 'Prime Minister'). The sentence suggests that Cowper may have been president of the Nonsense Club at the time.

Thursday. 18 October 1759. Joseph Hill.
The Rev. Wilfrid Cowper Johnson, Norwich.

Dear Joe,

I recieved a Letter from your Clerk yesterday containing an Account of a Treaty he has had with M.ʳ Fry a Limner about yᵉ House in R: L: S. I shall be obliged to[o?] if you will desire him to acquaint that Gentleman yᵗ we shall be glad to come to an Agreement with him. That we do not intend to Let the House however, without the Stables; and that for both together we cannot possibly take a less Rent than 60ᵗᵇ per ann: as to the Roof I imagine it cannot want a great deal of Repair, as it was made entirely new not much more than Ten years ago, but if it is any where defective shall have no sort of objection to making it good, upon the Terms M.ʳ Fry proposes. As to the Stables, I should imagine it would be rather beneficial to M.ʳ Fry to take them, even though he makes no use of them himself, as there are many people in yᵉ Neighbourhood, who would be glad of them, & wᵈ hire them at a Rent of 10ᵗᵇ or 12ᵗᵇ per ann: There are some Goods in yᵉ House such as Kitchen grate, Marble Tables, Bottle Rack, Looking glasses Lamp at the Door &c, which we intend to dispose of, and should imagine M.ʳ Fry would find it convenient to be the Purchasor; but they will be sold at all Events. I shall be in Town probably to-morrow, that is Friday Sen'night, and at any time after, shall be glad to treat with M.ʳ Fry about these matters in person.

I wish you Joy of our Successes in America, and shall Jump at a Letter from you.

Y.ʳ afftte Friend & Serv.ᵗ

W.ᵐ Cowper.

G.ᵗ Berk hamstead
Thurs: Oct. 18. 1759.

If M.ʳ Fry is not satisfied with these Terms, or should have any thing further to propose, I shall be glad if your clerk will be so good as to acquaint me with it, while I am here.

[XI]

Friday. 18 February 1763. Joseph Hill.
The Rev. Wilfrid Cowper Johnson, Norwich.

Dear Joe,

If the Wise acre had offer'd me 800ł for the House, I have a Conscience y^t would have fitted it exactly. As to Mr Hawkins he may hang himself upon the Sign Post whenever he pleases, but if he thinks I will wait to Chaffer and Haggle with such a Fusty Old-Cloaths-monger as He, he is mistaken. I shall write to him by this Post. to hasten his Resolution; He may know as well in 10 Minutes as in a Month, whether he will pay that Price for it or no.

Hawkin^s Lease did Lie upon the black Leathern Table when I left the Chambers, & there I dare say you will find it. There are but 8 Years to come, & I am as certain y^t he has no right to renew.

God bless you, & thank you for your Intelligence. We heard by another Wind this Morning y^t She had begun to drink Tar Water & y^t it agreed with her. Diî vortant bené![1]

Y^{rs} ever

Wm Cowper.

Feb: 18.
1763.

Shall I trouble you to put the Letter to Hawkins into ye Penny Post?

[XII]

Good Friday. 1 April 1763. Joseph Hill.
The Rev. Wilfrid Cowper Johnson, Norwich.

Dear Joe,

This Dawson is a sly Fellow; he has waited thus long in hopes y^t I would send for him, and sell him ye House for less than its' real Value; He now offers more than it is worth, yet seeing y^t he is a Scoundrel, I will take his Money.

Y^{rs} Affectionately

Wm Cowper.

April 1st 1763.

---

[1] Terence, *Hecyra*, I, ii, 121.

[XIII]

THIS parody of ancient and modern aesthetics, and the letter which precedes it, are signed with Cowper's initials, and may with considerable certainty be ascribed to him. The 'Dissertation' was sent to Cowper's friend Robert Lloyd for his *St James's Magazine*. Lloyd's note at the end of the issue for March 1763 probably refers to Cowper: 'The Essay from our old Friend came too late to be inserted.' His essay was published in April, and it alone seems to fit this description. Lloyd began this magazine in September 1762 but relinquished the editorship to the scoundrel William Kendrick in February 1764 owing to 'debts contracted during its progress'.[1] It continued only until June of that year. The magazine was an eighty-page monthly, devoted almost entirely to poetry and criticism. Walter Graham described it as an extension of an older type of periodical, the poetry journal, and 'quite the best thing of its kind up to this time'.[2]

Because of Cowper's remark at the end of the essay, 'in my next I shall present you with a perfect ode', Southey attributed 'An Ode. Secundum Artem' (vol. III, November 1763, pp. 187–9), to him. 'Evidently by the same person', Southey wrote, 'though signed with a different initial'.[3] The 'Ode' was signed 'L.', the poem preceding this, 'R. L.', and 'To the Public' before that, 'R. Lloyd', whose name appears on the title-page of the magazine ('by Robert Lloyd'). Hence 'L.' would be presumed to be Lloyd. J. C. Bailey[4] has shown by internal evidence, with what he rightly calls 'absolutely conclusive proof', that the 'Ode' is Lloyd's. Nevertheless, it remains in the Oxford text of Cowper's *Poetical Works* (pp. 288–9). It should be removed from the canon.

The 'Dissertation' appears to be an attack on Gray and Mason especially, and on the vogue of ode-writing, which had reached extraordinary heights in the years 1745–63.[5] Every versifier wrote

---

[1] Austin Dobson, 'Robert Lloyd', *At Prior Park and Other Papers* (London, 1912), p. 238.

[2] Walter Graham, *English Literary Periodicals* (New York, 1930), p. 179.

[3] Southey's *Cowper*, I, 95–6, 331–2. Southey first identified this contribution to the *St James's Mag.* as Cowper's.

[4] *Poems* (Bailey), pp. viii, 666.

[5] For a discussion of the development of the mid-eighteenth-century ode see George N. Shuster, *The English Ode from Milton to Keats* (New York, 1940), pp. 186–241; Norman Maclean, 'From Action to Image', *Critics and Criticism: Ancient and Modern*,

an ode. Horace Walpole complained that he was not able to do so, but of course his dog, Patapan, like any bright dog, did.[1] By 1760 the wits of London were burlesquing the mode. For example, Arthur Murphy wrote *An Ode to the Naiads of Fleet-Ditch* (London, 1761) and Andrew Erskine, *Two Odes. To Indolence, and to Impudence* (London, 1762). Cowper and his friends in the Nonsense Club were innovators in the burlesque tradition. They focused their parody on individual writers, particularly on Gray, whom they did not like.[2] Lloyd (to whom Cowper sent this essay) and Colman in 1760 had collaborated on *Two Odes* which ridiculed the work of Gray and Mason. The two young men indulged in all the characteristic fooling of the club. 'Ode I' (commonly called the 'Ode to Obscurity'[3]) attacked Gray whose two *Odes* ('The Progress of Poesy' and 'The Bard', but without titles in this edition) had been published at Strawberry Hill for Dodsley in 1757. To the Greek motto on Gray's title-page (translated) 'intelligible to the learned', from Pindar's second Olympian Ode, C. and L. add on their title-page the words immediately following in Pindar, 'the multitude will need interpreters'. As Gray invoked the 'Æolian lyre', C. and L. invoke the 'Cimmerian Muse' (Obscurity). The tailpiece to the first burlesque ode shows Pegasus pushing Gray from a mountain. This is in imitation of the close of Gray's second ode ('The Bard'):

> from the mountain's height
> Deep in the roaring tide he [the Welch Bard] plung'd
> to endless night.

C. and L.'s second ode is played off even more closely against Mason's 'Ode to Memory':[4] the same number of stanzas and lines, the same metre and rhyme patterns. They parody his footnotes, and on the half-title preceding their 'Ode to Oblivion', employ

---

ed. R. S. Crane (Chicago, 1952), pp. 408–60. Maclean begins the second period of ode-writing in the century at *c.* 1740, or with the publ. of Collins' *Odes on Several Descriptive and Allegoric Subjects* in 1746 (pp. 429, 436–7).

[1] Yale ed., *Horace Walpole's Correspondence* (New Haven, 1951), XVI, 257; (1954), XVIII, 221.

[2] *Letters*, I, 141. Eleven years before this 'Dissertation' was written, a less-sophisticated Cowper had found Mason's *Elfrida* 'an admirable thing' which met with his 'Sov'reign approbation' (to 'Toby', 1 April 1752: above, p. 183).

[3] It was thus advertised on its publ.: *London Chron.* 31 May 1760.

[4] In Mason's *Odes* (Cambridge, 1765).

exactly the same device of a lyre (though here degraded to a wood-cut) used in the engraved plate on Mason's title-page. As Mason in his last stanza invoked Milton, C. and L. end with an invoca-tion to Oblivion, 'FAT GODDESS, drunk with Falstaff's sack!'

Beyond this, there are in both of the burlesque odes many direct parodies of lines in Gray and Mason. Their favourite words are echoed with a burlesque effect—the same words that Cowper criticizes as foolish and fashionable. Some of these are peculiarly Gray's and Mason's, as a study of the odes in the periodicals or in Dodsley's *Collection* would prove. Others are in common usage. In the past twelve years Cowper and his friends had frequently relied on identical stereotyped words and phrases. And most of the poetic diction which he smiles at in 1763 will continue to occur in his poetry throughout his life.

The 'Dissertation' itself is probably a parody of the 'Advertise-ment' or 'Discourse' which introduced many of the odes published at this time. Sometimes the pedigree and theory of the ode were developed in notes to the poems (the most famous occurred a few years after the publication of this essay, in Gray's notes to his *Poems*, 1768). Cowper's satire is directed against essays like Young's 'Discourse on Ode', which was a high-water mark in mechanical thinking and rule-making. 'To sum the Whole', Young wrote, '*Ode* should be *peculiar*, but not *strain'd; moral*, but not *flat; natural*, but not *obvious; delicate*, but not *affected; noble*, but not *ambitious; full*, but not *obscure; fiery*, but not *mad; thick*, but not *loaded* in its Numbers, which should be most *Harmonious*, without the least sacrifice of *expression* or of *sense.*'[1] In 1745 Akenside prefaced his *Odes on Several Subjects* by an 'Advertisement' which read in part:

The author pretends chiefly to the merit of endeavouring to be correct, and of carefully attending to the best models. From what the ancients have left of this kind, perhaps the ODE may be allow'd the most amiable species of poetry; but certainly there is none which in modern languages has been generally attempted with so little success. For the perfection of lyric poetry depends, beyond that of any other, on the beauty of words and the gracefulness of numbers; in both which

[1] [Edward Young], 'On Lyrick Poetry' [or, according to the title-page, 'A Discourse on Ode'], *Ocean. An Ode* (London, 1728).

respects the ancients had infinite advantages above us. A consideration which will alleviate the author's disappointment, if he too should be found to have miscarried.

In the following year Joseph Warton wrote:

The Public has been so much accustom'd of late to didactic Poetry alone, and Essays on moral Subjects, that any work where the imagination is much indulged, will perhaps not be relished or regarded. The author therefore of these pieces is in some pain least certain austere critics should think them too fanciful and descriptive. But as he is convinced that the fashion of moralizing in verse has been carried too far, and as he looks upon Invention and Imagination to be the chief faculties of a Poet, so he will be happy if the following Odes may be look'd upon as an attempt to bring back Poetry into its right channel.[1]

William Cowper, like his friends Colman and Lloyd, could not resist a little mockery at the expense of so much high seriousness mixed with easy rules for success and a superabundance of fancy and fashion.

I have included in the notes to this essay examples of the epithets, expletives, and metaphors which Cowper cites. I have no definite information that he knew the work of any of the poets mentioned except Gray's,[2] but I include examples from their work as typical of the rash of ode-writing at this time. They are all taken from Odes (with the addition of Gray's *Elegy*) published between 1740 and 1763. Quotations are from: *The Poems of Gray and Collins*, ed. Austin Lane Poole, 3rd ed. (London, 1937); Mason, *Odes* (Cambridge, 1756) ['To Memory', 'To Independency', 'On Melancholy. To a Friend', 'On the Fate of Tyranny'], and 'Ode to a Water-Nymph', 'An Ode...at the Installation of... Newcastle', and 'Ode to an Æolus's Harp', in Dodsley's *Collection*, 4th ed. (vols. 1–3; 1st ed. of vol. 4: London, 1755), III, 297–300, IV, 269–75; also odes in his *Elfrida* (London, 1752) and *Caractacus* (London, 1759); Akenside, *Odes on Several Subjects* (London, 1745) and *An Ode to the Country Gentlemen of England* (London, 1758); Joseph Warton, *Odes on Various Subjects* (London, 1746); Robert Dodsley, *Melpomene...an Ode* (London, 1757); Michael Wodhull, *Ode to the Muses* (Oxford, 1760); James Scott, *Odes on Several Subjects* (Cambridge, 1761); [Richard Shepherd], *Odes Descriptive*

---

[1] Joseph Warton, 'Advertisement' to *Odes on Various Subjects* (London, 1746).
[2] We know that he had not read Collins' work before 1784 (*Letters*, II, 177).

and Allegorical (London, 1761). Dodsley's *Collection*, 5th ed. (vols. 1–3; 2nd ed. of vol. 4; 1st ed. of vols. 5–6: London, 1758), gives a good and large selection of odes. References to Cowper's later use of the epithets (from *Poems*) are given at the end of each note.

*   *   *

The St James's Magazine, II (April 1763), 118–25.

To the EDITOR of the ST. JAMES'S MAGAZINE.

SIR,

I hope I shall not be thought to depreciate the excellent professions of the Reading or Writing-Master, by attempting a third, which is no less necessary, and of equal importance to the literary world, The Penman, will, I know, fling his *copy* in my teeth, and challenge me with insulting his favourite BUCKINGHAM, who, in his treatise upon Writing and Writing-masters, affirms, that

Nature's chief master-piece is WRITING WELL.[1]

A sentiment, which I have often heard my friend GOOSEQUILL say, deserves to be written in letters of gold. Yet, though I honour my friend's zeal, when I consider that

Ten censure wrong, for one who *writes* amiss,[2]

If I can form a rule to be the standard of opinion, and guide to judgment, I shall not, I trust, repent me of my labours, in this discerning age, which leaves no merit unrewarded. It has hitherto been customary to persue that science, in which I flatter myself I am now a perfect adept, through public schools, and regular universities, by a laborious perusal of a set of musty Antients, and hum-drum old fellows, that a gentleman would be ashamed to be acquainted with; my method is more compendious, and as infallible, as thousands whom I have taught are ready to certify. Permit me therefore, through your Magazine, to offer the following dissertation, as a specimen of my abilities, and at the same time to inform the public, that I propose to teach the whole ART of

---

[1] [John Sheffield, D. of Buckingham], *An Essay upon Poetry* (London, 1682), p. 1; the poems begin: 'Of Things in which Mankind does most excell, | Nature's chief Master-piece is writing well.'

[2] Pope, *Essay on Criticism*, I, 6.

Poetry, upon a new plan, upon modern principles, illustrated with examples from modern poets, *at an easy expence,* and *without any loss of time.* Let the universities (the foreign ones I mean) say as much.

I am, Sir,

Yours, &c.

A Taste Master.

A Dissertation on the Modern Ode.[1]

An Ode, says the critic, is a very difficult species of writing. It requires a strength of fancy, sublimity of sentiment, curious elegance of diction, and though it seems perpetually flying off from its subject, an artful connection of parts, so as to make together one beautiful whole. These indeed might have been proper notions in their day, but at present sound only as the language of pedantry. For my part, I am not only convinced that it is no difficult species of writing, but will undertake to prove, that it is the easiest to attain, as being dependant upon certain rules, which, if duly observed, are an infallible guide to excellence.

I cannot but congratulate the present age upon the multitude of odes, single and in sets, which have generously been offer'd to our perusal; generously, I may say with strict propriety, and for *our* entertainment, since the authors seem to have had no interested views towards *Posterity.* The advantages, indeed, peculiar to this composition, are so many, and so obvious, that it is no wonder, every young muse should here first try her strength, where the honour is great, and the danger trifling.

But of the many advantages this species of writing is possessed of, I shall consider only three, and those by no means contemptible.

The variety of subjects it admits of,

The powers of description which it so eminently calls forth, and becomes so easily master of. And

The great convenience of its irregular measure.

The first advantage proposed is too evident to be contested. Let

---

[1] The 'Dissertation' was reprinted in the *Public Advertiser,* 16 Aug. 1763; at the end of the essay the source is given as follows: '[Loyd's Mag.].' To my knowledge it has not been reprinted since.

but the poet sit down and 'The world is all before him where to chuse'[1] both animal and intellectual. Though I would advise him by all means, in the infancy of his muse, to stick to the last, and try his hand upon the four CARDINAL VIRTUES; which, besides that they will give him an opportunity of consulting the *Head* and *Tail-pieces* of books for rich sentiment, will also help him to good store of imagery, as they have been reduced into emblems, and engraved in elegant designs by the greatest masters in those arts. Poetry and Painting we know are sisters, and as the painter often-times borrows his subjects from the strong imagination of the poet; the poet, in return, may draw his descriptions from the exact pencilling of the painter: Thus it is, those ingenious gentlemen excel, who versify at the bottom of a political print, and stand forth as the *writing* Raree-show men of wonderful Caricatures. In short, there is nothing in the creation that will not afford matter for an ode. It comes forth with equal propriety on the death of a king or a tom-tit, on a great minister, or a common whore, on the ruin of a nation, or the fall of a tobacco-box: And it has this superiority over all other kinds of poetry, that, whereas in them you must weigh the subject maturely, and turn it over and over to find out its strength, culling and rejecting, disposing and arranging it in proper methods, here we are happily delivered from all this trouble. Every object, in or out of nature, is matter enough for a modern to work upon, without fretting his imagination, or hazarding his judgment.

As for the DESCRIPTIVE, which we know is the first beauty in poetry, as it has often so eminently 'held the place of sense,'[2] mark how readily it follows; as thus—Whether the poet addresses himself to Wisdom or Folly, Mirth or Melancholy, he breaks out in a fine enthusiasm, with an 'Oh, or Hail,'[3] or some such pathetic expression, which naturally leads him to a description in at least fourteen lines, of the person and dwelling of no matter whom, which, with some observations upon her equipage and attendance, no matter what, make two stanzas, struck out from one word as it

---

[1] *Paradise Lost,* xii, 646.
[2] Pope, *Epistle to Dr Arbuthnot,* l. 148.
[3] Cowper himself would in later life begin fifteen poems with 'O' or 'Oh'. Maclean says that opening an ode addressed to a lofty allegorical conception with a 'Thou' or 'O thou' was a 'linguistic ritual' (*op. cit.* pp. 441–2).

UNCOLLECTED LETTERS AND ESSAYS

were; and all these beauties, according to the laws of the exactest critics, arise very naturally from the subject.[1]

But the greatest advantage is the variety of measure. It is no doubt very difficult to write correct rhime, and to include a sentiment in a couplet, is a *barbarous* confinement, and by no means sufferable amongst us, who have, it must be confess'd, so few to spare. This is again happily remedied in the modern ode, for there the poet may flow in the easy familiar, or rise into the epic, for half a dozen lines together; he may, in one verse, slide into a Lilliputian, and in the next straggle along in an Alexandrine, pairing them together like a dwarf walking by the side of a giant. He is not under the restraint of couplets, nor even rhiming alternately; if he finds it inconsistent with his sentiment to close the jingle at one line, he may leave it there for the present, as he is sure to catch it again at the turning of the next corner.

Such are evidently the advantages of Ode-writing. For which composition, I have with great pains drawn up certain infallible rules, whereby a student may learn to build the lofty Ode,[2] with as much regularity, and as true mechanical principles, as a mason or a bricklayer erects a wall: And as the laws of Epic Poetry have been extracted from the works of Homer, the laws relative to this species of writing, are drawn up from the performances of the modern professors of the art, and the most approved practice of Ode-mongers.

The first grand rule is the rule of Pathos.

In order to write pathetical (a most necessary ingredient in these compositions) never trouble yourself to express the warm emotions of the feeling heart, but get together a large quantity of Oh's and Ah's![3] and introduce them as—thus—Ah Me! Oh Thou! by

---

[1] Johnson wrote that from the 'accidental peculiarity of the ancient writers, the criticks deduce the rules of lyric poetry, which they have set free from all the laws by which other compositions are confined, and allow to neglect the niceties of transition, to start into remote digressions, and to wander without restraint from one scene of imagery to another' (*Rambler*, no. 158, 21 Sept. 1751).

[2] Parody of *Lycidas*, ll. 10–11: 'he knew | Himself to sing, and build the lofty rhyme'.

[3] Cowper had used 'Oh's' and 'Ah's' in at least fifteen of his short lyric poems written between 1750 and 1762 (in over half of those that remain). For example: *Ode...on the Marriage of a Friend* ('Ah me! how long bewilder'd and astray'); *On Her Endeavouring to Conceal Her Grief at Parting* begins 'Ah! wherefore should my weeping maid suppress | ... | Ah! why forbid the willing tears to flow?'—and the last stanza begins, 'Oh! then indulge thy grief, nor fear to tell' (*Poems*, pp. 277–8).

which means, as I have said before, you will slip more immediately into your subject, and show your knowledge of the Greek Οι μοι'ς and Αι Α'ς.[1]

And here I cannot help digressing a little, to take notice of the superiority which the Greek models (for we moderns now all write *professedly* on their plan) have over us in their pathetical exclamations, which they vary with the greatest elegance and propriety, adapting them to the soft manners of the female sex in the tender expletives of

$$\grave{\varepsilon} \ \grave{\varepsilon} \ \grave{\varepsilon} \ \grave{\varepsilon} \ \grave{\varepsilon} \ \grave{\varepsilon} \ \grave{\varepsilon} \ \grave{\varepsilon} \ \grave{\varepsilon} \ \grave{\varepsilon} \ \grave{\varepsilon} \ \acute{\varepsilon}^2$$

and to the hardy roughness of the male in the emphatical

Ωτο τοτο τοτο τοτο τοτο τοτο τοτο το. ÆSCHYL.[3]

Sounds infinitely superiour to the Oh's and Ah's, Alack's, and Alas's, of our days, which have no distinction of sexes.

I have mentioned the Greek poets as being the models our present writers endeavour to work after, but I desire not to carve out so much labour and inconvenience to the gentlemen professors of *modern-antient* poetry, as the necessity to reading those authors would subject them to. It is sufficient if they put at the head of the several parts of their odes (if they are introduced in the supplemental manner of chorusses to tragedies) STROPHE, EPODE, ANTISTROPHE, together with certain hard names of peculiar feet, such as *Trochaic's, Pyrric's, Iambics, Anapests, Cretics,*[4] or any other appellations of measure to be found in the second leaf of every schoolboy's Gradus. These will satisfy the *learned* reader with the abundance of the writer's erudition; and the *unlearned* one will be agreeably surprised to find his own common conversation, or (if he has a tendency towards rhime) his *common* versification made up of numbers he never knew the names of, instead of discovering with astonishment, like MONSʳ. JOURDAIN,[5] that he talks *Prose,*

---

[1] Roughly the same as the 'Ah Me! Oh Thou!' above.
[2] The original did not have an acute accent on the last 'ε'.
[3] The quotation is probably Cowper's exaggeration of l. 158 in *Choëphoroe*, ὀ'τοτοτοτοτοτοῖ: 'Woe! woe! woe!'
[4] The original read '*Creties*'. *Cretics* are metrical feet consisting of one short syllable between two long.
[5] Molière, *Le Bourgeois Gentilhomme*, II, iv.

will be happy to find he has been in the *capability* of verse all his life long, without knowing it. Yet however these gentlemen may have worn the garb of the antients, I am far from charging them with any internal resemblance. They have indeed got their model in clay, but have stolen no beam of light to inform it. But as it is necessary that we should *profess* working after the pattern of these celebrated masters, I shall give the student an infallible rule to proceed by in this case, without having recourse to their warehouses.

And this is my second great rule of *Classicality*.

Take MILTON, read his shorter poems,[1] and particularly LYCIDAS, COMUS and SAMPSON; wherever you meet with an epithet, more especially, if it be a compound one, put it in your notebook; for as MILTON copied the antients, the more you steal from MILTON,[2] of consequence the nearer you come to the antients.

This precept, in regard to epithets, deserves very particular attention, as upon a due observance in the choice of them depends the whole beauty of modern Poetry. There is besides an art of variation in the use of them, very necessary to be learnt, and which is proper to be explained in this place. The instances indeed, for the better illustration, are extremely familiar. The words Fountain and Stream have in all ages had attendant epithets to wait upon them, which were no more than *murmuring, querulous,* &c. but

---

[1] Cowper is satirizing the great vogue of Milton's shorter poems which had begun about 1740 after they had been neglected for nearly a hundred years. Poets like Gray, Mason, Collins, and the elder Warton praised Milton and his shorter poems especially; they 'imitated each of his poems in turn, borrowed words, phrases, or lines from him, and were so saturated with his works that many of their imitations and borrowings were undoubtedly unconscious' (Raymond Dexter Havens, *The Influence of Milton on English Poetry* (Cambridge, Mass., 1922), pp. 435–6; also pp. 419–38).

[2] Gray wrote to his friend Richard West, 8 May 1742, complimenting him on his *Ode* (to May) which was 'very picturesque, Miltonic, and musical' (Gray's *Corr.* I, 202). According to Havens, the reader may expect on the average at least one verbal borrowing from Milton on every page of Gray (p. 458). West's *Monody on the Death of Queen Caroline,* in Dodsley's *Collection* (London, 1748), II, 269–75, and Mason's *Musaeus, a Monody to the Memory of Mr. Pope, in Imitation of Milton's Lycidas* (London, 1747) imitate *Lycidas* in form and are filled with Miltonisms. Mason's *Il Bellicoso* and *Il Pacifico* are slavish imitations of Milton, and his odes, *For Music, To Independency,* and *To the Naval Officers of Great Britain* are also greatly indebted to *L'Allegro* and *Il Penseroso* (see Havens, p. 461). See also Scott's *To Wisdom* which begins 'Hence vain, deluding Joys' and ll. 11–12: 'But come thou Goddess sage, and mild, | Jove's first begotten darling Child!'

we, who love, not only to make persons of inanimate objects, but also to give them the powers of real life, are not content with a *Rill* (for that is now the fashionable expression)[1] that runs along *weeping* and *tinkling*,[2] unless it also *babbles* and *prattles*.[3] A stone must be a mouldring,[4] or perhaps for alliteration sake, a Smouldring one; oaks must be bound in *Ivy-chains*,[5] and a Tower will make a very insignificant appearance that is not *moss-grown*[6] as well as *cloud-capt*.[7]

The FIGURES which may easiest be introduced, are the ECPHONEMA[8] or EXCLAMATION, which, I believe, joined with the ANTITHESIS or SEE-SAW will be sufficient for the author to labour at, and the rest may fall in occasionally. As the HYPERBOLE is the greatest[9] fault in composition, I need not caution any modern practitioners against it, as we in general are so fearful of knocking out our brains against the stars, that like geese, we even duck our heads under a barn-door. Nor can I perceive any danger of our falling into those extravagancies from the flights of an over-

---

[1] 'Rill': Gray, *Elegy*, l. 111; *Progress of Poesy*, l. 4; Mason, *Elfrida*, 3rd Ode, p. 37, l. 10; *To a Water-Nymph*, in Dodsley, III, 299, l. 14; 300, l. 5; *Ode...Newcastle*, in Dodsley, IV, 270, l. 21; Colman and Lloyd, *Ode to Obscurity*, III, i, 12; *Ode to Oblivion*, I, 10; Warton, *To a Lady Who Hates the Country*, p. 38, l. 9; Wodhull, pp. 5, 14; Shepherd, pp. 6, 7, 22. Many poems, especially the odes, in Dodsley's *Collection* illustrate the excessive use of this word. Cowper later used it—for example, in *Charity*, l. 367; *Task*, I, 192 and IV, 64; *In Memory of John Thornton*, l. 38.

[2] 'weeping and tinkling': Mason, *On Melancholy*, ll. 13–14 ('As drops this little weeping rill | Soft-tinkling down the moss-grown hill')—these two lines contain four of the words which Cowper criticizes: *weeping, rill, tinkling,* and *moss-grown*; Colman and Lloyd, *Ode to Oblivion*, l. 10 ('tinkling, weeping rill'). Cowper, *Progress of Error*, l. 14 ('the chime of tinkling rills').

[3] See Gray, *Elegy*, l. 104 ('the brook that babbles by').

[4] 'mouldring': Gray, *Elegy*, l. 14; Mason, *On Melancholy*, p. 16, l. 14 ('Where Ivy chains each mould'ring stone'); *Elfrida*, 4th Ode, p. 51, l. 18 ('mould'ring clay'); Warton, *To a Gentleman upon his Travels thro' Italy*, p. 24, l. 7 ('mould'ring walls'); Wodhull, p. 19, l. 17 ('mould'ring pile'). Cowper, *Hope*, l. 351 ('mould'ring abbey walls'); *Task*, IV, 235 ('some rugged rock or mould'ring tow'r').

[5] 'Ivy-chains': Gray, *Elegy*, l. 9 ('ivy-mantled tow'r'). Cowper, *Charity*, l. 95 ('ivy mantled den').

[6] 'moss-grown': Gray, *Ode on the Spring*, l. 13 ('moss-grown beech'); Mason, *To Memory*, II, 21 ('moss-grown cave'); *Elfrida*, 1st Ode, p. 4, l. 13 ('moss-grown tow'r'); Colman and Lloyd, *Ode to Oblivion*, l. 6 ('moss-grown cell'). Cowper, *Shrubbery*, l. 18 ('moss-grown alley').

[7] 'cloud-capt': Gray, *Bard*, l. 57 ('cloud-top'd'); Colman and Lloyd, *Ode to Obscurity*, II, ii, 2 ('cloud-capt Ode'). Cowper, *Heroism*, l. 4 ('tow'r'd a cloud-capt pyramid').

[8] The original read 'ECPHOMENA'. *Ecphonema* is a rhetorical figure: 'to cry out'.

[9] Owing to a printer's error the original read: 'is the greatest is the greatest'.

heated imagination, whilst we go as cautiously to work upon a poem, as if it were, as indeed it really is, no more than a piece of mechanism.

There are, it is true, many niceties to be attended to in the well-ordering the musical part of these compositions; but, as every genius of sixteen is already a master of the proper pauses, cadences, &c. necessary to the perfection of jingle, any instructions upon this head would be altogether useless and impertinent. Allitteration is the artificial all in all of poetry. The Epithet must not only agree with the substantive; but even wear its livery, and ape the fashion of its master. Hence it must always begin with the same letter, and those verses are the most finished in which there are two substantives, two adjectives, and one verb. The verb standing in the middle to keep the peace, and the adjectives preceeding their respective substantives, as a bodyguard.[1] But a whole line, where every word begins alike,[2] is a master-piece of execution, and to be met with only amongst your first-rate geniuses. Though even this may be attained by a careful study of the alphabetical lists in BYSSHE's art of poetry,[3] and DYCHE's spelling-book.[4]

But that I may not be supposed to have drawn up rules which I am unable to practise, in my next I shall present you with a perfect ode, of which I shall only say with Horace,

Speret idem, sibi quivis.[5]

Yours, W. C.

---

[1] Gray, *Ode on the Death of a Favourite Cat*, l. 41 ('And heedless hearts, is lawful prize'); *Bard*, l. 31 ('Brave Urien sleeps upon his craggy bed'); *Elegy*, l. 8 ('And drowsy tinklings lull the distant folds'); Mason, *To an Æolus's Harp*, in Dodsley, IV, 274, l. 10 ('Bright June extends her fragrant reign'); *To Independency*, l. 15 ('Unsullied Honor decks thine open brow'); *To a Water-Nymph*, in Dodsley, III, 299, l. 3 ('The circling sea-nymphs told alternate tales').

[2] Gray, *Bard*, l. 49 ('Weave the warp, and weave the woof'); Colman and Lloyd, *Ode to Obscurity*, III, i, 6 ('The whiles he wins his whiffling way').

[3] Edward Bysshe, *The Art of English Poetry* (London, 1702); 9th ed. (1762).

[4] Thomas Dyche, *A Guide to the English Tongue*, 1st ed. (London, 1709); 45th ed. (1764). Or *The Spelling Dictionary*, 2nd ed. (London, 1725), 3rd ed. (1731).

[5] *Ars Poetica*, 240–1.

[XIV]

Saturday. 4 January 1766. Joseph Hill.
Address: To M⁏ Joseph Hill Cook's Court Carey Street near Lincolns Inn Fields London.
Postmark illegible.
Hertford County Record Office: Panshanger Collection.[1]

My dear Sephus:

E'er many Suns have risen and set You will receive a Draught of mine payable to M⁏ Reade Peacock,[2] for the Sum of 13. 12. 0.— For aught I know I may have drawn for more than I am worth, and if I have, I must refer you to your next Receipts to set that matter right. In the mean time if my Affairs here continue to proceed in the same even Course as at present, I comfort myself with the Thoughts of drawing no more this half Year, and then only for the Payment of M⁏ Unwin.[3]

Unwin the Younger is now in Town, and if you should happen to be at Ashley's[4] when he calls there, you will see one of the most aimable young Men I ever met with. I hope my Uncle will make much of him, for if he sees two more such before he dies, he will have better Fortune than falls to the Share of most men.

If I had built this House and chosen my Company, I could not have been better fitted, and so perhaps my Brother has told you; if he has not, I remember I told you so before,[5] and it will be well

---

[1] One sentence from this letter was publ. in Sotheby, Wilkinson and Hodge Cat., 20–2 May 1878, lot 107 [from the collection of William Hayley].

[2] Reade Peacock, a draper, was Cowper's first friend at Huntingdon. On 3 July 1765 Cowper had written to Hill: 'I have received but one visit since here I came. I don't mean that I have refused any, but that only one has been offered. This was from my woolen-draper; a very healthy, wealthy, sensible, sponsible man, and extremely civil. He has a cold bath, and has promised me a key of it, which I shall probably make use of in the winter. He has undertaken, too, to get me the *St. James's Chronicle* three times a week, and to show me Hinchinbrook House [the seat of the Cromwells], and to do every service for me in his power; so that I did not exceed the truth, you see, when I spoke of his civility.' By 27 Oct. 1766 his draper's bill had again mounted to about £16, and he feared that he had waited 'so long for payment that in a little time my credit and interest in that gentleman will begin to totter' (*Letters*, I, 27, 75, 82).

[3] The Rev. Morley Unwin, with whom Cowper lived. He was the father of William Cawthorne Unwin. Cowper's plans did not work out. On 10 March he had to advise the payment of the remainder of Dr Cotton's account, £65. In May he had to pay not only Mr Unwin's bill, but also his servants' wages and half a year's maintenance of Dick Coleman; the total, about £60 (*Letters*, I, 61, 64; see below, p. 220).

[4] Ashley Cowper, William's uncle.

[5] The letter is missing from the correspondence as publ. or as known to me in MSS.

if I don't repeat it in my next. I strike Root here every day deeper and deeper, as Vegetables are apt to do in a Soil which suits them. Not that I lead the Life of a Vegetable, Mr Animal! for I assure you I never conversed with any body that kept my Mind in better Training or more constant Exercise than Mrs Unwin does, but I make the Comparison by way of humble Acquiescence in the Imputation which you Londoners are apt to fasten upon us Rustics.

That I may not overload the Post Horse this slippery Weather, I conclude myself my dear Joe with my Love to all your Family and my own,

Y^r ever Affectionate Wm Cowper.

Hunt^n

Jan 4. 1766.   [xv]

Monday. 11 February 1766. Joseph Hill.
Sotheby, Wilkinson and Hodge Cat., 20–2 May 1878, lot 108 [from the collection of William Hayley].[1] Extract from catalogue.

It is my fixt purpose to live upon my income; in which resolution I am supported by reflecting, that I have nothing else to live upon.

[xvi, xix–xx]

THREE letters from Cowper to his cousin Maria Frances Cecilia (Madan) Cowper (1726–97) are included to show Hayley's method of editing. Each contains material hitherto unpublished. No editor after Hayley had access to the manuscripts of these letters; Southey follows Hayley (1803, I, 41–3, 56–8, 60–2), and Wright, Southey.

Hayley wrote to Lady Hesketh on 1 November 1805: 'from the Mass of his interesting Manuscripts, most kindly submitted to me, by his different Friends, for my Revisal & Selection, instead of being desirous of publishing all, he wrote, I suppressed perhaps *even more, than I printed.*'[2] His suppressions stretch from single words and sentences to paragraphs and whole letters. These bits which he omitted are frequently the most interesting: the frankest revelations concerning Cowper himself, his family and friends; the most personal expression of his religious beliefs or of the ludicrous

---

[1] An additional unpubl. letter to Hill, 23 Aug. 1766, is listed in the sale (lot 112), 'relating to business matters', but no quotation from it is given.

[2] Copy of letter written by Hayley, in his *Memoirs* (MS.), VI, 116.

foibles of the world about him; the darkest moments of his despair.[1] Some of the suppressions were necessary, Hayley believed, in order to spare any hurt to people who were still alive. For example, later in Cowper's correspondence he omits one of the finest small portraits.[2] It is a slashing and humorous glance at the Olney schoolmaster Teedon, 'the most obsequious, the most formal, the most pedantic of all creatures'. Cowper goes on to create a hilarious picture of this stodgy and affected pedant. 'I think that Sheridan would adore him', he writes;[3] and Sheridan would have adored Cowper's description even more. But this we must do without, and to go to the other extreme of Cowper's character, anything excessively Evangelical—for Lady Hesketh's sake. 'It is my wish', she wrote to John Johnson, 'that...nothing should be brought forward that should cause him to be considered as a Visionary! an Enthusiast! or a *Calvinist*! for I am *very sure* he was neither in reality.'[4] Hayley also disposed of notes of greeting or thanks and other small pieces of ordinary, daily life.

But Hayley went beyond this, which seemed to him necessary for the sake of the family and friends or for poetic reputation. He touched up a phrase here and there, improving and correcting what he thought had been perhaps written in haste. And sometimes he simply read and copied carelessly. These silent corrections and omissions are indicated in the notes to the letters of 4 April 1766 and 11 March and 3 April 1767. Only changes of words are given, however; none of Hayley's normalizations and modernizations (the style of 1800 instead of 1760), changes to lower-case, changes of punctuation, or his rearrangements of paragraphs.

The letters of Cowper's Evangelical period are permeated with scriptural allusions. I have only indicated a few of the more prominent references in the first of the three letters. In this the Holy Scriptures are referred to by direct quotations—whole

---

[1] Greatheed wrote: 'All the letters that I have entire touched on his dispair. These passages Mr Hayley has regulery [*sic*] omitted, and, I dare say that there are few if any among the letters published that have not similar chasms': [Greatheed], 'Memoranda respecting Cowper the Poet': John Rylands Libr. Eng. MS. 352/55, f. 4.

[2] Hayley (1803), I, 42–3.

[3] *Poems* (Bailey), pp. xxix–xxx.

[4] Hesketh, *Letters*, pp. 113–14; also her letter to Hayley, 16 Dec. 1803: Add. MSS. 30803 B, f. 153.

phrases or verses—with occasional modifications. By the time of the second letter to Mrs Maria Cowper (no. xix), a year later, the Bible has been digested into the Evangelical jargon, which was so displeasing to many people outside the group. Word after word has an emphatic Biblical ring, but few phrases remain in entirety. It is as if Cowper (here the typical Evangelical) has created his own texts, his own Scriptures, with an emphasis on those images and doctrines which peculiarly satisfied his needs and the beliefs of his group.

Textual notes in the following letter are from Hayley (1803), I, 41–3.

* * *

Friday. 4 April 1766. Mrs Maria Cowper.
Address: Mrs Cowper at the Park house near Hartford Hartfordshire
Postmark: 5 AP
Hertford County Record Office: Panshanger Collection.

My dear Cousin,

I agree with you that Letters are not essential to Friendship, but they seem to be a natural Fruit of it, when they are the only Intercourse that can be had. And a Friendship producing no sensible Effects is so like Indifference, that the Appearance may easily deceive even an acute Discerner. I retract however all that I said in my last upon this Subject,[1] having reason to suspect that it proceeded from a Principle which I would discourage in myself upon all Occasions, even a Pride that felt itself hurt upon a mere Suspicion of Neglect. I have so much Cause for Humility, and so much need of it too, and every little sneaking Resentment is such an Enemy to it, that I hope I shall never give Quarter to any thing that appears in the Shape of Sullenness or Self-Consequence hereafter. Alas! if my best Friend, who laid down his Life for me,[2] were to remember all the Instances in which I have neglected Him, and to plead them against me in Judgment, where should I hide my guilty Head in the Day of Recompense! I will pray therefore for Blessings upon my Friends even though they cease to be so, and upon my Enemies though they continue such.

The deceitfullness of the natural Heart, the Mystery of Iniquity

---

[1] See letter of 11 March 1766, first paragraph: *Letters*, I, 62.
[2] John xv. 13.

that works there,* is inconceivable. I know well that I passed upon my Friends for a person at least religiously inclined, if not actually religious, and what is more wonderfull, I even† thought myself a Christian. Thought myself a Christian‡ when I had no Faith in Christ, when I saw no Beauty in him that I should desire him,¹ in short when I had neither Faith, nor Love nor any Christian Grace whatever, but a thousand Seeds of Rebellion instead, evermore springing up in Enmity against him. Thus qualified for the Christian Life, and by the additional Help of a little Hypocritical attendance upon Ordinances, I thought myself as well off in point of Security as most, and though my Iniquities had set me on fire round about, I knew it not, and though they burned me, yet I laid it not to heart.§² But Blessed be God, even the God who is become my Salvation!,³ the Hail of Affliction and Rebuke for Sin, has swept away the Refuge of Lies.⁴ It pleased the Almighty in great Mercy to me,‖ to set all my Misdeeds before me, and to thunder into my very Heart with the Curses of his Broken Law in such manner that for near a Twelvemonth I beleived myself Sealed up under eternal wrath and yᵉ Sentence of unquenchable Vengeance.⁵ Then all my Christian Seeming, all my fair & specious Professions which had been my Support and Confidence before, became the Objects of my Horror and Detestation.¶ At length the Storm being past, and having answered all the gracious purposes of Him who sent it forth to convince me of Sin, of Righteousness, and of Judgment,**⁶ a quiet and peacefull Serenity of Soul succeeded, such as ever attends the Gift of a†† lively Faith in the all-sufficient attonement, and the sweet Sense of Mercy and Pardon purchased by the Blood of Christ. Thus did he break me

* the Mystery of Iniquity that works there: *omitted.*
† even: *omitted.*   ‡ Thought myself a Christian: *omitted.*
§ Thus qualified...to heart: *omitted.*   ‖ to me: *omitted.*
¶ and to thunder...Detestation: *omitted.*
** and having answered...Judgment: *omitted.*
†† a: *omitted.*

---

¹ Isaiah xliii. 2.   ² Isaiah xlii. 25.
³ Psalm lxviii. 19.   ⁴ Isaiah xxviii. 17.
⁵ See 'Lines Written during a Period of Insanity'; begins: 'Hatred and vengeance, my eternal portion'; ends: '*I*, fed with judgment, in a fleshly tomb, am | Buried above ground' (*Poems*, pp. 289–90).   ⁶ John xvi. 8.

and bind me up, thus did he wound, me and his Hands made whole.[1]

My dear Cousin! I make no Apology for entertaining you with the History of my Conversion, because I know you to be a Christian in the Sterling Import of the Appellation. This is however but a very summary account of the matter, neither would a Letter contain the astonishing Particulars of it. If we ever meet again in this World I will relate them to you by Word of Mouth, if not they will serve for the Subject of a Conference in the next, where I doubt not I shall remember and record them with a gratitude better suited to the Subject.

It will give me great Pleasure to hear from you; and though I know you are not fond of Writing, and do well remember the Complaints you used to make of the Necessity that obliged you to it, yet I shall hope that considering the much nearer Relation in which we now stand to each other than when we were only Cousins, being at length Members of the same Mystical Body,[2] I shall hope I say that your Love for a Brother will over come what your Affection for an ordinary Connection would probably yield to, & that you will find in your Heart to write to one who will remember you in his Prayers and hopes for a Place in yours.

How I shall rejoice to see the Major[3] and M.ᵣ Cleator![4] My love to 'em both and to all your Family.*

Y.ʳˢ my dear Cousin! affectionately

W.ᵐ Cowper.

April 4. 1766.

* It will give...Family [*last two paragraphs*]: *omitted.*

---

[1] Job v. 18.

[2] See Romans xii.

[3] Maria Cowper's husband William, a Major in the Hertfordshire Militia (*Madan Family*, p. 122), and himself a correspondent of Cowper (*Letters*, I, 51).

[4] I have not been able to identify him. The handwriting is difficult to read at this point. Cowper may have written 'Chator', in which case it is possible that this is the 'Mr. Chater', an Independent clergyman, who in 1783 was seeking a barn at Olney in which to preach. Cowper said: 'He is disposed to think the dissatisfied of all denominations may possibly be united under his standard; and that the great work of forming a more extensive and more established interest than any of them, is reserved for him' (*Letters*, II, 45). Presumably he is Thomas Chater, who in 1800 wrote *A Poetical Tribute to the Memory of William Cowper* (8vo, 1s.): see Robert Watt, *Bibliotheca Britannica* (Edinburgh, 1824).

APPENDIX A

[XVII]

Saturday. 3 May 1766. Joseph Hill.
The Rev. Wilfrid Cowper Johnson, Norwich.

My dear Sephus,

Excuse the Trouble I give you. An Old Friend of M⸢ʳ⸣ Unwin's died this Morning, and M⸢ʳ⸣ Unwin has occasion to send an Express to his Ex̄ōr at Bath. the Post-Master here says he can send it to London, but cannot get it through the General Post Office unless there be somebody to pay the Freight of it there. M⸢ʳ⸣ Unwin is not sure that any of his London Friends or Kindred are now in Town, and yᵉ thing requiring immediate Dispatch, for the Old Gentle-man can't be buried 'till the Express returns, I take yᵉ Liberty to trouble You with it. M⸢ʳ⸣ Unwin will account with Me, and I must[?] account with You for yᵉ Payment at yᵉ Post Office

Y⸢ʳˢ⸣ Wᵐ Cowper.

Hunt⸢ⁿ⸣ May 3. 1766

[XVIII]

Friday. 9 May 1766. Joseph Hill.
Address: To M⸢ʳ⸣ Joseph Hill Cookes Court Carey Street London.
Postmarks: HUNTINGDON 12 [?] MA
Houghton Library, Harvard: The Locker-Lampson–Warburg–Grimson Album: FMS Eng 870 (64A).[1]

My dear Sephus!

Faith was never yet the Fruit of Controversy; I have therefore no more than You, an Appetite to it, both because I have not Talents for such a Task, and because I should despair of any good Effect of it. I shall therefore content myself with supporting my Opinion of Faith in Christ by a Text or two from Scripture, and there leave, and take leave of the Argument.

We both beleive that our Saviour was the Messiah or the Sent of God. His Words upon the Subject are, He that beleiveth shall be Saved, He that beleiveth not shall be Damned.[2] You think I ascribe too much to Faith—Our Saviour ascribes All to it. No need of a Commentator upon Words so very explicit as these.

---

[1] This letter was listed without quotation in Sotheby, Wilkinson and Hodge Cat., 20–2 May 1878, lot 111 [from the collection of William Hayley], and Frederick Locker-Lampson, *The Rowfant Library* (London, 1886), p. 200. It was purchased at the Hayley sale by Locker-Lampson according to the marked copy of the sale in the B.M.
[2] Mark xvi. 16.

218

But how is it possible say you that Faith can be of such high Estimation in the Sight of God—Again our Saviour Answers—If ye Beleive not that I am He, Ye shall Die in your Sins.[1] But what does he mean when he says to us, Ye must beleive that *I am He*? Doubtless that We must beleive him to have taken away ye Sins of the World by ye Sacrifice of himself. But can this Persuasion Justifie us?—the Scripture says, in Him, they who *beleive* are *freely* Justified from all things.[2] and even the Just themselves shall live— how? by Works? nay but by Faith.[3] What then becomes of Works? say you; The Scripture says, that Faith *Worketh* by Love.[4] And every Man that merits the appellation he received in Baptism, can bear Testimony to this Truth from the Bottom of his Heart. So then the Word of the Almighty assures us that we are justified *freely* by Faith *working* by Love, and this in the plainest Language, in Terms the most express and certain.

But you think at this rate few shall be saved. Our Saviour says, narrow is the way and few there be that find it.[5] You see therefore that your Opinion in this Articl[e][6] coincides exactly with the Scripture.

My dear Joe! Variety Of Opinions in these things matters not. there is the same Variety in Matters of Science and Philosophy, but a Number of false Notions can never prove that there is not a true one. Let us humble our Hearts before God, and beseech him to *reveal his Son in us*,[7] according to ye Scripture Expression, and we shall soon see the Excellence of the Salvation wch Christ has purchased for us, and our own utter Insufficiency to be our own Redeemers.

I shall only add that admitting Christ to be ye Son of God and that He has himself annexed Salvation to Faith, wch he has certainly done, it is quite impossible to suppose y^t he has left no Account of that Faith behind him to which he has annext so great & precious a Recompense. We must take our Saviours Counsel to ye Jews therefore, & *Search ye Scriptures*, for in them we beleive y^t we have Eternal Life.[8]

---

[1] John viii. 24.   [2] Acts xiii. 39; Romans iii. 22–4.
[3] Habakkuk ii. 4; Romans i. 17; Galatians iii. 11; Hebrews x. 38.
[4] Galatians v. 6.   [5] Matthew vii. 14.
[6] Part of MS. covered by seal or torn in sealing and opening letter; also on following p.
[7] Galatians i. 16.   [8] John v. 39.

I shall be obliged to you if you will give my Love to Colman[1] when you see him next, & thank him for his Enquiries after me. The poem he wants is in a black Pocket Book or Letter Case amongst my Lumber in Town. If it can possibly be extricated from that Farrago of Stuff in wch it is at present dead & Buried, I shall be [glad to] have it restored to him accordg. to his Request.

I shall draw on you the 11th Ins^t for Mr Unwin's h[alf-yearly ren]t viz. 42^12.

I have little to say concerning myself, except that I am in good Health, and Happy; Neither have I known one uneasy Hour since into this House I came. My Brother also is well, and w^d send his Respects if he knew I was writing to you. My Love to all your Family and to the little Woman in Grosvenor Street[3] &c.

Yours ever

Wm Cowper.

Hunt^n.

May 9. 1766.

Pray let me know in your next the Name of the Ship to wch Sr Thos has consigned his Person.[4]

[XIX]

THE textual notes in the following letter are from Hayley (1803), 1, 56–8.

* * *

Wednesday. 11 March 1767. Mrs Maria Cowper.
Address: Mrs Cowper at the Park House near Hartford Hartfordshire
Postmark: 12 MR
Hertford County Record Office: Panshanger Collection.

My dear Cousin,

To find those whom I love, clearly and strongly persuaded of Evangelical Truth, gives me a Pleasure superior to any that this

---

[1] George Colman the Elder. Concerning the poem, see letter of 4 May 1767, below, p. 225.

[2] This was Cowper's first payment to the Unwins. He had moved into their home, 11 Nov. 1765 (Cowper's *Memoir*, p. 83). He continued his payments at half-yearly intervals (*Letters*, 1, 56, 61, 79, 83, and letter, below, p. 224, of 4 May 1767).

[3] This is presumably *not* the woman who in 1771 became Hill's wife, Sarah Mathews (1742–1824), who lived in Wargrave (*N. & Q.* 12th ser. v (1919), 259).

[4] Sir Thomas Hesketh, husband of Cowper's cousin Harriot Cowper ('Lady Hesketh'). He was a born sailor and kept at Southampton a yacht ('the good sloop the *Harriet*') on which Cowper had sailed (*Letters*, 11, 356–7).

World can afford me. Judge then, whether your Letter in which the Body and Substance of a saving Faith is so evidently set forth, could meet with a lukewarm Reception at my Hands, or be entertained with Indifference. Would you know the true Reason of my long Silence? Conscious that my Religious Principles are generally excepted against, and that the Conduct they produce wherever they are heartily maintained, is still more the Object of Disapprobation than those Principles themselves, and rememb'ring that I had made both the one and the other known to you, without having any clear Assurance that our Faith in Jesus was of the same Stamp & Character, I could not help thinking it possible that you might disapprove both my Sentiments and Practise, that you might think the One unsupported by Scripture, and the Other, whimsical and unnecessarily strict & rigorous, and consequently would be rather pleased with the Suspension of a Correspondence, which a different way of thinking upon so momentous a Subject as that we wrote upon, was likely to render tedious and irksome to you. I have told you the Truth from my Heart; forgive me these injurious Suspicions, and never imagine that I shall hear from you upon this delightfull Theme without a real Joy, or without Prayer to God to prosper you in the way of his Truth, his sanctifying and saving Truth.

The Book you mention lies now upon my Table. Marshall[1] is an old Acquaintance of mine; I have both read him and heard him read with Pleasure and Edification. The Doctrines he maintains are under the Influence of the Spirit of Christ, the very Life of my Soul, and the Soul of all my Happiness. That Jesus is a *present* Saviour, from the Guilt of Sin by his most precious Blood, and from the Power of it by his Spirit, that corrupt and wretched in ourselves, in Him, and in *Him only* we are complete,[2] that being united to Jesus by a lively Faith, we have a solid and Eternal

---

[1] Walter Marshall (1628–80), a presbyterian divine whose *Gospel-Mystery of Sanctification* (London, 1692; 7th ed. 1764) was an extremely popular work. The 6th ed. (1757) is introduced by a recommendatory letter from James Hervey (1714–58), dated 5 Nov. 1756 (p. x). Hervey, author of *Meditations and Contemplations* and *Dialogues between Theron and Aspasio*, was a particular favourite of Cowper at this time (see *Letters*, I, 70–1). Three days after this letter, Cowper wrote: 'I think Marshall one of the best writers, and the most spiritual expositor of Scripture I ever read....I never met with a man who understood the plan of salvation better, or was more happy in explaining it' (*Letters*, I, 90). [2] Colossians ii. 10.

Interest in his Obedience & Sufferings, to Justify us before the Face of our Heavenly Father, and that All this inestimable Treasure, the Earnest of which is in Grace, and it's Consummation in Glory, is *Given, freely Given* to us of God, without Regard to our Sins on the one hand, to hold it back, or to our imperfect Services on the other to bring it forward,* in short that he hath opened the Kingdom of Heaven to *all Beleivers,* these are the Truths which by the Grace of God, shall ever be dearer to me than Life itself, shall ever be placed next my Heart as the Throne whereon the Saviour himself shall sit, to sway all its Motions, and reduce that World of Iniquity and Rebellion to a State of Filial and affectionate Obedience to the Will of the most Holy.

These, my dear Cousin, are the Truths to which by Nature we are Enemies, they abase the Sinner and exalt the Saviour to a degree which the Pride of our Hearts, 'till Almighty Grace subdue† them, is determined never to allow. For the Reception of these Truths, of this *only Gospel,* it pleased the Lord to prepare me by many and great Afflictions, by Temporal Distress, by a Conscience full of the Terrors of Eternal Death, by the Fire of his Law. Thus humbled, I was glad to receive the Lord Jesus in his own appointed way; the Self righteous, Self justifying Spirit of Pride was laid low, and was no longer a Barrier, to shut in Destruction and Misery, and to keep out the Saviour.‡ May the Almighty reveal his Son in our Hearts continually more and more, and teach us to increase in Love towards him continually for having *given* us the unspeakable Riches of Christ.

My Love to my dear Friend the Major, & to all my little Cousins.[1] May the Lord Bless them & make them all true M[embe]²rs of his Mystical Body.§

Y[ʳˢ ever fai]²thfully Wᵐ Cowper

Mar: 11. 1767

* without Regard...it forward: *omitted.*
† subdue] Hayley: subdues.
‡ For the Reception...the Saviour: *omitted.*
§ My Love...Mystical Body: *omitted.*

---

[1] Living in 1767, two sons and two daughters: William (1750–98), Maria Judith (1752–1815), George (1754–87), Frances Cecilia (1764–1849): *Madan Family,* p. 243.
[2] Part of MS. torn away in opening seal.

[xx]

TEXTUAL notes in this letter are from Hayley, I, 60–2.

* * *

Friday. 3 April 1767. Mrs Maria Cowper.
Address: Mrs Cowper at the Park House Hartingfordbury near
Hartford
Postmark: 4 AP
Hertford County Record Office: Panshanger Collection.

My dear Cousin,

You sent my Friend Unwin[1] home to us, charm'd with your
kind Reception of him, and with every thing he saw at the Park.
Shall I once more give you a Peep into my vile and deceitful Heart?
What Motive do you think lay at the Bottom of my Conduct when
I desired him to call upon you? I did not suspect at first that Pride
and vainglory had any share in it, but quickly after I had recommended the Visit to him, I discovered in that fruitfull Soil the very
Root of the Matter. You know I am a Stranger here; all such are
suspected characters, unless they bring their Credentials with them.
To this moment I beleive it is matter of Speculation in the Place,
whence I came, and to whom I belong. My Story is of such
a Nature that I cannot satisfy this Curiosity by relating it, and to
be close and reserved as I am obliged to be, is in a manner to plead
guilty to any Charge their Jealousy may bring against me.*
Though My Friend you may suppose, before I was admitted an
Inmate here, was satisfied that I was not a mere Vagabond, and
has since that time received more convincing Proof† of my
Sponsibility! yet I could not resist the Opportunity of furnishing him
with Ocular Demonstration of it, by introducing him to one of
my most splendid Connections; that when he hears me called *that
Fellow Cowper*, which has happened heretofore, he may be able
upon unquestionable Evidence, to assert my Gentlemanhood, and
releive me from the Weight of that opprobrius Appellation. Oh
Pride, Pride! it deceives with the Subtlety of a Serpent, and seems
to walk erect, though it crawls upon the Earth. How will it twist
and twine itself about, to get from under the Cross, which is the

* My Story... against me: *omitted.*   † Proof] Hayley: proofs.

[1] William Cawthorne Unwin, who visited 'The Park' on 17 March (*Letters*, I, 89).

223

Glory of our Christian Calling to be able to bear with Patience and Good Will. They who can guess at the Heart of a Stranger, and you especially who are of a compassionate Temper, will be more ready perhaps to excuse me in this Instance, than I can be to excuse myself. But in good Truth it was abominable Pride of Heart, Indignation & Vanity, and deserves no better Name. How should such a Creature be admitted into those pure and sinless Mansions where nothing shall enter that defileth, did not the Blood of Christ applied by the Hand of Faith, take away the guilt of Sin, and leave no Spot or Stain behind it? Oh what continual Need have I of an Almighty, All sufficient Saviour!

I am glad you are acquainted so *particularly* with *all* the Circumstances of my Story, for I know that your Secresy and Discretion may be trusted with any thing. A Thread of Mercy ran through all the intricate Maze of those afflictive Providences, so mysterious to myself at the time, and which must ever remain so to all who will not see what was the great Design of them, 'till at* the Judgment Seat of Christ the whole shall be laid open. How is the Rod of Iron changed into a Sceptre of Love!

I thank you for the Seeds. I have committed some of each sort to the Ground, whence they will soon spring up like so many Mementos to remind me of my Friends at the Park. My Love attends Mr. Cowper and all my Cousins.

Y^{rs} ever Wm Cowper.†

April 3. 1767.

[XXI]

Monday. 4 May 1767. Joseph Hill.
The Rev. Wilfrid Cowper Johnson, Norwich.

Dear Joe,

The Day of Reckoning draws nigh. I shall draw upon you the Eleventh Inst^t for the Sum of Forty two pounds payable to Mr Unwin on Order, and soon after, for Payment of a Middle-sized Bill due to Mr Peacock the Draper. If these Draughts are inconsistent with the Discharge of my arrears to You, I shall insist upon satisfying them out of the Bank.

I have a Red Leather Trunk somewhere. If it is at your House,

* them, 'till at] Hayley: them; at.   † My Love...Cowper: *omitted.*

I shall be obliged to you for the Dispatch of it hither by the first convenient Opportunity; if Colman's Poem is any where to be found, I shall find it there, nor is that the only Valuable, or invaluable Trinket it contains, But the things I want most, are a pair of Gold Sleeve Buttons which were my Fathers.[1]

I beg you will give my Love to your Family, and believe me

Yours faithfully
Wm Cowper.

[XXII]

Saturday. 12 September 1767. Joseph Hill.
The Rev. Wilfrid Cowper Johnson, Norwich.

Dear Sephus,

A Man possessed of Lands in right of his Wife, dies, leaving his Son Exor. Do the Arrears of Rent down to the time of his Death belong to the Widow or the Son?

I am so important a Character in the present Circumstances of our Drama,[2] that I can't possibly be spared, and should undoubtedly turn the Tables upon you by inviting You to Olney, had we any Accomodation for you, but we are obliged to the Hospitality of a Friend for our own, & probably shall be so till Christmas.[3]

You will oblige me by a speedy Answer to the above Question,[4] & by delivering my Affectionate Respects to your Mother & Sisters.

Y^{rs} my dear Sephus
Wm Cowper.

Sep^t 12./67.

---

[1] The trunk in which Cowper's 'papers, &c.,...were all safely deposited' (*Letters*, I, 93) arrived before 16 July, when Cowper wrote: 'I found Colman's Poem in the Trunk, and have committed it to my Brothers care who will probably soon deliver it unto your Hands' (MS. in collection of the Rev. W. Cowper Johnson). I do not know to which poem Cowper refers.

[2] The removal from Huntingdon to Olney, 14 Sept.

[3] The friend was the Rev. John Newton. Mrs Unwin and Cowper were unable to move into their own house on 'the Parade, that is on the south side of the Market Place', until 15 Feb. 1768 (*Hist. MSS. Comm., 15th Report*, Appendix, Pt I (Dartmouth MSS.), pp. 183–6).

[4] On 21 Sept. Cowper sent thanks to Hill for his 'information in the law matter', but on 10 Oct. he was again asking a legal question about rents due to a widow when lands had been held by a man in right of his wife (*Letters*, I, 98–9). The questions arose owing to the death of the Rev. Morley Unwin.

B

UNCOLLECTED POEMS: EARLY AND LATE

[1]

THE following poem is possibly Cowper's. It is signed with his initials (often used by him as a signature) and it appeared in a magazine with which he might well have had connections: *The Student, or the Oxford Monthly Miscellany*.[1] This was the first publication in which Bonnell Thornton was concerned. The journal was published at Oxford for John Newbery, and according to Alexander Chalmers, 'SMART was the principal conductor, but THORNTON and other wits of both Universities occasionally assisted. THORNTON's first attempt appeared in the first number, "The Comforts of a Retired Life", an elegy in imitation of Tibullus. Mr. THOMAS WARTON was also a writer in the poetical department.'[2] Smart's contributions, however, did not appear until the Cambridge wits joined the staff in June 1750, but from that time on he contributed frequently to the *Student*.[3] Young writers outside the Oxford group had been encouraged to contribute and within a few months so many pieces had come from Cambridge men that the title of the journal was changed so that they might have, the editors said, 'an equal share of whatever merit may accrue from our work'.[4] Contrary to Chalmers' opinion, instead of Smart, Thornton appears to have been the prime mover in the undertaking, and may have served as the editor. According to Boswell, Thornton and Colman were the principal writers.[5] At least one

---

[1] This title was used for vols. i–v (Jan.–May 1750); thereafter, *The Student, or, the Oxford, and Cambridge Monthly Miscellany* (to July 1751). The magazine was publ. on the last day of the month. [2] Alexander Chalmers, *The British Essayists*, xxx, xxi.
[3] G. J. Gray, 'A Bibliography of the Writings of Christopher Smart, with Biographical References', *Trans. Bibl. Soc.* [London], vi (1900–2), 275–6; Robert Brittain, 'Christopher Smart in the Magazines', *Library*, 4th ser. xxi (1941), 320–36.
[4] Advertisements in the *Gen. Adv.* 10 Jan. and 30 June 1750, quoted in Charles Welsh, *A Bookseller of the Last Century* (London, 1885), p. 311.
[5] Boswell, *Johnson*, i, 209. However, Eugene R. Page believed that it was 'highly unlikely' that Colman was concerned in the *Student*. 'He was only eighteen years old

contribution may be attributed to Lloyd,[1] but for the most part the poems and essays are unidentifiable. The announcement of the magazine said that nothing was published which had been printed before, or without the consent of the author.

Not only for these reasons may the poem, 'A Reflection on the Year 1720', very well be Cowper's, but especially because of internal evidence: the description of the castaways and the storm over the sea, which is characteristic of Cowper. The images here bear a striking resemblance to others in Cowper's poetry. The metaphoric pattern of sea, storm, and castaway is the most common and most important in his work (see chapter VII).

*   *   *

The Student, or the Oxford Monthly Miscellany, 1 (31 January 1750), 34–5.

A REFLECTION *on the Year* 1720.[2]
By one of the south-sea directors.
Deus nobis hæc otia fecit. VIRGIL. [3]

THE clouds grew big, the thunder roll'd on high,
And missive fires swift darted thro' the sky;
The winds impetuous swept the ravag'd plain,
And dreadful tempests ruffled all the main;
The sea in mountains rais'd her foaming waves;
Wide gap'd the deep abyss, our watry graves;
Devouring harpies hover'd in the air,
And all around one scene of black despair.
On our devoted bark the tempest bore,
And threaten'd ship-wreck on a savage shore;
In vain the pilot did his art essay,
The rudder broke, the sails all torn away;

---

at the time and was still a student at Westminster. This theory probably arose because of the fact that in later years he and Thornton collaborated' (*Colman*, p. 26). Page appears to have done no real research on the matter: I therefore believe that Boswell's word is to be preferred to his. Colman was writing verses at Westminster (*Colman*, pp. 15–16), and he may well have sent some of them to Thornton, who had sought contributions from his old schoolmates. Colman matriculated at Christ Church, Oxon., 5 June 1751 (*Colman*, p. 19).

[1] 'On the Prefixing the Names of the *Muses* to the *Student*', *Student*, II, 273.
[2] The year the South Sea Bubble broke.
[3] Eclogue I, 6.

No creek, no friendly port, no shelter near,
Nor angry heav'n our ardent pray'rs would hear;
We, hapless, bulging on a rocky coast,
But for some pitying God had been for ever lost.
Now to that God my grateful voice I raise,
To speak my earnest thanks, and sing his praise.
To him I owe my life and little store,
My present ease, and this indulgent hour.
Near P——¹ village stands an ancient seat,
Far from the guilt and envy of the great.
Hither remov'd from business, care, and strife,
Blest with content I lead an happy life;
To wife and children, (rescued from the storm)
The kindest offices of love perform.
To her, the faithful friend in my distress,
For ever I'll my gratitude express
In dearest acts of lasting tenderness.
To these I virtue's steady precepts teach,
With generous principles their minds enrich;
To fly from base corruption's gilded bait,
And rather to be good than rich and great;
To serve their country and their country's friends,
Nor prostitute their votes to servile ends.
Here on the Thames I oft with pleasure gaze,
Whose silver stream in rich meanders strays
Thro' flow'ry meadows and delightful plains,
Where Ceres' bounty glads the lab'ring swains.
There distant hills adorn'd with lovely groves;
There shady walks to feast our mutual loves;
Here bleat the sheep, and there the cattle graze;
And shelter'd birds sing their harmonious lays.

---

¹ Probably Purley, a mile or two from Pangbourne. Purley Hall, an early seven-teenth-century mansion near the Thames, was the seat of Francis Hawes (d. 1764), an 'especially unscrupulous' director of the South Sea Company. He was the father of Frances Anne Hawes (1713–88), the notorious Lady Vane of Smollett's *Peregrine Pickle* ('The Memoirs of a Lady of Quality'). See *G.M.* xxxiv (1764), 450; *V.C.H....* *Berks*, iii, 417, 421; Lewis Melville [pseud. for Lewis S. Benjamin], *The South Sea Bubble* (London, 1921), p. 248; L. M. Knapp, *Tobias Smollett: Doctor of Men and Manners* (Princeton, 1949), p. 123, n. 76. I cannot suggest a reason why Cowper could have written this poem, but he may have known Hawes through his friend Joseph Hill of the Chancery, who had connections with Reading, not far from Purley.

The varied scene does nature represent,
As she appear'd when man was innocent.
Here is a welcome to a faithful friend,
With whom my days in tranquil ease I spend,
Talk o'er our troubles past, and my whole thoughts unbend.
   Thus blest on silken wings life flies away,
Nor wish I now, nor dread my latest day;
For by the change I only can remove
From fading joys below to endless joys above.

W. C.

[II]

THERE is a possibility that Cowper either wrote or revised the epitaph on the monument to General James Wolfe (1727–59) in the church at Westerham, Kent. A manuscript of this epitaph in Cowper's autograph was among the collection of his books and relics which went to John Johnson ('Johnny of Norfolk'), the son of Cowper's cousin, Catharine Donne Johnson. John Johnson divided Cowper's personal effects among his sons William, John, and Henry. The manuscript of the epitaph on Wolfe descended to John the younger, and then to his son the Reverend Henry Barham Johnson, whose widow finally sold it with her other Cowper items. Later the manuscript was sold by Maggs Brothers Ltd, who printed it in their catalogue: *Mercurius Britannicus No. 81* (July 1943), lot 59: price £5. 5s.

The monument was erected in Westerham (where Wolfe was born) in 1760 by 'some gentlemen in the parish'.[1] The only attribution of the authorship of the epitaph known to me is in Mrs Annie Elizabeth Wolfe-Aylward's *Pictorial Life of Wolfe*. She writes that 'the inscription is by the then Vicar, The Rev. George Lewis'.[2]

It is reasonable, of course, to suppose the manuscript is only a copy taken from the inscription as published in the *Gentleman's Magazine* in 1760, or from the tablet itself. But until the author is

---

[1] *G.M.* xxx (April 1760), 201. The text of the epitaph was printed on that page of the *Magazine*; also in Fawkes and Woty's *Poetical Calendar*, VIII (1763), 122.

[2] A. E. Wolfe-Aylward, *The Pictorial Life of Wolfe* (Plymouth, [1927]), p. 109, note beneath a photograph of the tablet in the Westerham Church. George Lewis (1712–71), Vicar of Westerham (1749–71): *Rec. Old Westm.* and *Suppl.; Alumni Oxon.*

more definitely identified, Cowper should remain a candidate. He frequently wrote epitaphs,[1] and his interest in Wolfe is well-known. Cowper wrote to Hill in 1782, recalling their days in the Temple: 'When poor Bob White brought me the news of Boscawen's success off the coast of Portugal, how I did leap for joy! When Hawke demolished Conflans I was still more transported. But nothing could express my rapture when Wolfe made the conquest of Quebec.'[2] And in *The Task* he wrote:

> Wolfe, where'er he fought,
> Put so much of his heart into his act,
> That his example had a magnet's force,
> And all were swift to follow whom all lov'd.[3]

Both William Cowper and George Lewis may have had a special connection with Wolfe's campaign through Dean Spencer Cowper. His wife's nephew, George Townshend, succeeded to the command at Quebec on the death of Wolfe (13 September 1759). Lewis was at Westminster with Spencer Cowper, and a contemporary at Oxford.[4] The Dean may have asked one of the family poets, or the Vicar, to provide an epitaph.

Cowper's manuscript differs from the copy in the *Gentleman's Magazine* (*G.M.*) and the tablet at Westerham (W.) only in spelling and punctuation. For example, in the first line:

W.] GEORGE   [*G.M.*] *George*   W.] His   [*G.M.*] his
W. and *G.M.*] laurel'd   W.] Head   [*G.M.*] head

The manuscript does not include the line from the *Aeneid*, VI, 546, at the bottom of the monument (printed also in the *Gentleman's Magazine*): 'I DECUS I NOSTRUM'.

*   *   *

---

[1] See, for example, *Poems*, pp. 363, 407, 420; and Cowper made alterations on epitaphs written by others: an example, that on the tomb of John Howard, the prison reformer, by John Bacon. J. Field, ed. *Correspondence of John Howard* (London, 1855), pp. 203–4.

[2] *Letters*, I, 436.   [3] *Task*, II, 248–51.

[4] But at a different college—Christ Church, not Exeter, which was Spencer Cowper's college. George Townshend (1724–1807) was 4th Vct and 1st M. Townshend.

Epitaph on Gen. Wolfe on a plain block of white marble in the church
of Westerham in Kent, erected at the expence of the parishioners.

Whilst George in sorrow bows his laurell'd head,
And bids the artist grace the soldier dead,
We raise no sculptur'd trophy to thy name,
Brave youth! the fairest in the list of fame.
Proud of thy birth, we boast the auspicious year,
Struck with thy fall, we shed a general tear,
With humble grief inscribe one artless stone,
And from thy matchless honours date our own.[1]

[III]

I N the manuscript of Hayley's *Vindication* there are copies of six
of Cowper's poems, in part or in whole, from Theadora Cowper's
small collection of the original manuscripts of his early verse.
Theadora had sent copies of these poems in her letters to Hayley.
Her whole collection was later published, rather poorly, by James
Croft in *Poems, the Early Productions of William Cowper* (1825).
The poems in Hayley's *Vindication* are: (1) 'William Was Once',
(2) 'The Symptoms of Love', (3) 'This Ev'ning Delia', (4) 'Bid
Adieu, My Sad Heart' (in the *Vindication* it is called: 'At Parting
in Hertfordshire'), (5) 'See Where the Thames', (6) 'How Quick
the Change'. Theadora changed some of the lines in one or two
of these poems in order to conceal references which she regarded
as personal. She also omitted a few stanzas for the same reason.
'The Symptoms of Love' is given here as found in the manuscript
of Hayley's *Vindication*, because the fifth stanza is new.[2]

*   *   *

THE SYMPTOMS OF LOVE[3]

I

Would my Delia know if I love, let her take
My last Thoughts at Night and the first when I wake
With my Prayers and best Wishes preferr'd for her Sake

---

[1] The verses are quoted from the Maggs Brothers Cat. I do not know the present
location of the MS.

[2] The poem is printed from Croft in *Poems*, p. 270.

[3] Hayley's *Vindication* (MS.), ff. 24–5.

2

Let her guess what I muse on when rambling alone
I stride oer the Stubble each day with my Gun
Never ready to shoot till the Covey is flown

3

Let her think what odd Whimsies I have in my Brain
When I read one Page over and over again
And discover at last that I read in vain

4

Let her say why so fixt and so steady my Look
Without ever regarding the Person who spoke
Still affecting to laugh without hearing the Ioke

5

Why when I would see how the dull Minutes pass
I apply to my Watch with a serious Face
And return it again just as wise as I was

6

O why when with Pleasure her Praises I hear
That sweetest of Melody sure to my Ear
I attend and at once inattentive appear

7

And lastly when summon'd to drink to my Flame
Let her guess why I never once mention her Name
Tho' *Herself* and the Woman I love, *are the same.*

[IV]

THE search for Cowper's translation of the *Henriade* began with
Hayley. He said that Cowper had written, 'as he informed me
himself, two entire Cantos of the Poem'.[1] The first report of the

---

[1] Hayley (1803), I, 28–9; also Hayley to Theadora and Lady Hesketh, 20 July and
21 Oct. 1801, and Lady Hesketh's reply that she knew Cowper transl. a part, 'but
never the whole, *at least I believe not,* and my Sister knows little about it' (Add. MSS.
30803 A, ff. 148, 171, 173). Their searches continued until 1805: Lady Hesketh to
Hayley, 10 April 1805: Cowper Mus., Olney. Joseph Hill, Cowper's friend, told

translation had come earlier, in a review of *The Task* in the *Gentleman's Magazine*, which was almost surely written by John Duncombe, close friend of William and John Cowper at Berkhamsted, and associate of the latter also at Cambridge, where they were Scholars and Fellows of Corpus Christi College. The review states that 'the four first books of the Henriade (in Smollett's edition) 1762, were well translated by him [John Cowper]; the four following books by his elder brother, the present author; the ninth by E. B. Greene, Esq. and the tenth by Mr. Robert Lloyd'.[1] When William Cowper read this notice, he wrote to Lady Hesketh:

> It is astonishing to me that they know so exactly how much I translated of Voltaire. My recollection refreshed by them tells me that they are right in the number of books that they affirm to have been translated by me, but till they brought the fact again to my mind, I myself had forgotten that part of the business entirely. My brother had twenty guineas for eight books of English *Henriade*, and I furnished him with four of them.[2]

This is as authoritative a statement as any we have concerning the Cowpers' translation of Voltaire's epic. The work has, in spite of these clues, remained unidentified to the present time, except for H. P. Stokes's comments in his *Cowper Memorials*, where the item from the *Gentleman's Magazine* and Cowper's reply to it are mentioned.[3] H. S. Milford, editor of the Oxford text of Cowper's poems, writes that the translation is 'not extant'.[4] And nowhere in any biography of William Cowper, or any collection of his poetry, is the text of the translation quoted or the exact location named.

The question of the correct text was complicated because Hayley had not seen the announcement in the *Gentleman's Magazine*,

---

Hayley that William had been induced to undertake the transl. by his brother, 'for a very small reward'. Hill believed that William's part was the 2nd and 4th cantos; 'but of this I am not quite certain; they were both of them [William and John Cowper] very sick of their tasks': Joseph Hill to Hayley, 19 Feb. 1802: copy owned by the Rev. W. Cowper Johnson, Norwich.

[1] *G.M.* LV, Pt ii (Dec. 1785), 986. A N.B. on the first page of the 9th canto reads: 'The author of this translation is obliged to Edward Burnaby Green, Esq; for the following canto' (*Henriade*, p. 205).

[2] To Lady Hesketh, 16 Jan. 1786: *Letters*, II, 448.

[3] Stokes, *Cowper Memorials* (Olney, 1904), pp. 19–20, 119.

[4] *Poems*, p. xxvi.

and believed that the translation by the Cowper brothers was that which had 'appeared in a Magazine of the year 1759', which he could not find.[1] Two writers of letters to the editor of the *Gentleman's Magazine* incorrectly informed him that the translation he was looking for was in the *Grand Magazine of Universal Intelligence*, published in ten parts between September 1759 and May 1760.[2] And one correspondent wrote in 1809 to give him the information contained in the review of 1785 (*Gentleman's Magazine*), and quoted the first twenty-two lines of the seventh canto. But in the following year Hayley wrote to the editor of the *Magazine* himself, still inquiring about the missing periodical of 1759.[3]

The translation for the *Grand Magazine* had actually been written by Edward Purdon, whose miserable fame is recorded in the epitaph on him by Goldsmith. The latter's *Memoirs of M. de Voltaire* had been written in connection with Purdon's work.[4] As late as 1836–9 H. F. Cary and Robert Southey believed, because of Hayley's remark that the translation had been published in a magazine, that that in the *Grand Magazine* was Cowper's.[5]

Robert Lloyd, who contributed the tenth canto to the Smollett or Cowper translation, may also have translated the rest of the *Henriade*. His translation of the first canto appears in his *Poems*

---

[1] Hayley (1803), I, 28–9. Later he 'indeed found in a Magazine of that period [1759] a version of the Poem, but not by the Cowpers', Hayley said; 'yet their version probably exists comprized in a periodical publication:—but my own researches, and those of a few literary friends, kindly diligent in enquiry, have hitherto been unable to discover it' (II, 393). One of the literary friends was Samuel Greatheed, who told Hayley that he remembered the monthly appearance of the books of the *Henriade* in the 'Royal Magazine for 1759 & 1760'. Later, on searching through the volumes of the magazine, Greatheed was unable to find them. He must have confused the *Royal Mag.* with the *Grand*—see below (Greatheed to Hayley, 26 Aug. 1800, 1 Oct. and 17 Dec. 1801, 3 Sept. 1802: Fitzwilliam MSS.). The *Henriade* does not appear in any set of the *Royal Mag.* which I have seen.

[2] The transl. begins: 'I Sing the Monarch who o'er Gallia reign'd, | And by the sword his glorious right maintain'd.' Letters concerning the transl. are in *G.M.* LXXVII, Pt ii (1807), 716–17; LXXIX, Pt ii (1809), 605.

[3] *G.M.* LXXIX, Pt ii (1809), 1094–5; Hayley to John Nichols, 3 Sept. 1810: Nichols, *Illustrations*, IV, 744.

[4] James Prior, *The Life of Oliver Goldsmith* (London, 1837), I, 288, 304–8; Temple Scott, *Oliver Goldsmith Bibliographically and Biographically Considered* (New York, 1928), p. 48; R. S. Crane, 'The Text of Goldsmith's *Memoirs of M. de Voltaire*', *M.P.* XXVIII (1930), 212–19.

[5] H. F. Cary, ed. *The Poetical Works of William Cowper* (London, 1839), p. viii; Cary had informed Southey in Aug. 1836, and he accepted Cary's information, though he knew of the original statement (1785) in the *G.M.* See Southey to Gorham, 15 Feb. 1836, and to Baldwin, 4 Aug. 1836: *Selections* [from Southey's letters], IV, 435–6, 462.

(1762) and again in his collected *Poetical Works* (1774).[1] Translations had earlier been printed, almost as soon as the poem itself had been published (1728). They came as part of the special interest in Voltaire during, and immediately after, his visit to England in 1726–9.[2] The first was John Ozell's translation of the first canto, published in 1729, followed three years later by John Lockman's translation of the whole into blank verse.

On 1 February 1761 Smollett advertised proposals for printing by subscription *The Works of M. de Voltaire. Translated from the French. With Notes, Historical and Critical.* 'One Volume in Twelves, elegantly printed', was promised on the first of every month until the whole of Voltaire's works, as translated from 'the last *Geneva* Edition', had been completed.[3] Volume 1 was published on Monday, 2 March.[4] Actually, the thirty-five volumes[5] were published from 1761 to 1765; the *Henriade* was volume XXIV of the series, which came out irregularly. 'In order to make a pleasing variety' the proprietors gave 'sometimes a volume of prose and sometimes a volume of dramatic or poetical pieces.'[6] In the first volume the editors were said to be 'Dr. Smollet, and Others'. The second and remaining volumes bore the name of T. Francklin on the title-page in addition to that of Smollett, who seems to have annotated only the prose works. Francklin translated and edited the drama and the poetry, excluding the *Henriade*.[7]

Thomas Francklin, an enthusiastic Old Westminster, who had a chapel near Ashley Cowper's house in Bloomsbury, had several possible connections with the Cowper family. As the Regius Professor of Greek at Cambridge (1750–9), he had most likely known the excellent young classical scholar, John Cowper, and

---

[1] Lloyd, *Poems* (London, 1762), pp. 138–62; begins: 'Thy chieftain, France, to try'd illustrious worth, | By right of conquest king, by right of birth, | I sing.'
[2] See H. B. Evans, 'A Bibliography of Eighteenth-Century Translations of Voltaire', in *Studies in French Language, Literature and History Presented to R. L. Græme Ritchie* (Cambridge, 1949), p. 49. [3] *Lloyd's Evening Post*, 20–3 Feb. 1761, p. 184.
[4] *London Chron.* 21–4 Feb. and 28 Feb.–3 March 1761, pp. 188, 214.
[5] An extra vol. (XXXVI) was added in 1769; a vol. of Voltaire's letters, transl. by Francklin, was publ. in 1770. Second and third eds. of the individual vols. appeared between 1762 and 1771. A later ed., 1778–81, was enlarged to 38 vols., including Voltaire's later works and a life by Condorcet. See Eugene Joliat, 'Smollett, Editor of Voltaire', *M.L.N.* LIV (1939), 429–36; Evans, p. 53; B.M., Libr. of Congress, and Yale Univ. Libr. Cats. [6] 'Advertisement' at the end of vol. X (London, 1762).
[7] Joliat, p. 431; L. M. Knapp, *Tobias Smollett: Doctor of Men and Manners* (Princeton, 1949), p. 240.

might well have asked him to translate a portion of Voltaire's poetical works. John, in turn, had subdivided his task among his brother and his friends.

'Smollett and Francklin's edition is a very acceptable piece of work', says Professor Joliat. 'It had the merit of being the first to present to English readers a complete and authorized version (up to 1765) of Voltaire, and accordingly was more popular than any other English translation of the latter's works.'[1] It was republished as late as 1901 and 1927.[2] Mr H. B. Evans, without knowing that the Cowpers were the authors, has called their work on the *Henriade* one of the rare examples of good translating of Voltaire in the eighteenth century.[3]

William Cowper's four cantos (v–viii) appear on pp. 103–200 of *The Henriade. By Mr. De Voltaire* (London, 1762). Quotations from his translation are given in chapter vii, above.

[v]

THE five poems which follow are from a volume of Cowper's verse in his autograph, now in the Henry E. Huntington Library (HM 12588). This volume contains forty-eight poems on 124 leaves (small quarto), the versos of which are usually blank. The poems were written between 1773 and 1781; most of them were published in the volume of *Poems*, 1782. The following have not previously been published.[4] They are given here without annotation. The title of the third may be translated, 'A Song of Victory'.

* * *

EPIGRAM ON

THELYPHTHORA.

Oh rare Device! the Wife betray'd,
The Modest, chaste, Domestic Woman,
To Save a worthless, Wanton Jade,
From being, what she would be, Common.

[HM 12588, f. 3.]

---

[1] Joliat, p. 435.

[2] *The Works of Voltaire* (Paris and London, 1901)—*Henriade*, xxx, 1–160; (New York, 1927)—*Henriade*, xxi, 1–160.   [3] Evans, p. 52.

[4] I am grateful to Mr Tyrus G. Harmsen, Cataloguer in the Dept. of MSS., Henry E. Huntington Libr., for his help in connection with this and other MSS. in the libr.

ON THE VICTORY GAINED BY SIR GEO: RODNEY OVER
THE SPANISH FLEET OFF GIBRALTER IN 1780.

For which he has* since been rewarded with
The Lieutenant Generalship of the Marines.

From Shades of Tartarus & Realms of Woe
The Trojan Hero pluckd the Golden Bough.
Of all that Rodney ever Earn'd in Fight,
His fairest Wreath was gather'd in the Night.
'Twas not indeed a Golden Branch he won,
But George's Bounty soon shall make it one.
            [HM 12588, f. 17.]

                ΕΠΙVIΚΙΟV.

Who Pities France? her Enterprizes cross'd,
Her Hopes confounded, & her Treasures lost—
Her Eastern Empire shaken to the Ground,
Her Western, tott'ring at the Trumpets Sound.
Aspiring, tho' not prosperous in Arms,
Has she not fill'd all Nations with Alarms?
Has she not taught the thankless Child, how best
To Aim a Poignard at the Parents Breast?
Conferr'd a Grace she had not to bestow,
Tied Independence round a Rebels Brow,
Helped him to Pick a Gem from Englands Crown,
In Hopes one Day to fix it in her Own?†
Who Pities France? So Prosper All who dare
Awaken, unprovok'd, the Flames of War,
So Prosper All, who deem Repose well sold,
And Blood well barterd, in Exchange for Gold.
            [HM 12588, ff. 29, 31.]

* has] was *deleted.*
† *This line has been partially cut from the page in trimming the volume for binding; the reading is uncertain.*

APPENDIX B

A PRESENT FOR THE QUEEN OF FRANCE.[1]

The Bruiser e'er he Strikes a Blow,
(Such is his Friendship for his Foe)
Cordially shakes him by the Fist,
Then Dubbs him his Antagonist,
And Bangs him Soundly if he can,
To Prove himself the better Man.
So Queen of France in Loving Mood,
Feeling a Thirst for British Blood,
E'er she began her Tilting Match,
Sent Queen of England first a Watch.
As who should say, Look sharp, take care,
Ma trés Aimable et ma Chere,
For you and I must go to War.
The Inference is short and sweet,
Tho' Navies Join, & Armies meet,
And Thousands in the Conflict fall,
There was no Malice in't at all.
 Now what shall Englands lovely Queen,
Whose Act is never base or mean,*
What shall our Gloriana send
In Recompense to such a Friend?
For something at her gracious Hands
Ee'n Charity itself demands,
To Comfort, Gratify and Sweeten
France, so unmercifully Beaten.
 The Muse brings forth with little Labor,
A Present for our Royal Neighbor.
 Most Christian Heroine, behold,
Beset with Eastern Gems and Gold,
Your Friends who Stiled you *Great and Good*
Sov'reigns of† yonder Sea of Blood,
Which *Great* & *Good* with much good Will,

* *The end of this line has been partially cut from the page in trimming; the comma is supplied.*
† Sov'reigns of] Escapd from *deleted.*

---

[1] At the request of Lady Hesketh, Hayley did not include this poem in his *Life of Cowper* (1803), for she considered it 'utterly unworthy' of Cowper: Lady Hesketh to Hayley, 28 July 1802: Add. MSS. 30803 B, f. 60.

You have Assisted them to Spill,
In charitable Hope to Sever
Them & their only Friends for Ever.
Behold a Gift you must delight in,
The Congress—after so much Fighting
A little ruefull to be sure—
The Congress, Ma'am, in Miniature.
Let these your Cabinet adorn,
And as you View them Night and Morn,
Reflect that *Great* and *Good* belong
Not to the King that does the Wrong;
Those Titles He Asserts alone,
Who Just and Equal on his Throne,
Manfully Vindicates his own:
Yet will not, dares not, Use his Might
To Violate anothers Right.
[HM 12588, ff. 55, 57, 59.]

PATIENCE RECOMMENDED
TO WIVES THAT HAVE DEAF HUSBANDS.

Thus says the Lady to her Spouse;
How I detest this odious House!
It is not large enough, & was it,
Yet this low Room, and that dark Closet,
Those Hangings with their worn out Graces,
Long Beards, long Noses, & pale Faces,
Are such an Antiquated Scene,
They almost kill me with the Spleen.
—Sir Humphry Shooting in the Dark,
Makes Answer quite beside the Mark.—
No doubt, my Dear, I bid him come,
Engaged myself to be at Home,
And shall Expect him at the Door
Precisely when the Clock Strikes Four.
  You are so deaf, the Lady cried,
And Raised her Voice, and Frown'd beside,
You are so sadly deaf, my Dear,
What shall I do to make you Hear?

239

Dismiss poor Harry? he replies—
You are by far more nice than wise.
For one slight Blunder all this Stir?
A Wiser man than He might Err.
—Well—I Protest 'tis past all Bearing—
"Child! I am rather hard of Hearing—"
"Yes truly—one must Scream and Bawl,"
"I tell you, you can't Hear at all."
Then with a Voice exceeding low—
No matter if you Hear or no.
  Alas! and is domestic Strife,
That sorest Ill of Human Life,
A Plague so little to be feard
As to be wantonly incurr'd,
To gratify a fretfull Passion
On ev'ry trivial Provocation?
The kindest and the happiest Pair
Will find Occasion to forbear,
And Something ev'ry Day they Live
To Pity, and perhaps, Forgive.
But if Infirmities that fall
In common to the Lot of all,
A Blemish or a Sense impair'd
Are Crimes so little to be Spar'd,
Then Farewell all that must create
The comfort of the Wedded State,
Instead of Harmony, 'tis Jar,
And Tumult and intestine War.
  The Love that cheers Life's latest Stage,
Proof against Sickness & Old Age,
Preserv'd by Virtue from Declension
Becomes not weary of Attention,
But Lives, when that Exterior Grace,
That first Inspir'd the Flame, Decays.
'Tis gentle, delicate, and kind,
To Faults compassionate or blind,
And will with Sympathy endure
The Evils that it cannot Cure.
But angry, coarse, and harsh Expression,

Shews Love to be a mere Profession,
Proves that the Heart is none of His,
Or soon Expells him if it is.
[HM 12588, ff. 95, 97, 99.]

[VI]

THESE four lines of verse were written by Cowper at the end of
a letter which he had received from Walter Bagot in February
1786.[1] They were impromptu verses on a few sentences in the letter:

I c⁴ point out to him [Dr Paul Henry Maty (1745–87), Assistant
Librarian of the British Museum and Editor of the *New Review*[2]] many
very many beauties not only in your Task but also in your former book
of Poems—but my judgment may be overruled by friendship and our
Stars, for without pretending to, nay! despising Astrology, I cannot
help thinking that there is—'tho'
Nescio quod, certe est quod me tibi temperat astrum.

* * *

Long shine the star, what Star soere it be,
That tempers and inclines thine heart to me,
For if a Star can temper and incline
The heart to friendship, thou hast also thine.

[VII]

ON 3 January 1790 Cowper wrote to Samuel Rose: 'I have been
too busy to write to any body, having been obliged to give my
early mornings to the revisal and correction of a little volume of
Hymns for Children, written by I know not whom. This task

---

[1] Walter Bagot to Cowper, 10 Feb. 1786: Morgan MSS. MA 86, vol. II, f. 6.
[2] Cowper had written to Bagot, 23 Jan. 1786: 'Lady Hesketh...writes me word
that Dr. Maty of the [British] Museum has read my *Task*. I cannot even to you relate
what he says of it; though, when I began this story, I thought I had courage enough
to tell it boldly. He designs however to give his opinion of it in his next monthly
Review....' Maty gave *The Task* a favourable review ('a work in general very good')
in the *New Rev.* for Jan. 1786, IX, 31–7.

I finished but yesterday, and while it was in hand wrote only to my cousin and to her rarely.'[1] Before 29 March the book had been published, and Cowper had discovered the author, the Reverend Rowland Hill (1744–1833), a popular Evangelical preacher at the Surrey Chapel, South London. On that date he wrote to Hill:

> The moment when you ceased to be *incog*. I ought to have written you at least a few lines of apology for the liberties I had taken with your hymns, but being extremely busy at that time, and hoping that you would be so charitable as to pardon the omission, I desired Mr. Bull to be my proxy, charging him to make my excuses, and to assure you that I was perfectly satisfied with your making any alterations that you might see to be necessary in my text. If anything fell from my pen that seemed to countenance the heresy of *universal redemption*, you did well to displace it, for it contradicted the Scripture, and belied me.
>
> I am much obliged to you for the little volumes which I received safe on Saturday; and because I suppose that your end will be best answered by dispersion, if I should have occasion for half a dozen more, will order them from your bookseller without scruple.[2]

This publication has not previously been identified by writers on Cowper.[3] It was *Divine Hymns Attempted in Easy Language for the Use of Children* (London: T. Wilkins, 1790). Cowper had undoubtedly been asked to serve as an editor of it by his friend the Reverend William Bull, who had also been associated in the publication of the hymnal. In the early part of 1790, Hill had written to Bull to announce the book:

> At last the famous publication is out—Cowper, Bull, Hill, & Co., 'parturiunt montes, nascitur', &c.: and now the paper is so paltry, the pointing so bad, and the typographical blunders so capital, that I have not ventured to advertise them. My printer is a poor man, and it is charity to employ him, but he's the biggest blunderer in all the world, myself not excepted. I intend, if I can, not to advertise till the next edition, and that shall be more correct. Mr. Cowper will find almost all his judicious amendments strictly attended to; the omissions are so small, that I think he himself would judge them scarce worth apology. I think you know them all. I have mentioned the corrector's name in the preface, just as you have directed. . . . The hymn-books you receive

---

[1] *Letters*, III, 415–16.
[2] *Letters*, III, 450.
[3] Although John Julian in his *Dictionary of Hymnology*, rev. ed. (London, 1908), p. 524, wrote that 'the person referred to as having revised the *Divine Hys.*, 1790, was the poet Cowper'.

with this you have already more than paid for by your friendly assistance. The half-dozen, more decently bound, are for Mr. Cowper; will you send them to him the first opportunity.[1]

In his Preface to the *Divine Hymns* Hill wrote that he would not have 'ventured to have *published* what I have now *printed*, had not almost all of them been revised and corrected, by one whom I am not permitted to mention, but whose name and character as a poet, would do the highest credit to this little publication'.[2] On another page Hill added a note to point out that 'Hymn 24, and 37, were also added by the gentleman[3] that corrected the publication'. These hymns are: 'A Hymn for a Child that Has Ungodly Parents' and 'A Hymn for Sunday School Children'.[4]

By 1810 the hymnal had reached a seventh edition, and there were revised editions in 1819 and 1833. It was used by the congregation of the Surrey Chapel until 1841.[5] After Cowper's death Hill acknowledged him by name as the reviser of the first edition.[6] The 'Hymn for Sunday School Children' was first included among Cowper's works in the 1808 edition of his *Poems*:[7] the other hymn, in *New Poems* by Cowper (1931).[8] The verses from the Bible (not included in the later editions) and the only verbal variant between the first edition (1790) and the Oxford text are indicated below; changes in spelling or punctuation are not shown.

*   *   *

---

[1] Rowland Hill to William Bull, undated: William Jones, *Memoir of the Rev. Rowland Hill* (London, [1837]), pp. 575–6; quoted also in Josiah Bull, *Memorials of the Rev. William Bull* (London, 1864), pp. 192–3.   [2] *Divine Hymns* (1790), p. iv.

[3] Owing to one of the many printer's errors, the original read 'gentlemen'; this was corrected ('gentleman') in subsequent editions.

[4] *Divine Hymns*, p. vii, note, and pp. 36–7, 58–9.

[5] Edward W. Broome, *The Rev. Rowland Hill: Preacher and Wit* (London, [1881]), p. 45.

[6] *A Collection of Hymns for Children* (London, 1808), p. v; *Hymns for Children* (London, 1819 and 1833), p. v.

[7] Cowper, *Poems* (London, 1808), II, 378–9: 'Hymn for the Use of the Sunday School at Olney.' The hymn seems to have been printed a little earlier in a collection which contained over twenty of Cowper's poems. This was James Plumptre, *A Collection of Songs* (London, 1806–8), 3 vols.: vol. III (1808, Preface dated '*December the 9th*, 1807.'), pp. 369–70—'*A HYMN.* | *For the Children of a Sunday School* | BY W. COWPER.' A note on p. 369 reads: 'Written for the children of the Sunday-School at East-Dereham, in Norfolk, and now first published.'

[8] (London: Oxford U.P.), pp. 16–17, from Bodleian MS. Eng. misc. d. 135, f. 51 (among papers relating to Cowper, collected by John Bruce. Bruce copied the poem from a vol. of Cowper's poems in the autograph of John Johnson, now in the Henry E. Huntington Libr.: HM 12587, vol. II, ff. 9–10).

[1790:]

A HYMN FOR A CHILD THAT HAS UNGODLY PARENTS.

If a son seeth all his father's sins which he hath done, and considereth, and doeth not such like, he shall not die for the iniquity of his father, he shall surely live.   EZEK. 14, 18.

A HYMN FOR SUNDAY SCHOOL CHILDREN.[1]

Better is a poor and wise child, than an old and foolish king.

ECCL. iv. 13.

l. 14] elder

[VIII]

AMONG the Private Papers of James Boswell in the Yale University Library there is a broadside (about 3 × 11 inches, printed on one side of the sheet), which is another printing of the 'Good Song' in the Oxford text of Cowper's *Poetical Works*, pp. 673–4, published there from a similar broadside. (Earlier reprinted in *New Poems* (1931), pp. 6–9.) It is impossible to determine which sheet is the earlier printing. Variations other than spelling and punctuation are noticed below.

*   *   *

SONG, / TO THE TUNE OF

[There are roman numerals between each stanza; and a refrain is added after each. Stanza 1 is given as an example.]

HERE's a Health to right honest JOHN BULL,
    When he's gone we shan't find such another;
And with Hearts and with Glasses brim full,
    Here's a Health to OLD ENGLAND, his Mother!
        And with Hearts, &c.

l. 12] Since *Betters* he knows he shou'd have,
l. 15] our Trade is,
l. 21] had
l. 25] the Loom
l. 26] made us

---

[1] *Poems*, p. 477. Milford mentions another printing of the hymn (*Northampton Mercury*, 7 Aug. 1790): in the notes, p. 662.

l. 29] makes
l. 36] Or LIBERTY Lengthen our Coat?
l. 39] 'Tis they who'd get all by the Plunder,—
l. 41] Then away! such nonsensical Stuff,
l. 47] the Work's

[There is no printer's ornament at the end as on the sheet which was the source for the Oxford text.]

C

UNCOLLECTED CONTRIBUTIONS
TO MAGAZINES: 1789–93

[I]

TOWARDS the end of 1788 Cowper's publisher, Joseph Johnson, asked Cowper to assist him by writing several reviews for his journal, the *Analytical Review*. Cowper agreed to do this in the hope that it would divert his mind from depression. However, he soon wrote to Samuel Rose:

> I do not at present feel myself so much amused by my new occupation as I hoped to be. The critic's task is not a pleasant one, unless he can find something to commend; and it has not yet been my fortune to stumble on an opportunity of much encomium. There are already three authors in my cupboard; ay, four, who will have small cause to bless their stars that it has been my lot to judge them. On Saturday I read the first book of the *Athenaid*, and it is a sad thing, but a true, that I must read it again before I shall understand it. . . .Apollo and all Parnassus know, or ought to know, that I enter on his work with the best disposition in the world to be charmed with it.

Two weeks later Cowper had not yet written the review of the *Athenaid*, but by 17 February he had finished the first two volumes of Glover's work (for one review) and was waiting with his analysis of the last volume (for a second review) until Johnson had told him just what kind of reviews he wanted. 'Send me a line', Cowper wrote to Johnson, 'to inform me of what you most wish, whether analytical revisals or critical, and I will proceed with the 2 poems that I have not yet reviewed accordingly.' On the 25th he told Lady Hesketh: 'My hands are at present less full than usual. Having lately sent Johnson as much Review work as will serve to satisfy him for a time, I allow myself a little vacation from these labours, which, however, I must soon resume.'[1]

Most of these contributions to the *Analytical Review* have not

---

[1] *Letters*, III, 341–2, 351, 357; *U. & U.* p. 54.

been identified.[1] The reviews of the *Athenaid* were, of course, known from the references in Cowper's letters. Southey printed a large part of the first review in an appendix to the seventh volume of his *Works* of Cowper, where he also identified and gave selections from the reviews of Timothy Dwight's *Conquest of Canäan* and Erasmus Darwin's *Loves of the Plants*.[2] Because of a remark in a letter to Samuel Rose, 4 October 1789, Robert Pratt attributed to Cowper a review of *The Poems of Ferdosi*.[3]

In a letter to Rose, 24 June 1792, Cowper wrote:

I have now Dr Darwin's last publication before me, which, having reviewed the first, I chose to review likewise, inconvenient as it is to me at present to be call'd away from Milton. Johnson left it to my option. You have seen it I conclude or will see it soon, and should any striking remark present itself either to you or to M[rs] Rose in the perusal, I shall be happy to have it for the credit that it will reflect upon my own. I seem in truth, whatever I was once, to be now exceeding dull, and to have lost my wits just when I should have them most about me.[4]

On 1 January the review had not yet been completed. He wrote to Teedon:

I have had a small matter to do for Johnson in the literary way this half-year, and through mere incapacity and lowness of spirits, have been obliged to neglect it. In other days it would have cost me but a single morning. Last night I received a letter from him requiring it speedily; and this morning I awoke out of a dream that has disabled me more than ever.[5]

---

[1] Cowper made a list of the books he reviewed, which was later in the possession of Lady Hesketh. This she forwarded to Hayley in 1801. Both of them believed that the reviews should remain unidentified, and Lady Hesketh requested that the list itself be burned (Lady Hesketh, 1 and 14 Nov., and Hayley, 7 Nov. 1801: Add. MSS. 30803 A, ff. 178-9, 181).
[2] 'Notes and Illustrations', Southey's *Cowper*, VII, 310-21. Darwin's work was vol. II of his *Botanic Garden*, but published first.
[3] From the letter to Rose: 'I feel some impatience to see the Analytical which has not reached me yet, especially since I find that I am not an outside passenger, but shall loll with dignity in the body of that vehicle.' See Robert A. Pratt, 'Two Letters of William Cowper', *T.L.S.*, 18 Nov. 1931, p. 916.
[4] M. C. Bates, 'Cowper to Hayley and Rose, June 1792: Two Unpublished Letters', *Harvard Libr. Bull.* XI (1957), 93.
[5] *Letters*, IV, 356.

Cowper was able to complete the writing of the review, however, and it was published in the March issue of the magazine.[1] Apparently it was the last piece that he sent to the *Analytical Review*.

The various reviews which have been named as his are signed either 'G. G.' or 'P. P.'[2] Johnson had but few reviewers during the years 1789–93, and these usually reviewed books in one or two fields only. Not many signatures—almost always initials—are used in these volumes. The eleven reviews signed 'G. G.' or 'P. P.' deal with poetry exclusively: the writer may be regarded as the poetry editor of the magazine for the year from March 1789 to April 1790, when all except the last (and most difficult to write, the review of Darwin's book) appeared. Personal references, the style of the reviews, and the characteristic sense of whimsical humour show the author of all eleven to have been Cowper. There are parts of some of the reviews which may stand with his excellent letters of the same period.

A list of the reviews in the *Analytical Review* which are clearly Cowper's, and a selection of items of special interest follow. The titles and descriptions of the books under review are given as published in the magazine.

*　　*　　*

(a) Vol. III (March 1789), pp. 323–35:
[Richard Glover (1712–85)][3] *The Athenaid, a Poem*. By the Author of Leonidas. Three Vols. 12 mo, 815 pages, price 9s. sewed. Cadell. [Signed: 'G. G.']

---

[1] The MS. of the review is in the Harvard Coll. Libr.: *46M-298 (tipped in a copy of Cowper's *Poems* (1782), *46-2071); see my note, 'Cowper and Darwin's *Economy of Vegetation*', *Harvard Libr. Bull.* XI (1957), 317–18. A comparison of the MS. with the publ. review reveals slight changes in the text, and many quotations from Darwin's work inserted in the latter.

[2] Southey suggests that 'G. G.' may possibly allude 'to a *sobriquet*, by which he seems to have been known in his family circle'. This was 'Gingerbread Giles', as Cowper signed himself in a letter to Lady Hesketh, 24 Dec. 1786. Southey's *Cowper*, VI, 47; VII, 314. The source for the name was probably 'Giles Gingerbread' (the 'little boy who lived upon learning'), John Newbery's famous children's story (first published c. 1765). 'P. P.' may possibly refer to some other of Newbery's stories for children, which frequently had alliterative titles (e.g. the 'History of Master Peter Primrose [1752]', who had obtained through reading 'some knowledge of men and things').

[3] According to Leslie Stephen, in the *D.N.B.*: 'His ponderous "Athenaid"...is much longer and so far worse than "Leonidas", but no one has been able to read either for a century.'

(b) Vol. III, Appendix (April 1789), pp. 538–55:
[Continuation of (a). Signed: 'P. P.']

(c) Vol. III, Appendix (April 1789), pp. 531–4:
[Timothy Dwight (1752–1817)] *The Conquest of Canäan, A Poem, In Eleven Books.* Printed at Hartford in New-England, in 1785; and Reprinted in London for J. Johnson in 1788. 12 mo. 363 pa. pr. 3s. 6d. sewed. [Signed: 'P. P.']
[Selection:]

We do not expect from a poet the fidelity of an historian. Wherever he finds his subject, he claims a right to shape it to his purpose; may lead his reader to the catastrophe by such ways as please him most; may bring his characters into action and slay them at his own time, or may employ such as never existed. Poetry cannot be without Fancy, and Fancy can content herself with no materials as she finds them.

The poet before us, availing himself of this privilege, has modelled the sacred narrative to his mind, and in such manner that he who would learn by what steps the Israelites became possessed of the promised Land, must still seek his information in the bible.

(d) Vol. IV (May 1789), pp. 29–36.
[Darwin] *The Botanic Garden. Part II. Containing the Loves of the Plants, a Poem; with Philosophical Notes.* 4to. 184 pages, and 8 plates. Price 12s. in boards. Lichfield, Jackson. London, Johnson. 1789. [Signed: 'P. P.']
[Selection:]

Much critical knowledge is conveyed, and much philosophical too, in these dialogues [between the Poet and the Bookseller], but it is impossible not to observe how very inferior a part is assigned in them to the Bookseller, whose short questions serve merely as a trigger to shoot off the poet's charge of deep and abstruse intelligence. They remind us of a fable which we got by heart in our infancy, and which we therefore still remember. A certain carver exhibited the figures of a man and a lion, the lion under the foot of the man. It chanced that a lion passing that way observed them, and being naturally offended at the man's partiality to his own kind, told him, with some asperity, that the man should have been undermost, had a lion been the carver. We doubt not but Booksellers may be found who will know how to make the application.

(e) Vol. v (September 1789), pp. 47–51.
Ger. Nicolai Heerkens Groningani Aves Frisicæ. Rotterdami apud C. R. Hake. 1787. The Friesland Birds of G. N. Heerkens of Groningen. 8vo. p. 297. [Signed: 'G. G.']
[Selection:]

...the writer of this article is acquainted with a person [undoubtedly John Newton], formerly Captain of a ship in the Guinea-trade, and a gentleman of the most unsuspected veracity, who has assured him, that once, on his return to England, at a great distance from any land, the rigging of his ship was suddenly almost covered with swallows that settled on it, needing rest. They were in fact so wearied with their long flight, that the sailors took many of them in their hands.

(f) Vol. v (October 1789), pp. 206–10.
The Poems of Ferdosi. Translated from the Persian; by Joseph Champion, Esq. Vol. i. 4to. p. 448. Price 12s. in Boards. Cadell. 1788. [Signed: 'G. G.']
[Selection:]

His [Ferdosi's] task was to versify the imperial annals of Persia; and if those annals abounded with fictions so clumsy and improbable, that a child of ordinary discernment would be disgusted by them, the bard was to be pitied who had fallen on such a theme; and if he could embellish it by poetic art so as to make it agreeable, was entitled to the highest encomiums. Such encomiums, after rehearsing a specimen of his work, Ferdosi accordingly received, together with a promise from the sultan of a golden dinar (a dinar is nearly eight shillings and six-pence in value) for every line of his composition on the important subject. Hear this, ye bards of Europe, and regret that ye are not bards of Asia! For, the single instance of Churchill excepted, who if our memory does not deceive us, was most magnificently paid by Flexney (though Flexney was no sultan, but a bookseller) we are rather apprehensive that poetry is a soil not remarkably grateful to the pains bestowed upon it.

The merits, therefore, of Ferdosi we admit; but when we seek in this version of him, those strokes of genius and of art that distinguish the true poet from the poet made such only by the desire to be one, we find them not, but are presented instead with an *universal blank*. The animated oriental has escaped in the transfusion, and only a vapid residuum is left for the unfortunate English reader, and for us, of all English readers most unfortunate, the reviewers.

(*g*) Vol. v (November 1789), pp. 356–9.
[William Lawrence Brown (1755–1830)] *An Essay on Sensibility. A Poem. In six Parts.* 8vo. 183 p. Price 4s. sewed. G. Nicol. 1789. [Signed: 'G. G.']

(*h*) Vol. v, Appendix (December 1789), pp. 578–9.
[Ebenezer Rhodes (1762–1839)] *Alfred, an historical Tragedy. To which is added, a Collection of Miscellaneous Poems, by the same Author.* Sheffield, Gales; London, Robinsons. Small 8vo. p. 174, pr. 4s. sewed. 1789. [Signed: 'G. G.']
[Selection:]

This volume, as the prologue to Alfred informs us, is the work of a mechanic. Considered as such, it is well written, as are the poems that follow it. But it is a certain truth, and we wish it were laid to heart by multitudes whom it much concerns, that no Englishman *can* be master of his own language who understands no other. And it is equally true, that without critical skill in the language in which he writes, it is impossible that any man should be a poet. Our language has now attained to a purity which it had not in the days of Shakespear, and we expect that purity in verse. The instance, therefore, of our immortal dramatist (could it be established as an instance) would furnish no argument against the validity of our doctrine.

(*i*) Vol. vi (February 1790), p. 194.
[Author unknown] *Poetical Essays.* By a young Gentleman of Hertford College, Oxford. 4to. 45 p. pr. 2s. 6d. Robinsons, 1789. [Signed. 'G. G.'][1]

---

[1] Most of this review is quoted above, pp. 155–6.

(*j*) Vol. VI, Appendix (April 1790), pp. 536–42.
The Vision of Columbus. A Poem. In Nine Books. By Joel Barlow, Esq.[1] 12mo. 244 p. Pr. 3s. sewed. Printed at Hartford, in New England. Reprinted in London for Dilly. 1788. [Signed: 'G. G.']
[Selection:]

The first book is chiefly occupied in a display of American scenery, without dispute the noblest in the world,...poetry seems never more unsuccessfully occupied, than when describing a modern battle; if the various movements and evolutions of such a scene are difficult to be understood in prose, much is that difficulty increased in verse, and the field inveloped in smoke and dust is hardly more obscure than the language that represents it....

We beg leave, by way of hint to the *young* men of our own country, to remark, that this poem, and the Conquest of Canaan by Mr. Dwight, respectable works both, and on well-chosen subjects, are the productions of two *young* Americans.

(*k*) Vol. XV (March 1793), pp. 287–93.
[Darwin] *The Botanic Garden. Part I. Containing the Œconomy of Vegetation. A Poem. With Philosophical Notes.* 4to. 338 pages. and ten Plates. Price £1 1s. in boards. Johnson. 1791. [Signed: 'P. P.']

[II]

COWPER's return of interest in periodical writing from 1789 to 1793 was a return to the kind of writing he had done forty or fifty years earlier when he was a templar. During the time he wrote for the *Analytical Review* he also sent two letters to the *Gentleman's Magazine*, which were parodies of the queries in the *Magazine*. Cowper himself may have answered some serious inquiries straightforwardly in the same magazine in 1758.[2] During the years many of its solemn controversies about trivial matters had indeed become a joke. A burlesque on them was just the sort

---

[1] Barlow (1754–1812), like Dwight, was one of the 'Hartford Wits'.
[2] Above, pp. 185–90.

of thing which would appeal to Cowper's fancy. He wrote to Lady Hesketh, 12 March 1791:

Thou mayst remember perhaps that long since (not less I suppose than a year and a half) I sent some ridiculous queries to the *Gentleman's Magazine*, in hopes that either the answers to them or some grave gentleman's censure of them, would afford me an opportunity to kick up a controversy about them, for the amusement of myself and my friends...they appeared and were answered not only in the *Magazine*, but soon after in several newspapers also; but nothing occurred that furnished me with the occasion of wrangling that I had sought. At length, however, in the last *Magazine*, a musty and insipid antiquarian has thought proper to animadvert on the frivolous nature of my queries with an air of great gravity and self-importance. I have accordingly entered the lists; that is to say I have this very morning written and sent to the post a letter to Mr. Urban, complaining of the undue severity of old square toes' stricture, and proving him to be altogether as ignorant and a more frivolous writer than myself. Now, therefore, at last I hope that my end will be answered, and that there will be some sport between us. On my part at least nothing shall be wanting, for it will be delightful to me to plague him, and the occasion presents itself just at a time when I have leisure to improve it.[1]

And to Mrs Throckmorton, on the 15th, he wrote:

I shall now tell you a piece of news, for which if the thing pleases you as much as it has pleased me, you will thank me. The queries that I sent to Mr. Urban are at last censured, censured severely, and censured by the man of all the world whom I should have most wished to censure them, a grave, fusty, worm-eaten antiquarian. I have already sent up a reply in which I have given him a good dressing, and should it but make him as angry as I think it cannot fail to do, we shall have rare sport all the summer. I had actually given up all hope of such good fortune, and the arrival of it now at so late a day is therefore doubly agreeable.[2]

The letter from the 'grave, fusty, worm-eaten antiquarian' is in the *Gentleman's Magazine* for February 1791 (vol. LXI, Pt i, pp. 103–4), over the signature 'E'. Its censure is directed in part against the queries of 'Indagator' in the *Magazine* for September 1790 (vol. LX, Pt ii, p. 801), which was dated 10 September, almost exactly a year and a half before Cowper's letter to Lady Hesketh

---

[1] *Letters*, IV, 39–40.   [2] *Letters*, IV, 43.

on 12 March 1791. 'Indagator's' letter has been correctly identified by Mr Kenneth Povey as Cowper's.[1]

Annotations to these letters, I think, are for the most part superfluous. Besides, I should not like to fall into the sins of the scholar whom Cowper is burlesquing.

* * *

[*Gentleman's Magazine*, LX, Pt ii (September 1790), 801.]

Sept. 10.

Mr. URBAN,

ANECDOTES concerning the late Dr. Daffy, author of the celebrated elixir that bears his name, will be esteemed a favour, if any of your numerous correspondents can supply them. I have been informed that, not long since, two elderly ladies, descendants of the Doctor, were living in some part of the city, but, having no calls to London, cannot myself ascertain it. It has to my knowledge been asserted, that no such Doctor in reality ever existed, but that these two ladies were the inventresses of that excellent cordial, and are, in the aggregate, Doctor Daffy. Should this prove to be the case, it will be somewhat singular; and it seems almost as singular that it should be doubtful whether it is the case or not. Is it possible that the very existence of such a benefactor to the publick should be problematical?

I should be equally obliged to any of your correspondents who can inform me what became of the pebbles with which London and Westminster were formerly paved, when the new pavement was substituted in their stead. It is certain that they must have been displaced; but whither could they be conveyed? into what gulph were they thrown? or where stand they piled like a mountain? They would make admirable causeways for foot-passengers in all the country towns and villages that want them.

When was the popular and wholesome beverage, called *porter*, first introduced, and who invented it? and why is such a blessing as the secret of making it permitted to be engrossed by a few, and the benefit confined almost solely to the metropolis? Thousands of lives are every year prematurely terminated in the country by

---

[1] Povey, 'Further Notes for a Bibliography of Cowper's Letters', *R.E.S.* VIII (1932), 317.

254

the use of what is called *good old sound* beer (the most noxious liquor in the world), which would doubtless be preserved were porter universally drunk instead of it.

Why are fried beef and cabbage called *bubble* and *squeak*? The name, if I am not mistaken, was given to that dish within my memory, but for what reason I could never learn. Names that pretend to be descriptive of, and to predicate the subject, and yet perform no such matter, are very uncommon.

What was the real character of Joe Miller, of jocular memory? Was he himself a jester, and famous in his day for saying what we call *good things*? or was he only an humble collector of the jokes of others? Is there any life of him extant? When did he live, and where was he buried?

Whence originated an expression in use almost in every part of Great Britain—*an't please the pigs*? Why is the pleasure of the pigs to be consulted, as it is by many people, on all the ordinary occurrences of the day, so that they hardly undertake any thing without a previous reference to their permission? A gentleman of my acquaintance being told lately that the South-islanders, whose favourite food is pork, had extirpated all the sheep, which had multiplied among them prodigiously, replied, *they did it, un-doubtedly, to please the pigs*.

I flatter myself, Mr. Urban, that none of your ingenious correspondents will esteem any of these queries too trivial for an answer, since the gratification of curiosity is always desirable; and no periodical publication gratifies it so often as yours.

INDAGATOR.

* * *

Cowper had received unsatisfactory replies in October and December 1790 (vol. LX, Pt ii, pp. 876, 1075–6, 1086–7, 1194–5), and in January 1791 (vol. LXI, Pt i, p. 16), and would receive one still later, in June (p. 520). He had started a discussion on the derivation of words and odd sayings, which was sometimes enter-taining; but he was not really pleased until he read 'E's' reply. It was dated from Stoke Newington, 17 February, and began with a note of thanks to 'your respectable correspondent D. H. for the notice he takes of me in the Supplement, p. 1190'. 'D. H.'—that is, Richard Gough,[1] a close friend of the Editor of the *Magazine*, John Nichols—had written in that place (vol. LX, Pt ii, p. 1190):

> Mr. Nichols will not be displeased to be told, that *Robert Drury* was a *Leicestershire* man....It appears also, that Drury's father left him two hundred pounds and the reversion of a house at Stoke Newington.— The Historian of Stoke Newington, in Bibl. Brit. Top. will accept this hint.

The historian (and 'E') was James Brown,[2] who was born at Stoke Newington in 1750, and lived there until 1799. He spent his life in 'musty' antiquarian pursuits. The letter containing his reply to Cowper is here quoted in part:

> The stories about cant-words are beneath the dignity and reputation of the Gentleman's Magazine; foolish phrases about 'pleasing pigs,' and the like, have been descanted on, which I profess I never heard before; and that the people who deal most in such nonsense are the most uneducated and vulgar of mankind. I am obliged to your Magazine for much both of entertainment and information continually, and wish to guard it against descending to any thing mean and low.
>
> I am obliged to you for the pleasing view and account of Sir Walter Raleigh's house at Islington;[3] but how do you know it was his? I see no coat of arms mentioned, that answers to any of the quarters in his (See Gent. Mag. June 1787.). The family of Carew was connected with his, and bears Or, 3 Lions passant in pale sable; but neither does that appear in the plate of the aforesaid Magazine.

According to Mr Povey, '"Indagator's," or Cowper's, rejoinder was not printed or even acknowledged.'[4] However, in the March issue of the *Gentleman's Magazine* there is a letter which is almost surely his. It is dated 12 March, the day on which he told Lady Hesketh he had written the letter.

---

[1] According to Gough himself, he 'opened a correspondence with Mr. Urban in 1767...under the signature of D. H.; which signature he retained to the last....' Quoted in John Nichols, 'A Prefatory Introduction', *General Index to the Gentleman's Magazine, from the Year 1787 to 1818* (London, 1821), I, lxvi.

[2] James Brown (1750–1839), only s. of James Brown of St Albans and Stoke Newington (1709–88), who was well-known as a traveller and as a student of the Persian language (see *D.N.B.*). The younger Brown was the author of 'Sketches of the History and Antiquities of the Parish of Stoke Newington, in the County of Middlesex' (London, 1783), published anonymously, and included as Pt ix of *Bibliotheca Topographica Britannica*, in vol. II: *Antiquities in Middlesex and Surrey* (London, 1790). (He was identified as the author in Nichols, *Anecdotes*, I, 160; VII, 51, 522; IX, 71; and *Illustrations*, VIII, 686.) Brown frequently contributed to the *G.M.* and assisted Nichols in the writing of his *Anecdotes*. He published several historical works concerning St Albans. See *G.M.* N.S. XI (1839), 322–3.

[3] *G.M.* LXI, Pt i (Jan. 1791), 17.   [4] Povey, *loc. cit.*

[*Gentleman's Magazine*, LXI, Pt i (March 1791), 216–17.]

March 12.

MR. URBAN.

I WAS greatly pleased to see, in p. 17. the drawing of Sir Walter Raleigh's house at Islington.[1] I wish your correspondent may pursue the research of antiquities in that village, which, I am persuaded, would afford much gratification to the Antiquaries, as perhaps it has been a path untrodden by being too near home. Let me recommend "A Walk in and about Islington." Despise it not, because the plodding cit there seeks to inhale a little fresh air, or his holiday-'prentice and sweetheart regale with tea and hot rolls at White-conduit-house. Give me leave to point out to Mr. P.[2] King John's-court, at the farther end of the Lower-street, now lett in tenements to poor people, but which bears evident marks of having been a stately mansion, if not a royal palace. There are several armorial bearings in the apartments on the ground-floor, in particular one:—Gules, a chevron Or, three escallop-shells Azure, between 3 griffin-heads, erased of the third, upon a chief Azure, a cross crosslet Or.—What have these arms to do with King John?—Yet so runs the tradition.

A house in Cross-street is called Qu. Elizabeth's Palace, the front of which has undergone many alterations, but an antient lodge still exists at the end of the garden towards Canonbury-fields, called the porter's lodge; though I have my doubts of this belonging ever to her Majesty, as the other to King John, the arms on the lodge being a chevron 3 cross patée, between 3 herons (I believe) a hand Gules*. This certainly denotes only baronetage, nothing royal.

Another house in the Lower-street is denominated Oliver Cromwell's.—The Priory at Highbury is recorded to have been destroyed by Jack Straw: a public-house there was formerly called Jack Straw's Castle, in commemoration of that rebel, I suppose. Part of old Canonbury house and park wall still remain. A house in the beginning of the town, near the new turnpike, formerly

* The arms of the *Fowlers*, Baronets. EDIT.

---

[1] See n. 3, p. 256.
[2] Who had sent in the drawing and description of Sir Walter Raleigh's house.

Mrs. Denne's, afterwards Mrs. Charron's boarding-school, is supposed to have been built by some great person.

I should also be glad to know what foundation there is for the traditionary tale of Lady Owen (who endowed the alms-houses which bear her name, and lies in the church) rising to her fortune and rank by a *random-shot* from an arrow of Sir Thomas Owen, which she received not in her heart, but a less noble situation, as she was going to milking? This wound Cupid revenged with one of his arrows, that made a still deeper impression on Sir Thomas.— I have heard that there were three arrows on the top of the school-house founded by her, in remembrance of the event; but they were gone before my time.* If Mr. P. or any other of your correspondents, can give an answer to these queries, it will gratify the curiosity of (and perhaps entertain) more of your readers, than

EUSEBIA.

P.S. I have heard that Sir Walter Raleigh's portrait hung up at the Pyed Bull. Whether that is a proof of much weight for ascertaining the house to be his residence, I know not. As parochial dinners are often held there, to those who find a gratification in smoking, it might heighten the flavour of their tobacco, to know they enjoyed their favourite weed in the very house of the first who brought it over to England.

I cannot agree with your correspondent E. in thinking the etymology of phrases so much below your Magazine: though they may be now inelegant, from the fluctuation of language and fashion, yet they throw light on the old customs they allude to, and have survived. Your old and valuable correspondent Paul Gemsege did not think them beneath his notice.[1] I was pleased with the derivation of *spick and span new*:[2] may not *brand new* spring from the same origin? it is an old word for a sword. To "talk of the devil"[3]

* These we well remember. EDIT.

---

[1] 'Paul Gemsege', an anagrammatical signature used by the antiquary, Samuel Pegge (1704–96)—see Nichols, *Anecdotes*, v, 53. His letter concerning the cant word *Tontine* appeared in the January number, p. 27.

[2] Letter from 'P. T.', *G.M.* lx, Pt ii (1790), 1194: 'Says one ancient Britain to another, Is your spear new? no, it is *spike new*; that is, he had got a new spike to his old spand (handle or haft); Is yours new? says another, no; but it is *spand new*; Is yours new? yes, *spick* and *spand new*.'

[3] A note by 'L. E.' concerning the etymology of this phrase had appeared in the February number, p. 136.

I have always heard tacked, "and his imps appear," when the person you have been speaking-of enters.—But I fear you will think my postscript as long as a letter.

EUSEBIA.

* * *

Under the mask of 'Eusebia'—with respect or awe for the good, with a character known for piety—Cowper had written about something he could be certain would make 'E' strike again. Although he probably did not know who 'E' was, he almost surely did know (from the *Gentleman's Magazine* itself) that he was the historian of Stoke Newington. This parish adjoined Islington, about which Cowper, as 'Eusebia', wrote. Most likely his information came from recollections of the place during his days in London, when he knew such suburbs very well.[1] And he could get precise information from *The History and Antiquities of Canonbury-House at Islington* (London, 1788), by John Nichols.[2] In fact, Nichols' long list of queries at the end of this history—'submitted to the Inhabitants of ISLINGTON, preparatory to an intended Topographical Description of the Parish, its Antiquities, &c.'[3]— is an example of the kind of antiquarian interest which Cowper is parodying. By muddling certain items from Nichols' work, Cowper could be sure that 'E', who was an authority on that part of Middlesex, would reply. And 'E' did.

[*Gentleman's Magazine*, LXI, Pt i (May 1791), 401–2.]

Apr. 27.

Mr. URBAN,

I AM surprized that your correspondent Eusebia, p. 217, in writing about the old house in Lower street, Islington, to which she gives the name of King John's Court (a name common, though I know not why,

---

[1] See *Letters*, I, 14, 16. Canonbury House was the residence of John Newbery during the years 1760–7, and many of the poets and hacks in his employ, before and during these years, lived there. Cowper may very well have visited some of these men since he associated with many of the younger poets while he lived in London. Smart lived at Canonbury House, 1753–7; Goldsmith was there, 1762–3. See Charles Welsh, *A Bookseller of the Last Century*, pp. 46–58; Edmund Blunden, 'A Boswellian Error', *Votive Tablets* (London, 1931), pp. 160–6.

[2] It followed Brown's work in *Bibl. Top. Brit.* vol. II. In connection with Cowper's comments, see especially Plate II, and pp. 3, 9, 29, 30–1, 53–4.

[3] Nichols, *Canonbury-House*, pp. 75–6. For example, Query 11: 'What chantries, altars, shrines, lights, images, gilds, or roods, appear to have been in the old church; or what reliques, miracles, and legends?' Query 15: 'A further account of Mrs. Owen's alms-houses and school?'

17-2

to almost all the antiquated remains of palaces, abbies, and nunneries, about London), should not have mentioned the name which I have always heard ascribed to that building, though I freely own I have none but legendary and traditional ground for it: I have heard it called *Hunsdon House*, and supposed to be the property and residence of Henry Carey, first cousin to Q. Elizabeth, and by her created Lord Hunsdon. I remember to have seen over the door a great HD; which for several years has been, and, for aught I know, still may be, covered by a board, whereon is an inscription. The arms of that noble lord were, Argent, on a bend Sable three roses of the field. If your correspondent can find that coat in the house, it will do much toward confirming my tradition. What family the arms she has mentioned, of which she has certainly given an imperfect and erroneous account, belong to, I know not.

As to Jack Straw's castle at Highbury, I know nothing of any public-house so denominated; but I remember a certain spot, on which Mr. Dawes afterward built his house, or laid out part of his garden, which had the appearance of being a factitious mount, surrounded by a deep trench; and *that* I always understood to be Jack Straw's castle.

Several particulars in your correspondent's letter seem plainly to shew, that she has never seen your intelligent Printer's History of Canonbury, which is very extraordinary, as she seems so zealous for the honour of Islington: it would, indeed, have given her no knowledge as to the "situation in which *Mrs.* Owen received *Judge* Owen's arrow," which the lady seems very desirous to be informed about; but it would have been of use to correct several little *errata* in her letter, and to shew her the improbability of this history.. . .

E.

The correspondence seems to have ended here. By May and June Cowper's time was taken up in finishing his *Homer*; there was no opportunity for pranks. He would have been greatly amused, however, if he had lived to know that James Brown, and other readers of the *Gentleman's Magazine* in 1790–1, were not the only ones to be fooled by his mocking queries. They were referred to very seriously by John Nelson in the most authoritative history of Islington.[1]

---

[1] John Nelson, *The History and Antiquities of the Parish of Islington*, 2nd ed. (London, 1823): see, for example, pp. 188–9. Nelson's book is the best source of information on the places mentioned in the letters.

NOTES ON COWPER'S RELATIVES
AND FRIENDS

THE following list of relatives and friends gives supplementary facts, dates, and major sources of biographical information. In many cases there is no work which contains a survey of their lives. Most of Cowper's associates at Westminster School (chapter III) are not given below; information concerning them may be found in *The Record of Old Westminsters*. This record, *Alumni Cantabrigienses*, and *Alumni Oxonienses* are not mentioned among the sources. Persons cited in the *Dictionary of National Biography* have an asterisk (*) after their names.

BAGOT, Walter (1731–1806), Rector of Blithfield and Leigh, Staffs, from 1759: [William Bagot, 2nd Bn], *Memorials of the Bagot Family* (Blithfield, 1824), p. 89; Joseph Welch [and C. B. Phillimore], *The List of the Queen's Scholars of St. Peter's College, Westminster* (London, 1852), pp. 34, 351–2; Sophy Louisa Bagot, *Links with the Past* (London, 1901).

BENSLEY, James (1733?–65), Trinity Coll., Camb. (B.A. 1755, M.A. 1758, Fellow 1756), I.T. (1752), Lincoln's Inn (1756): *G.M.* xxxv (1765), 199. Robert Lloyd's three epistles 'to J. B. Esq.' (two of them in 1757) were probably written to Bensley: Lloyd, *Works*, ed. William Kenrick (London, 1774), I, 96–100, 101–3; II, 37–50.

BOURNE, Vincent* (1695–1747): John Mitford, 'Memoir', in Bourne, *Poematia* (London, 1840).

CHURCHILL, Charles* (1732–64): Wallace C. Brown, *Charles Churchill* (Lawrence, Kansas, 1953); Joseph Lee Walsh, *The Literary Career of Charles Churchill to 1763*, unpubl. Ph.D. diss. (Yale Univ., 1935).

COTTON, Nathaniel* (1705–88), author of *Visions in Verse* (London, 1751), 9th ed. (1776); *Various Pieces in Verse and Prose* (London, 1791), ed. by his son, Nathaniel: *G.M.* LVIII, Pt ii (1788), 756, 834; LXXVII, Pt i (1807), 398, 500–1; Pt ii (1807), 631–2; Alexander Chalmers, *The General Biographical Dictionary* (London, 1813), x, 317–20; Clutterbuck, I, 85; William Urwick, *Nonconformity in Herts* (London, 1884), 204; F. H. Fulford, *William Cowper at St. Albans* (St Albans, 1902); Charles E. Jones, 'A St. Albans Worthy: Dr. Nathaniel Cotton, 1705 to 1788', *St Albans and Herts Archit. and Archæol. Soc.: Transactions* (1936), pp. 57–63 (portrait of Cotton reproduced, p. 57; photograph of his 'Collegium' in 1910, p. 58).

COWPER, Ann Donne (1703–37): It appears that in 1726–7 she was engaged to Samuel Hudson, of Great Yarmouth, Norfolk, and Leghorn, Italy, who died early in 1727: T. H. King, 'Cowper's Mother and an Early Lover', *N. & Q.* CXLVII (6 Sept. 1924), 167.

COWPER, Ashley (1701–88), m. Dorothy Oakes: *Madan Family*, p. 242. He was a friend of Hogarth (Lady Hesketh to Hayley, 22 July 1802: Add. MSS. 30803 B, f. 58). In addition to Theadora, Harriot, and Elizabeth Charlotte, Ashley had several other children, all of whom died very young: Charlotte at 'about four Years old' and a 'Son [Spencer?, who d. 1740], about six Years old'—see [Ashley Cowper], *Poems and Translations* (London, 1767), pp. 140–4. Also, Anthony Ashley, who d. shortly after birth (1730); Ashley (b. 1739); and Theodora Emily (b. 1731): Duncan Warrand, *Hertfordshire Families* (London, 1907), pp. 146–7; Add. MSS. 28101 (Ashley's 'Family Miscellany'), f. 3.

COWPER, Elizabeth Charlotte (d. 1805): At the time of her marriage to Sir Archer Croft (1731–92), 24 April 1759, she was described as the 'youngest daughter of Ashley Cowper, esq.' (*Grand Mag. of Univ. Intelligence*, II (1759), 278). Sir Archer was of Croft Castle, Hereford; succeeded to the baronetcy in 1753; officer in the Court of Chancery: G.E.C., *Complete Baronetage* (Exeter, 1904), IV, 50.

COWPER, Harriot (1733–1807), m. Sir Thomas Hesketh (1727–78), of Rufford, near Ormskirk, Lancs, who matriculated Christ Church, Oxon., in 1743; was created bt in 1761: G.E.C., *Complete Baronetage* (Exeter, 1906), V, 121.

COWPER, John (1694–1756), Christ's Coll., Camb. (1711–13); Merton Coll., Oxon. (B.A. 1715/6, M.A. 1718); Fellow of Merton; D.D. from Camb. (1728); Chaplain to the King (from 1728): *Court and City Register*; Duncan Warrand, *Hertfordshire Families* (London, 1907), p. 145 (Cowper families: pp. 131–51). His portrait is reproduced in Wright, *Life* (1921), p. 33. A MS. commonplace book with notes on Berkhamsted, belonging to John Cowper and his two sons, is in the Earl of Crawford and Balcarres's collection. For the Rev. John Cowper's verses see *Madan Family*, pp. 79, 86; Nichols, *Poems*, VIII, 93; [John Duncombe, ed.] *Letters from...Dr. Thomas Herring...to William Duncombe* (London, 1777), pp. 69–70. According to the annotated copy of [Ashley Cowper, ed.] *The Poetical Miscellany* (London, 1744) [B.M. 992.k.20–1], he wrote the following poems in that collection: 1, 28–9 ('On Miss R[ope]r Having the Tooth-ach'), 39–40 ('The Client's Warning-Piece'), 88 ('The Parallel'), 364–74 ('An Epistle...to his Gr—ce the D—ke of Ch—nd—s').

COWPER, John (1737–70), s. of the above-mentioned: H. P. Stokes, *Cowper Memorials. Records of the Rev. John Cowper* (Olney, 1904); William Cowper, *Adelphi. A Sketch...of the late Rev. John Cowper* (London, 1802), reprinted in Stokes, pp. 63–86; John Cowper to Mrs Maria F. C. Cowper, 17 and 23 Sept. 1764: Cowper Mus., Olney. According to a note by S[amuel] G[reatheed], 4 Nov. 1800, William's account of his brother's last illness and conversion had been published before the well-known posthumous edition of 1802. Greatheed wrote: 'Mr Cooper sent one copy of this account to Mr Newton and another to Archdeacon Histor of Bucks, who had I think known his Brother intimately. He left no copy for Himself....While M^r C lived at Weston I met with part of it in print, in the late Revd David Simpsons "Deathbed Evidences of the Gospel". I showed him the book, and having read [it,] he said to the best of his recollection it was accurate, so far as it went. He expressed no dissatisfaction at finding that it had been made Public' (Cowper Mus., Olney: MS. vol. entitled 'A Collection of Materials towards a Life of Cowper'—probably collected by Greatheed). I have not been able to locate a copy of Simpson's book. John Cowper's library was sold by James Robson in 1771: 'A Catalogue of Very Valuable Books in all Languages and Sciences, containing, the Curious Library of the Rev. Mr. Cowper': B.M. 128.k.7(1).

COWPER, Mary: *see De Grey, Mary Cowper.*

COWPER, Spencer* (1669–1728), the poet's grandfather; M.P. for Beeralston (1705–10) and Truro (1715–27); Attorney-Gen. to the Prince of Wales (1714–17); K.C. (1715); Chief Justice of Chester (1717); Justice of the Common Pleas from 24 Oct. 1727.

COWPER, Theadora Jane (1734?–1824): according to the inscription on her tomb in the churchyard, Petersham, Surrey—'THEODORA JANE COWPER departed this Life the 21st October 1824 in the 90th year of her age' (information from the Rev. R. S. Mills).

CROFT: *see Cowper, Elizabeth Charlotte.*

DE GREY, Mary Cowper (1719–1800), dau. of William Cowper (1689–1740), of Hertingfordbury, Clerk of the Parliaments: *Madan Family*, p. 243.

DE GREY, William* (1719–81), 2nd s. of Thomas de Grey of Merton, Norfolk; admitted M.T. 26 Jan. 1737/8; Bencher 1758; Treas. 1766.

DONNE, Ann: *see Cowper, Ann Donne.*

DONNE, Harriot Rival (1736–?), m. Richard Balls, of Catfield, 1759: Catharine B. Johnson, *William Bodham Donne and his Friends* (London, 1905), p. 334; *Letters*, IV, 82.

DUNCOMBE, John* (1729–86), only child of William Duncombe; Corpus Christi Coll., Camb., B.A. (1749), M.A. (1752), Fellow (1751–8); one of the six preachers at Canterbury Cathedral (from 1766): Nichols, *Anecdotes*, VIII, 271–8; Kippis, *Biographia Britannica* (London, 1793), V, 509–12; David Bonnell Green, 'Three Cowper Letters', *N. & Q.* CCI (1956), 532. Vol. VI of Nichols, *Poems*, is largely a collection of poems by or about people related to J. Duncombe, or his friends. His portrait appears in the picture by Susannah Highmore (who became his wife), of Richardson reading the MS. of *Sir Charles Grandison* to his friends: see C. L. Thomson, *Samuel Richardson* (London, 1900), p. 226.

DUNCOMBE, William* (1690–1769), youngest s. of John (1645–1728), of Stocks, and brother to John (1680–1746), of the same place; clerk in the navy office (1706–25): Nichols, *Anecdotes*, VIII 265–70; Kippis, V, 504–9; Boswell, *Johnson*, III, 314. His portrait is the frontispiece to Nichols, *Poems*, VI. He was listed as of 'Dunstable Houghton', and owner of the following properties in Berkhamsted in 1755: 'Combes ffarm, 4 Mess[uag]es in Northchurch, [and] Lagley ffarm': B.M. Lansdowne MSS. 656, f. 6.

HESKETH: *see Cowper, Harriot.*

JOHNSON, James* (1705–74), Bp of Gloucester, 1752, and Worcester, 1759.

LLOYD, Pierson (1704–81), Chancellor of York, 1780.

LLOYD, Robert* (1733–64), captain of the 'School' at Westminster (1750), elected 'Head' to Camb. (1751): Welch and Phillimore, *The List of the Queen's Scholars*, pp. 357–8; Nichols, *Anecdotes*, II, 330–2; Austin Dobson, 'Robert Lloyd', *At Prior Park and Other Papers* (London, 1912), pp. 210–42; Irving McKee, *The Literary Career of Robert Lloyd*, unpubl. Ph.D. diss. (Yale Univ., 1935).

LUDFORD, Ann and Thomas; Ann was the only dau. of the Rev. Edward Taylor, Rector of Finningley, Notts. She m. first, Thomas Bold, a distiller of London, who d. *c.* 1727. She afterwards m. Ludford in 1731. She d. 15 May 1743, aged fifty. Thomas, her 2nd husband (1708–76), was the s. of Samuel Bracebridge, Esq. (he afterwards assumed the name and arms of Ludford), of Ansley Hall, co. Warwick. Ann and Thomas Ludford were buried in the North Cloister of the Abbey. Joseph L. Chester, ed. *The Marriage, Baptismal, and Burial Registers of…St. Peter, Westminster* (London, 1876), pp. 375, 421.

MADAN, Martin* (1725–90): *Madan Family*, pp. 104–21, 273–302.

MADAN, Penelope: *see Maitland, Penelope Madan.*

MAITLAND, Penelope Madan (1730–1805), dau. of Col. Martin Madan and Judith Cowper, and wife of the Hon. Gen. (later Sir) Alexander Maitland, s. of the 6th E. of Lauderdale: *Madan Family*, pp. 124–5, 253.

MORRITT, John Sawrey (1738?–91), purchased Rokeby Park, Yorks (1769). His s. John Bacon Sawrey (1771–1843), friend of Wilberforce, Scott, Southey, and Davy, made it one of the show places of the country (among the contents of the house, 'the Rokeby Venus'). Morritt is the source for the full story of John Cowper and the gypsy, a famous bit of Cowperiana—Southey to Henry Taylor [April? 1836]: Bodleian MS. Eng. lett. d. 8, f. 196. (Southey writes that Morritt was 'John Cowpers most intimate friend.— & the only witness to the dreadful circumstance [the encounter with the gypsy], which it is impossible to disbelieve & perhaps as impossible satisfactorily to account for in any way'.) See *Letters*, I, 125; Southey's *Cowper*, VII, 256–60; Wright, *Life* (1921), pp. 13, 99. On J. S. M. see F. S. Moller, *Alumni Felstedienses* (London, 1931), p. 23; Nichols, *Anecdotes*, VIII, 565; [Thomas Forster], *Epistolarium or Fasiculi of Curious Letters* (Bruges, 1845), p. 181.

COWPER'S RELATIVES AND FRIENDS

PITTMAN, William (1702–65), M.A. King's Coll., Camb. (1729), Fellow (1724–33), D.D. (1743); Vicar of Kensworth, Herts (1743–65); Chaplain to the D. of Bridgewater. He left the Markyate Street School 'in a very flourishing Condition Chr.ˢ 1751 having just Published a Compendious Introduction to the Latin Grammar collected from the best Grammarians both Antient and modern with Useful observations on the whole[.] He also Published Florilegium Poeticum ex Ovidio Tibullo Propertio Martiali...': Anthony Allen, *Skeleton Collegii Regalis Cantab* (MS. King's Coll., Camb., written *c.* 1750), vol. IV, f. 2145. (I have not been able to find copies of these two books by Pittman.) See also *Eton Reg.* p. 271; *V.C.H....Bedford*, II, 314; Cussans, III, 100; John Venn, *Annals of a Clerical Family* (London, 1904), p. 68.

PLAYFORD, Ann, d. 29 June 1743, aged seventy-two, and was buried in the North Cloister of the Abbey. She was a dau. of Thomas Baker, Gent., of Oxford. She m. Henry Playford (1657–1709?) in 1688. Chester, p. 364, n. 1, and pp. 346, 353, 357. I am indebted also to Mr L. E. Tanner for information received in conversation.

POPE, Robert (Robin) (d. 1767): John Wolstenholme Cobb, *Two Lectures on...Berkhamsted*, 2nd ed. (London, 1883), p. 72.

REDMAN, Jones (1695?–1763): *Eton Reg.*; *G.M.* XXXIII (1763), 257; Cussans III, 91. Poems by Redman are found in Nichols, *Poems*, VI, 304–11; one by John Cowper, the poet's father, 'To Dr. Redman, Who Sent the Author a Hare', Nichols, *Poems*, VIII, 93.

ROBERTS, Samuel (d. 1832): Wright, *Life* (1921), p. 360; *Letters*, I, 23; IV, 256, n. 2, and 495, n. 1; *Memoir*, pp. 73–4.

ROWLEY, Clotworthy (1731–1805), adm. Trinity Hall, Camb., in 1750; M.P. for Downpatrick (1771–1801): *G.M.* XXXIII (1763), 257; *Inner Temp. Rec.* IV, 565; V, 44, 156, 211, 418; information received from Mr Brian Spiller; *Letters*, III, 194. In 1794 his address was 'Old Court, near Brayshead [Wicklow] Ireland': Lady Hesketh to Rowley, 21 May 1794: Cowper Mus., Olney.

SUTTON, Richard (1733–1802), Under-Secy. of State (1766–72), a Lord of the Treasury (1780–4), M.P. for St Albans (1768–80), Sandwich (1780–4), and Boroughbridge (1784–96), created a bt (1772); he sat twice (1767 and 1773) for portraits by Sir Joshua Reynolds; he was afflicted with gout during most of his later life: *G.M.* LXXII, Pt ii (1802), 687.

THORNTON, Bonnell* (1724–68): John Wooll, *Biographical Memoirs of... Joseph Warton* (London, 1806), pp. 268–9; Alan Dugald McKillop, 'Bonnell Thornton's Burlesque Ode', *N. & Q.* CXCIV (1949), 321–4; Wallace Cable Brown, 'A Belated Augustan: Bonnell Thornton, Esq.', *P.Q.* XXXIV (1955), 335–48.

UNWIN, Mary Cawthorne* (1724–96) and Morley (1703–67); their s., William Cawthorne Unwin (1744–86); dau., Susanna, later Mrs Powley (1746–1835): Wright, *Life* (1921), pp. 63, 360. A most important source of information concerning the family is the letter from S. Greatheed to Hayley, 4 Oct. 1800: Fitzwilliam MSS.

265

INDEX

Purdon, Edward, 234
Purdy, Richard L., 183
Purley, Berks, 228

Quarme, George, 131
Quennell, Peter, 145
Quinlan, Maurice J., 144

Raleigh, Sir Walter, 257-8
Ramsgate, Kent, 53
Redman, Jones, 11, 265
Reynolds, Frederick, 32-3
Rhodes, Ebenezer, 251
Richardson, Samuel, 69
Richardson, William Westbrook, 76
Richmond, see Lennox
Roberts, Samuel, 163, 166, 265
Rockingham, see Watson-Wentworth
Romney, George, 126
Rose, Samuel, 72, 241, 247
Rothschild, family of, 191
Rottingdean, Sussex, 131
Rousseau, Jean-Jacques, 84
Rowe, Nicholas, 3, 26
Rowley, family of, 46-7
Rowley, Clotworthy, 46-7, 51, 83, 137-8,
    146, 166, 180 n., 265
Russell, Sir Francis, Bt, 49
Russell, Sir William, Bt, 49, 106

St Albans, 124, 130, 138, 160-3, 165, 261
St James's Chronicle, 87, 117, 212 n.
St James's Magazine, 87, 89, 185 n., 200-11
Salinger, J. D., 34
Salter, Thomas, 53
Sargeaunt, John, 23
Scott, James, 203-11 passim
Seare, John, 146, 191-2
Selwyn, William, 38
Shakespeare, William, 64, 86, 251
Sharpe, Gregory, 75
Sharpe, John, 75
Sheffield, John, 1st D. of Buckingham,
    204
Shepherd, Richard, 203-11 passim
Sheridan, Richard Brinsley, 214
Sign-Painters Exhibition, 86-7
Simpson, David, 138, 263
Smart, Christopher, 74, 87, 94-5, 226,
    259 n.
Smollett, Tobias, 10, 113, 122, 233-6
Southampton, 54, 66, 131-2
Southey, Robert, 110-11, 139-43, 200,
    214, 234, 247

Spedding, James, 139
Spencer, John, 1st E. Spencer, 45
Spencer, Lady Georgiana Cartaret (after-
    wards Lady Cowper), 45
Spender, Stephen, 34
Spenser, Edmund, 64
Stainsby, John Alexander, 64
Stanhope, Philip, 15
Steele, Sir Richard, 32, 100
Steevens, George, 117
Stephen, James, 139
Sterne, Laurence, 145
Sternhold, Thomas, 185, 189
Stoke Newington, Middlesex, 256-60
Stokes, H. P., 233
Student, 87, 94, 226-9
Suett, Mrs, 19
Sunderland, Judith, Cts of, 45
Sutton, Sir Richard, Bt, 23, 42-7, 55,
    83, 147, 177, 265
Sutton, Sir Robert, 43-5
Swift, Jonathan, 58-9, 195

Taplow, Bucks, 131
Tasso, Torquato, 55
Taylor, Henry, 139, 141
Teedon, Samuel, 97 n., 214, 247
Temple, Inner and Middle, see London:
    Temple
Tennyson, Alfred, 1st Bn Tennyson, 106
Tewin Water, Herts, 130
Thicknesse, Philip, 33, 179
Thomson, James, 59
Thomson, William, Lieut.-Col. (d. 1768),
    130
Thornton, Bonnell, 15, 51, 78-101 passim,
    117, 146-7, 179, 226, 265
    portrait of, Plate IV
Thornton, John, 52, 135, 139-42
Thornton, Mrs John, 171
Thrale, Hester Lynch (afterwards Piozzi),
    86 n.
Throckmorton, Mrs John, 253
Thurlow, Edward, 1st Bn Thurlow, 36-7,
    49, 52, 60-3, 79-81, 83 n., 119-20,
    138, 153, 178
'Toby', see Price, Chase
Torriano, Giovanni, 195
Torrington, see Byng
Townshend, George, 1st M. Townshend,
    230
Trevelyan, G. M., 30
Tring Park, Herts, 191-2
Trollope, Anthony, 33

INDEX